OFFICE AUTOMATION

A Survey of Tools and Techniques

OFFICE AUTOMATION

A Survey of Tools and Techniques

DAVID BARCOMB

DIGITAL PRESS

Design by David Ford
Printed in U.S.A.
10 9 8 7 6 5 4 3
Documentation number EY-AX015-DP
ISBN 0-932376-16-9

Trademarks mentioned in the text are listed at the back of the book.

The text of this book was created on a DEC Word Processing System and, via a translation program, was automatically typeset on the DECset-8000 Typesetting System. The illustration on the cover was created on a Genigraphics system by the Computer Images Department, Educational Services, Digital Equipment Corporation.

Library of Congress Cataloging in Publication Data

Barcomb, David, 1937–
    Office automation.

    Includes index.
    1. Office practice—Automation.   I. Title.
HF5548.2.B332   651.8   81-15276
ISBN 0-932376-16-9   AACR2

PREFACE

When I began to write this book, I had two goals in mind. One was to demystify the topic of office automation and make it understandable and accessible to those whom it should serve. The other was to survey the functional elements of office automation in an introductory and explanatory fashion. The functional approach, in fact, seemed the best route to the goal of demystification, because it concentrates on realities, on tools and techniques that are tested and available now.

My method, therefore, is to introduce the key elements of office automation, to explain each one in concrete terms, and finally to indicate how the various functions relate to one another and mesh together in integrated systems. I have also included a brief chapter on basic communications technology for nontechnical readers and a general discussion of some key issues in implementation. I have not, however, examined the broad underlying concepts and networks of developing technologies that provide the theoretical framework of office automation. Those topics, and the profound implications they will have for the future, lie beyond the parameters of this first practical introduction to office automation.

I have generally directed the book to readers with a managerial background and have tried to suppress the technical jargon of the information specialist. Even so, the subject matter should appeal to system designers and analysts, programmers, and workers and students interested in data processing and information management.

The reader should be aware that I occasionally mention specific models or organizations or services in the book as examples of the functions or components under discussion. It is not my intention in doing so to endorse or recommend any product or service or to exclude other products or services in the same category.

Although my goal is to remove the veil of mystery from office automation, readers looking for glamor and futuristic functions need not be disappointed. Much of what has been thought of as years away is already here, in use, and easily available. In fact, you are holding the result of some of it.

Most of this book was produced with an automated system. I used a communicating word processor to outline, write, edit, and transmit the original draft of the manuscript. Routine communications between author and publisher were transmitted by an electronic mail system that is part of an integrated office information system. Some of the illustrations are computer generated. Finally, the type you are reading was automatically set by a photocomposer from word processed copy by means of a translation program.

Because of the unique means employed in its creation, this book has involved the cooperation of many people. I wish to thank the following individuals and organizations for the loan of equipment, use of software packages, and access to timesharing systems: Digital Press for the use of a word/data processing system, and the Digital Equipment Corporation for the use of its internal integrated office automation system; Jack Gilmore, Bob Travis, and Green Adair, all of Digital Equipment Corporation, for assistance in implementing various software packages; Ken Krechmer, formerly of Racal-Vadic, and Racal-Vadic, Inc., for use of the Vadic VA355 modem and model 871 telephone handset; Meredith Fischer of the Qwip Division of Exxon Enterprises for her efforts in providing use of the Qwip facsimile unit; Computer Transceiver Systems, Inc., and Art Bajart of Public Relations–Communications, Inc., for the use of an Execuport 4000G portable terminal; and Lawrence Turner of the Taylor Merchant Corporation for use of the 77R-GLM pocket microfiche viewer.

I am also indebted to Mary Lou McKeen of General Electric's Boston Genigraphics Service Center for creating the block diagrams in Chapter 11 and to Sharri Magid and Kevin Sanders of Digital Equipment Corporation for use of the table comparing capabilities of various facsimile models.

For valuable contributions throughout the writing and production of this work, I extend thanks to: Don Elias of Digital Equipment Corporation for initiating the project; Dr. David Potter, Augmentation Resources Center, Tymshare, Inc., for access to individuals and scarce documentation pertaining to integrated systems; John McNamara of Digital Equipment Corporation for reviewing the chapter on communications; Morris "Mo" Green, for providing access to research material and reviewing the chapter on micrographics; Dan Hochman, one of the pioneers in digital fax, for permission to use personal documents; John MacDonald, for reviewing the manuscript from the managerial point of view; Samuel Fordyce, NASA Headquarters, Washington,

D.C., for copies of unclassified materials on teleconferencing experiences; the staff at Digital Press for encouragement and assistance; and my wife, Janice, who helped with the word processing.

I also wish to thank the individuals and organizations cited throughout the book who shared the results of their office automation efforts but preferred to remain anonymous; those who reviewed the outline and later versions of the manuscript, signficantly improving this work; and the hundreds of fellow practitioners and researchers in office automation without whose contributions office automation and this book would not exist.

David Barcomb
Cherry Hill, New Jersey
November 1981

To my wife, Janice, and our daughter, Lisa

CONTENTS

FOREWORD

In summing up this informative, timely, and important contribution to the literature of office automation, David Barcomb reminds us, "There is no magic in office automation; the magic is in the people who use it effectively."

Those are wise words indeed. Too many people view office automation as a replacement for people. We hear and read about the electronic office and the paperless office. Regarding the latter, we are reminded of the statement by Bob Murray, vice president of the Diebold Group. Said Bob, "You show me the paperless office and I'll show you the peopleless office. But you show me first."

We share that view. Not too long ago there was much talk of the "checkless society." Today's reality is a society creating millions more checks than anyone ever dreamed of. But technology has provided the means to effectively and efficiently handle the processing.

And so it will be with the office of the future. Not paperless. Not peopleless. But rather an office adapting today's technology to the needs of the worker. Paperwork will be simplified, not eliminated. People will be present but more productive. Technology will be more humanized. The office will become an effective management information center, and people will play the major role.

Arnold E. Keller
Vice President and Publisher
Infosystems

I

INTRODUCTION

TO

OFFICE

AUTOMATION

Each of us experiences unfamiliar circumstances that cause us unnecessary concern: the first day of a school year, the first meeting of a new organization, or the first day on a new job. We feel ill at ease because of strange surroundings or unknown customs. Once we find old friends or meet new ones and learn the prevailing social or professional customs, we feel more comfortable.

Office automation is like that: its unfamiliar terminology and processes may cause apprehension, but familiarization removes the strangeness. We soon see that much of office automation is new ways of using old principles, practices, and equipment. Those elements that really are new are soon understood.

In a broad sense, *office automation* is the incorporation of appropriate technology to help people manage information. (Technology is considered "appropriate" when it utilizes the most abundant domestic resources and conserves capital and skilled personnel.)[1]

Office automation is a subset of *automation*, a term said to have been coined by D. S. Harder of General Motors Corporation in 1936.[2]

New ways of using old principles.

The word *office* specifies the sector. But what is an office? To a typist it may be a room full of desks and typewriters. To a salesperson it may be the front seat of a car or a motel room. To a truck driver an office is the cab of a truck. To a reporter it can be a newsroom or even a telephone booth. All of these have one common element: they are all places where people manage information. In this examination of office automation, an office will be regarded as any place where managerial, professional, and clerical workers are engaged primarily in handling business information.

Office automation uses integrated information systems that exist now and are possible and practical, as distinct from systems that are presently unattainable or impractical. The dividing line is reality. The "office of the future" is the source of ideas that lead to progress. Office automation is the realization of those ideas. This book deals with tools and technology that exist today.

Office automation is a concept, an approach to a new way of handling information. It is not a project with a defined point of completion, nor is it the installation of any single functional element. Rather, office automation is the linking of multiple components or elements in such a way that information, once entered, can be processed and channeled from point to point with a maximum of technological assistance and a minimum of human intervention.

Office automation, then, is not a turnkey product or service that can be purchased, predesigned and preassembled, and simply put in place. It is more than a new type of office system or new technologies or hybridized hardware. A range of available tools must be coordinated and tailored to the needs of a particular organization. If improperly selected and implemented, office automation degrades information systems, causes turmoil, and adds to expenses.

In the 1950s knowledge workers (people engaged primarily in processing information) began to use the computer as a tool for handling numbers. Identifiable, repetitious patterns involved in accounting, inventory control, and similar activities dealing with masses of numbers were systematized and programmed for computerized processing, relieving people from repetitious drudgery. Using an array of technology, including computers, office automation today does much the same for knowledge workers engaged in data, text, audio, and graphic information processing. All four modes of conveying information exist in most offices—as computer input, typed reports, the telephone, and graphs, respectively. Yet none of these modes has been optimized for purposes of information management.

Basically, data processing forms half of the information management picture; office automation fills the other. A conventional data processing system puts data through multiple processing steps prior to arriving at a result. As processing occurs in a computer, the system recognizes specific circumstances and calls appropriate programs and subroutines into play to meet those needs.

In office automation, people are counterparts to data processing systems. As people process information, they recognize specific circumstances and call into play appropriate tools to meet those needs, ultimately arriving at a result. Data processing converts data (raw facts) into information; office automation assists people as they process (classify, select, and/or arrange) information and convert it to knowledge and action.

Office automation incorporates technology to serve rather than be served by people, for people are more valuable than equipment. Toward that end, system planners are incorporating human-factors-engineering principles into the design of both hardware (equipment) and software (programs), resulting in so-called "friendly" or "user friendly" systems.

Of a total United States work force of more than 90 million, there are nearly 33 million knowledge workers.[3] Of the $1.241 trillion in wages and fringe benefits paid in the United States in 1978, as much as $800 billion, or roughly two-thirds, went to office workers.[4] But production workers, as well, are required to fill out forms. In fact the U.S. work force as a whole devotes 60 percent of all working hours to information management and only 40 percent to actual production of goods.[5]

Yet, technologically, knowledge workers have been neglected. Table 1.1 lists the conventional tools with which workers manage information

Mignon typewriter of 1904. Note revolving typewheel and matrix indicator. Photo courtesy of Millers Falls Paper Company.

in offices and the dates of their invention: there has not been a major technological change in office tools since 1946. In some cases, old technology has been adapted to new uses. Except for data processing and photocopying, there has been little concentration on office systems technology. Now, however, technology is flooding the office environment, and with it has come a marked improvement in the design and implementation of tools for information management.

Anyone who considers his or her office modern uses most or all of the tools listed in Table 1.1 to solve information problems. Yet some of these tools generate still more problems. In many offices, for example, people waste time standing in line waiting to use the photocopier. Locating "convenience" copiers closer to users or providing copiers that operate at much higher speeds gives rise to other problems, for copying expands to fill the equipment capacity available. When monks labored for days to copy a short document, no one would have suggested sending "information copies" to a distribution list of forty people. Today it is common practice. Over 250 billion copies spew from copiers and duplicators each year, with convenience copiers responsible for 50 to 100 billion of that total.[6]

Old and New Systems Perspectives

Narrowly defined, a system is simply a methodical, organized procedure. Systems of this sort are essential to daily productivity. Conventional office systems work from a partial or fragmented approach addressing a small area of the total information landscape. They are

TABLE 1.1 Tools of the contemporary office with their dates of invention or discovery.

3200 B.C.	Ink (Egypt)
A.D. 105	Paper (China)
1040	Movable type (China)
1335	Mechanical clock with dial
1565	Pencil (first written reference to)
1642	Calculator
1714	Typewriter
1809	Fountain pen
1823	Computer (mechanical)
1839	Microphotography
1843	Facsimile
1876	Telephone
1888	Ball-point pen
1899	Magnetic tape recording
1937	Xerography
1946	Computer (electronic)

oriented to a specific task or set of tasks, and solutions are formulated in terms of a specific user. Generally, if such systems reach beyond their own departments, they do so only within the vertical managerial chain to which the user belongs.

Office automation adopts a broader point of view that takes into account the following principles:

- Some information management functions are systematic or semisystematic.
- Some information management functions and most data and information are common to numerous users.
- Conventional systems are actually subsystems.
- An entire organization (firm, association) is itself a system made up of many subsystems.
- Ultimately, all organization systems are linked.

Good automated office systems are modular and highly flexible. They give their users as much freedom of choice as possible. They also provide mobility. Users can carry portable communicating terminals with them wherever they go, so that even away from their offices they can in seconds access electronic files and locate specific documents according to subject, author, or date. Terminal users can rapidly communicate with a dozen people in the same building or on the opposite side of the earth. One person can take part in ten meetings in different cities in one day without leaving his or her office.

Office automation has four indispensable components: philosophy, equipment (or technology), systems, and people. The most important component is people; it is they who convert information to knowledge. No brilliance of systems design, no level of capital outlay, no cleverly written report can compensate for the failure of system planners to provide easy-to-use, nonthreatening systems technology. An archaic malady of conventional data processing systems involves just such an omission. In the early years of data processing, computer memory was quite expensive. To limit memory use and conserve costs, designers and programmers encoded commands as concisely as possible, and terminal operators were (and still are) required to learn what amounts to a new language. Memorizing one or even several such enigmatic commands would be no problem, but operators continue to be faced with user handbooks filled with page after page of them.

Today labor is expensive whereas computers are becoming relatively inexpensive. With more computer capacity available, programs can be written to permit the use of natural-language commands, which are much easier to remember and still provide the same system response. Good office automation systems, both computerized and non-computerized, are "friendly," or approachable.

Even friendly automated office systems occasionally malfunction or, in computer parlance, "go down." In a conventional office, if a pen runs out of ink the user can get a new one from a desk drawer or supply cabinet. In an automated office the user is not always able to solve a problem without a technician. This drawback, however, is being addressed. For example, one computer manufacturer provides three plug-in electronic boards. If the device in which they are used fails, the user simply replaces one board at a time until the machine resumes operation, usually within five minutes. The faulty parts are then replaced by the manufacturer.

Major System Elements

Office automation has matured as a concept. One significant integrated office automation system has been operational for fifteen years and certain patterns have emerged over time. Because there are functions basic to virtually all knowledge workers, the same functional elements tend to recur in the system designs of office automation planners. These elements, embracing the four information conveyance modes of data, text, audio, and graphics, are:

- Word management (data, text, audio, graphics)
- Electronic mail systems (data, text, audio, graphics)
- Electronic filing (data, text, audio, graphics)
- Micrographics (data, text, graphics)
- Teleconferencing (data, text, audio, graphics)
- Integrated office automation systems (data, text, audio, graphics).

Each of the above elements is discussed in subsequent chapters.

Benefits

The following list shows some of the benefits that businesses and knowledge workers can derive from the proper implementation of office automation technology.

- Optimize staffing
    Enhance human capabilities
    Conserve human resources
    Compensate for manpower shortages
    Minimize drudgery
- Increase productivity
    Improve accuracy
    Speed up throughput
    Speed up turnaround
- Gain competitive edge
    Improve timeliness of information
    Improve decision making
    Conserve natural resources
- Increase scope of control
    Enhance individual and organizational flexibility
    Make information portable
- Decrease expenses
    Reduce capital investment in structures
    Reduce or cap off payroll costs

Office automation puts to work the almost daily breakthroughs in communications technology to promote the rapid and efficient transfer of information in the service of human knowledge. Intelligent selection and effective use of the new communications tools requires understanding the important issues that confront modern business, the best way to introduce the new tools to enhance the operation of a business, and the nomenclature and apparatus of communications technology. Chapters 2 and 3 discuss these topics.

NOTES

1. Rowan A. Wakefield and Patricia Stafford, "Appropriate Technology: What It Is and Where It Is Going," *1999: The World of Tomorrow*, edited by Edward Cornish (Washington, D.C.: World Future Society, 1978), p. 134.

2. *Encyclopaedia Britannica*, 14th ed., s.v. "Automated Systems."

3. *Information Please Almanac, 1980* (New York: Information Please Publishing, 1979), p. 56.

4. "'Office of the Future' Almost Here?" *Infosystems*, June 1979, p. 30.

5. "The U.S. Productivity Crisis," *Newsweek*, September 8, 1980, p. 56.

6. Raymond R. Panko, "The Outlook for Computer Mail," *Telecommunications Policy*, June 1977.

Wisely improve the Present.

Henry Wadsworth Longfellow
Hyperion, Book IV

KEY ISSUES
AND
IMPLEMENTATION
STRATEGIES

Any organization that wants to make office automation a successful reality must overcome formidable obstacles, including fear or uncertainty and both external and internal bureaucratic pressures. These manifest themselves in financial, communications, social, and organizational issues. Except when international communications are involved, technology per se is not an issue.

Financial Issues

To buy, complete, and file a single business form costs about ninety times as much as the blank form itself; that estimate excludes photocopies and any subsequent processing. In 1977 the annual cost to maintain document files was nearly 15 cents per page, including labor, depreciation on file cabinets, and cost of floor space; by 1980 that figure is estimated to have risen to almost 20 cents per page.[1] In conservative figures, the cost to obtain and complete the forms in a full file cabinet up to 18,000 pages is nearly $25,000. The average cost of maintaining that file is, at present rates, over $3,500 per year. In the first five years of its existence, each innocent-looking file cabinet costs $42,300. That figure is rising yearly and is only a fraction of the total cost. The total life-cycle cost of those forms would include purchase, transportation, storage, issuance, completion, signing, placement in an envelope, addressing, internal routing to and through mail room, postage, reading, photocopying, forwarding, filing, retrieving, archiving, and ultimate disposal.

In 1963, records management authority Emmett Leahy estimated that 1 million pages were being generated in offices every minute of the day: 1.44 billion pages every twenty-four hours, or 525.6 billion pages per year.[2] The figure is even higher today. The 1977 U.S. volume of forms alone (exclusive of photocopies and documents prepared on plain paper) was set as high as 400 billion pages.[3] Of the total paperwork generated in the United States each year, between 175 billion and 250 billion pages make their way into file cabinets.[4] Furthermore, only 3 to 10 percent of all documents filed are ever again referred to for any reason. Of the small percentage of documents that are retrieved, between 80 and 90 percent have been generated within the two years preceding retrieval.[5]

In addition to a firm's internal record-keeping, government at every level is requiring more and more information from business. As early as the 1950s, any firm regulated by a federal commission had about twice as many records as a firm of comparable size not under the jurisdiction of a federal commission, and the four million small business firms in the U.S. at that time were committing between 5 and 29 percent of their total labor hours to federal reporting.[6] Today there are more than a thousand federal statutes and regulations dealing with record retention and more than 4,700 separate reporting requirements for private enterprises.[7]

At 1979 wage levels, it cost at least 3 cents to research and write each word or number in the average report; one government agency placed its costs at $3.36 per word or number.[8] These figures convert to a range of $17 to $2,000 per page.

From 1952 to 1970 the cost of a one-page business letter nearly tripled, from around $1.15 to a little over $3.00. Between 1970 and 1981 that cost more than doubled to $6.63. One business consultant has found at least one instance in which business letters cost $18.00 per page.[9]

Productivity

In the U.S. in recent years Labor Department statistics show that the white-collar labor force has been growing nearly five times as fast as

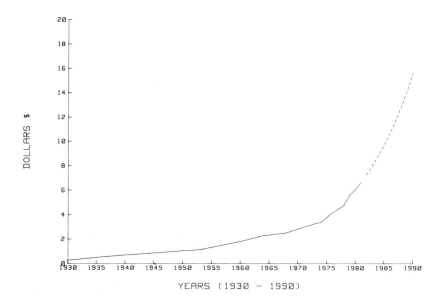

Computer-generated graph, showing the rising cost of an average business letter, 1930–1990. Produced by Hewlett Packard with HP 9845B computer, HP 9872C pen plotter, and HP Forecasting and Graphics Software. Data to 1981 from Dartnell Institute of Business Research.

the blue-collar labor force. In fact, over 50 percent of the U.S. work force now process information rather than produce material goods. Yet, while industrial productivity rose about 85 percent during the decade of the seventies, office productivity increased only 4 percent.[10] Office productivity will become of even greater concern in the future; it is predicted that by the end of the century 72 percent of U.S. workers will be engaged in indirect services.[11]

One reason for the productivity lag in offices seems to be a reluctance to apply technology. Traditionally, the office has been tolerated as a necessary expense; as little capital investment as possible has supported administrative and clerical operations. In 1900 the capital equipment investment per factory worker was $8,000 and the capital equipment investment per office worker was $300. Today the first figure is about $64,000 and the second is about $3,000. There is a direct correlation between capital investment and productivity in major industry groups. Yet only now is that correlation being recognized and acted upon to the benefit of both employers and knowledge workers.

In a standard business organization, profit is the normal motive, and administration has long been identified as a drain on profit. Information management is inherent in administrative activity: without it there could be no sound business operations. A product or service results in a profit only after intermediate steps, many of which involve collecting, organizing, storing, and communicating information.

The basic ways to improve profit are to increase volume or profit margins or productivity while decreasing expenses. In the case of a hypothetical firm, net earnings could be tripled by selling three times the volume of its product (difficult), tripling profit margins (a noncompetitive posture), or some combination of the two. The third possibility is improving productivity. An increase in profits resulting from improved productivity would be a reduction in expenses and an addition to net earnings. Although it is impossible for a firm to exert absolute control over external factors affecting its business (number of salesmen in competitive firms, size of advertising budget of competition, etc.), it is possible to control many internal factors, and thus to control productivity.

Productivity is output divided by input. Input can be nearly any factor—hours, people, dollar outlay—so long as it is consistent. Productivity improvement is a comparative measure. For example, if two purchasing agents manually produce 20 internal memos per day, the output (20) is divided by the input (2). Now, if the same two persons can produce 25 internal memos per day with automated tools, their output (25) divided by the input (2) is 12.5. The difference between the earlier and later outputs (2.5) divided by the original output (10) shows a productivity change (an improvement) of 0.25, or 25 percent.

Such measurement is simple to apply in a production environment, where output can be counted. It is not so easily applied to managers and professionals, whose output often involves abstract values as well as quantity, making measurement more difficult. Paradoxically, productivity declines as the level of education rises.[12] As those with the highest level of education, principals should be the focal point of productivity improvement within the office. There are usually twice as many of them as there are nonprincipals, they receive twice as much compensation, and their costs are roughly four times as high.[13]

The productivity of principals can be measured directly or indirectly. The indirect method is the simpler: it measures the productivity of subordinates, which presumably reflects the ability of the principal.[14] The direct method is based on time utilization. Time utilization involves shadow functions, activities that are attendant to but make no direct contribution to the intended task.[15] Such functions include misdialing and redialing telephone numbers, making additional calls because of busy signals or unavailability of the intended recipient, searching for misplaced documents, and proofreading documents more than once. For the typical manager, shadow functions account for at least 30 minutes of nonproductive time each day.

Unscheduled interruptions from telephone calls, visitors, or impromptu meetings result in loss of train of thought and in time spent to resume thought processes. An average interruption results in 8 minutes of lost time; most managers lose at least 60 minutes per day in this way. In addition, time lost in the process of letter or memo creation—giving instructions to the typist, reviewing the final copy, and signing—amounts to about 5 minutes per letter. Transferring information from one medium to another also takes a toll; to write a note as a result of a telephone call takes approximately 1 minute, about 16 minutes per average day per principal. Retrieval of paper documents from file drawers, book cases, binders, etc., takes at least 2 minutes per document; ten retrievals a day involve 20 minutes.[16]

This loss of productive time, amounting to 136 minutes or 28 percent of the average eight-hour working day, can be reduced by the proper application of office automation tools. A study by a well-known consulting firm states that a 19 percent improvement in managerial productivity is possible;[17] other sources claim improvements of 20 to 25 percent.

Clerical productivity is much easier to determine, because non-principals deal primarily in quantifiable tasks. Conventional techniques can be used to measure the relative productivity of a typewriter and a word processor, or the number of information retrievals and the average time per retrieval in a manual and a computer-aided environment. Office automation can considerably improve the productivity of non-principals and relieve them of the tedium of performing a number of repetitive tasks.

Many statistics are available about individual office automation elements, but none are publicly available about the return on investment of integrated office automation systems. It is clear, however, that office automation systems can provide significant returns. In one case known to the author, a teleconferencing installation was amortized in three months; management enjoyed a return of about 900 percent in the first year. Not all automated tools show such direct and spectacular results, but undoubtedly potential gains exist for those businesses that are courageous and resourceful enough to commit the necessary sums and effort to implement the new technology.

Communications Issues

Prior to the mid-nineteenth century, mail sent from the East to the West Coast traveled by ship around South America. The advent of the Pony Express shrank the sea passage of several weeks to a land passage measurable in days. On the heels of the Pony Express came the telegraph. Now it is possible to dial directly to telephones at many points around the world and communicate instantaneously. When letters took weeks to travel several thousand miles, it didn't matter whether it took ten minutes or ten days to locate information requested in the correspondence. Today, with someone waiting on a long-distance telephone line thousands of miles away, a prompt response is essential.

Social Issues

Women's liberation, equal opportunities in employment, perception of secretarial and clerical jobs as low-status, and declining educational standards are exerting pressure on information management systems: a person who can get eight dollars an hour as a computer programmer or as a hardhat employee on a construction job has little incentive to settle for an entry-level clerical or secretarial position at half that amount, especially if the position entails menial tasks such as doing the boss's Christmas shopping and serving coffee.[18] As a result of these trends, since 1975 the number of qualified applicants for secretarial positions has declined. In 1978 an estimated 439,000 secretarial positions became available, but 88,000, or 20 percent, could not be filled with qualified applicants. By 1985 the cumulative shortage of qualified secretaries could reach 700,000, with a total clerical shortage of up to 3 million.[19]

Filling management positions at the entry and middle levels poses less acute, but similar problems. During the 1960s, when many people chose alternative lifestyles and philosophies, the "system" was considered contemptible, "big business" was considered "bad business," and there was widespread aversion to pursuing degrees in business and management. Those attitudes have abated, MBA degrees are back in style, but managerial personnel ranks are leaner.[20]

Today's concerns about office automation resemble those about data processing in its early years. Data processing, contrary to expectations that it would spawn soup lines, created a massive, worldwide industry. Office automation, like data processing, can benefit rather than create problems in industry. It is not only a means of overcoming today's shortage of competent secretarial and managerial personnel; it also offers great potential for career advancement.[21] Fifteen years ago positions such as word processing manager and other similar supervisory and management opportunities for women did not exist. Today these rewards are a reality; more will come.

Organizational Issues

A major change in office staffing has resulted from the introduction of word processing systems. The concept of administrative support is based on the performance of secretarial and clerical functions by a team instead of the one-to-one manager-secretary relationship. Its purpose is the improved management of human resources and, ultimately, cost control or reduction. Support personnel assume the routine duties of the principals they support and in return gain access to career paths into management. Delegation of routine duties frees managers and professionals for more productive work.

Administrative support originated in the 1960s, when word processing equipment was relatively expensive and the only way to attain a reasonable return on investment was to centralize operations. The transfer of typing duties to centralized service groups created a problem: what to do with the secretarial time formerly dedicated to typing?

A variety of solutions emerged, all based on one premise: delegate some of the routine administrative and clerical duties of managers and professionals. By the mid-1970s, however, it was clear that retaining the traditional principal and secretary relationship was inefficient, even though the secretary had assumed the position and duties of an administrative assistant. Typing accounts for 20 percent of the secretarial day, and waiting for work accounts for another 18 percent; this 38 percent of the working day, approximately three hours, exceeds the time required to perform the delegatable duties of virtually any principal. Moreover, if all secretaries became administrative assistants at higher wage scales, and staffing increased in the word processing centers, the result would be additional expenses.

A more rational, flexible approach now provides support where and when it is needed. Though still based on increased status and a career path for secretaries, it utilizes human resources more efficiently. The International Information/Word Processing Association has defined the new career path positions as:

- Administrative secretary (entry level)
- Senior administrative secretary (experienced)
- Executive administrative secretary
- Supervisor of administrative secretarial center
- Manager of word processing/administrative support systems.

The most significant change is the elimination of the former one-to-one relationship between secretaries and principals. Another significant change has come about through the dispersion of word processing equipment as a result of lower prices. Most administrative support now involves all former secretarial tasks except occasional typing assignments in emergencies or on subjects of a highly confidential nature.[22]

Usually an administrative support team consists of two or more administrative secretaries and sometimes a messenger or photocopying specialist, all overseen by one working supervisor. Each secretary on such a team supports three or four principals, with primary responsibility for at least two and secondary responsibility for the others supported by the team. This arrangement provides principals with trained backup support, even during vacations and periods of illness. A principal whose needs require close, personal attention may be assigned a specific secretary with primary responsibility for that principal and secondary responsibility for others. At least one other team member is always trained as backup to the primary team member.

One organizational concept is of large administrative support centers or "pools"; these distribute work loads more evenly than smaller units and provide the greatest efficiency. Even in large centers secretaries are assigned primary support roles for specific individuals. Usually a large center comprises a number of teams, often located with word processing operations and under joint supervision. The supervisor or manager of the group is directly responsible for distribution and scheduling of the work load. However, the location of large central groups far from the principals they support causes inconvenience and a thin and impersonal bond between principal and secretary.

Minicenters, sometimes called "puddles," consist of one or two teams and are located closer to the offices of the principals they support. Such an arrangement strengthens interpersonal relationships. Word processing support is generally located with the minicenters. A third arrangement locates a team directly outside the offices of the principals it supports. Word processing support may be provided within the same group, in a minicenter, or in a word processing center.

Among the documented examples of successful administrative support teams are several involving small teams located close to principals.

Administrative support center equipped with a multiterminal shared-resource word processing system. Note letter-quality printers at left and beside terminal on right, acoustic coupler on top of the storage and processing unit, and disk pack being placed in disk drive. Photo courtesy of Digital Equipment Corporation.

In the home office of a petroleum company, 9 administrative support and word processing minicenters per floor on three separate floors, or a total of 27 units, support 1,100 principals. Each minicenter is tailored to the specific needs of the principals supported. The quality of support has improved, and the firm reportedly is enjoying annual savings of $1.7 million compared with the previous secretarial arrangements.[23]

Teams established by and operating within individual departments pose no organizational problem; they function in much the same manner as before. Centralized administrative support, however, requires pragmatic organizational and personal considerations. Diminished interpersonal communication between secretaries and principals may result in lower secretarial job satisfaction.[24] Principals, too, often prefer to have one secretary whom they can consider their own, whether for job effectiveness or because they consider a private secretary to be a status symbol. Against these perceived drawbacks must be weighed such benefits as improved productivity, reduction of staffing, continuity and flexibility of support to principals in times of illness or approaching deadlines, assumption of certain management tasks by a supervisor, and, for secretaries, career paths into management.

Human Factors

When integrated office automation systems are installed, managers (especially executive management) and professionals are often reluctant to enter their own messages or operate their own terminals. Many are unable to type and feel that, even if they could, to perform such tasks themselves would not be cost efficient. Many also regard typing as demeaning. Managerial resistance may disappear in time as a result of the confluence of two factors: (1) many younger people coming into management or the professions have learned to type at school, and (2) the increasing use of personal computers spreads familiarity with terminals. Another incentive lies in system design. A terminal operated by means of a ten-key numeric pad, perhaps even the telephone keypad as in some systems, will encourage users at least to receive and retrieve information even if they do not enter any by keying. One obvious advantage of the simplified keypad over a full keyboard arrangement is its ease of use for intermittent users who are not exposed to more complex systems consistently enough to master them.

Health Effects of CRTs

Every electronic and electrical device radiates energy; even electrical wiring emits electronic waves. The widespread use of electronic digital computers has led to a number of studies on the effect of prolonged use of cathode ray tube or video display terminals (CRTs or VDTs). The National Institute for Occupational Safety and Health (NIOSH) has taken readings for all types of emitted radiations from such equipment and has concluded that they present no threat to human health. NIOSH did find, however, that employees using VDTs have more health complaints than workers who do not use VDTs; among the primary complaints were eyestrain, headaches, backaches, and irritability. To minimize these effects, NIOSH has recommended that employees who use VDTs take regular rest periods and have their eyes examined before they begin using VDTs and periodically thereafter; that VDTs be designed so that keyboards and screens are separate and adjustable; that lighting in the work area and within the terminal be controlled to eliminate glare; that operators' chairs be comfortable; and that equipment be tested for radiation after it is serviced.[25]

Computer manufacturers are responding to the reports of stress-related complaints with a variety of designs incorporating improvements in ergonomic engineering. They are not only making quieter and more flexible machines with better lighting qualities, but are attempting to produce devices that are convenient and easy for noncomputer specialists to use. There is a real effort to make computers friendly and nonthreatening to their operators.

Implementing Office Automation

Office automation conceives of the office as a system within a larger system, the organization as a whole. But with no coordination, successful implementation at the organizational level is unlikely. Active executive support helps to prevent or eliminate much of the obstructionism that usually accompanies pervasive changes. There must be a centralized plan to give office automation a well-defined role within the organization and to orchestrate its implementation. Such planning involves a hard look at the organizational structure and at the goals and functions of the entire system.

Ignoring the organizational issue has costly consequences. In some cases different groups and departments will acquire office automation tools independently, and the result is a jumble of incompatible equipment and systems. One large U.S. corporation has installed four incompatible networks of facsimile units; planners in other firms complain of inheriting multiple brands of incompatible word processors and even incompatible models of the same manufacture. In other cases one department will assume leadership of the implementation effort on the assumption that to control office automation within the organization will bestow power, promotion, and financial reward. The result is numerous interdepartmental jurisdictional disputes with bitter consequences. Early settlement of the organizational issue by senior level management will prevent almost all such disputes.

Who should lead the office automation effort? Departmental nominees include data processing, word processing, office systems, records management, and management information systems. Almost every department involved with information handling has its champions. But office automation will not fit easily and neatly into most existing organizational structures. Because so many disciplines are involved, no one department or person can possibly be expert in all. Besides, parceling out the effort to preexisting departments defeats realistic prospects for centralized coordination.

One very successful approach is to form an entirely new group to plan and control office automation. This group should be guided by an upper management steering committee representing the major departments within the organization.[26] The steering committee should be a standing body that provides policy guidance to the office automation department. The members of the committee not only represent the interests of their various entities, but also understand the roles of their respective groups and are an authoritative means of cutting interdepartmental red tape.

Members of the office automation department itself should be drawn from preexisting departments with functional expertise in individual disciplines. User policy and maintenance jurisdiction should reside with the office automation department to ensure continued compatibility of equipment and systems. When office automation tools are needed, the office automation unit can draw on its members' respective strengths while broadening its general knowledge. The unit provides the necessary degree of coordination without infringing on the jurisdiction of the operating units. This structuring has proved successful, for it is nonthreatening to the functional groups.

In addition to its primary roles, the office automation department will in some ways function as a pseudo-vendor. No one vendor or dealer can supply all the products and services needed for office automation. Therefore, the department will obtain components from several sources, coordinate them into an end product, and market them to the internal end users.

An office automation department should consist of individuals who possess expertise in at least one of the areas listed below.

- Administrative management
- Audiovisual communications
- Cost/benefit analysis
- Data communications
- Data processing
- Human factors engineering

- Micrographics
- Office services supervision
- Office systems (manual or automated)
- Organizational development
- Primary organizational function (e.g., experience in manufacturing in a manufacturing firm)
- Procurement (specifically, capital equipment selection)
- Records management
- Software development
- Telecommunications
- Word processing

A Flexible Master Plan

Once an office automation organization has been established, senior management and/or the steering committee should develop a master plan for information management. The office automation (OA) department, working with the steering committee, should then establish a strategy for implementation, including both a specific short-term strategy that will produce visible progress for the sake of credibility and intermediate and long-term planning flexible enough to accommodate technological innovations. The prospect of technological change should not delay an office automation effort; virtually every device will eventually be improved, and delaying implementation only puts off the inevitable and deprives an organization of present tangible benefits. The planners must pick a starting point that will permit later enhancements. Because developing that plan can be a long process, it may be necessary to conduct evaluations or tests of products concurrently so that the effort does not lose impetus.

At the same time, planners must continue to emphasize the paramount importance of the long-term goal, which is communications. In this respect, planners should keep in mind that effective communications networks that can be expanded and also interconnected are essential to any successful integrated automated system. If a system functions well, the burgeoning demands upon it may exceed the capacity provided by the planning unit.

A master plan for implementing office automation involves realistic financial considerations by senior management. The product—the office automation system, with its subsystems, procedures, and policies—will be unique and therefore will require some applied research. Senior management should be prepared to accept the expense of halting parts of a project or even an entire project in the interest of a better result. Moreover, demand will occasionally outstrip vendors' capacity to provide certain tools or the communications networks capacity. Delays will then be unavoidable. Consequently, budgeting for office automation departments is nearly futile; it is better instead to budget for personnel, space, and facilities services while maintaining a flexible attitude toward funding rentals, leases, and vendor services.

When a company undertakes an office automation effort, the question of job security soon crosses the minds of most employees. Unless that question is answered, lack of cooperation, tacit undermining, a talent flight, and other undesirable results may occur. Senior management's information strategy should include written assurance from the chief executive that office automation will not result in loss of jobs. A plan for job transfer and attrition will reduce employees' concerns and help build a cooperative attitude. Similarly, the steering committee should constantly monitor companywide employee displacement; the personnel department (represented on the committee) should give interview priority to displaced employees, who should not be arbitrarily moved to another capacity. In one organization, over 9 percent of displaced employees obtained promotions and raises as a result of internal movement. Such facts, when publicized by management, may help enlist employee support.

The personnel and office automation departments should work closely to keep one another aware of and fill new positions that become available as a result of system implementations, for example, word processing trainee, word processing operator, and electronic mail manager. The personnel department will need to investigate wage scales in their firm and in the area and establish and approve new job descriptions.

Implementation

Devising a strategy for implementing office automation, like any other strategy, requires answering three questions: Where are we now? Where do we want to go? And how do we get there from here? There are no simple answers, because every organization is unique.

The first step is to determine the current status of information management and communications throughout the organization. What are the existing resources? Who operates them? Where do they exist? From what location are they controlled? Are they appropriate? Are they adequate? Do some functions cut across more than one department? Can they be coordinated more effectively in a different structure? What are the significant problems and who has them? Rank the problems according to volume, relative to their importance to the organization. Talk with management to determine areas of concern. Then obtain details from supervisors and other employees. Although the process sounds complex and time-consuming, it isn't; patterns of need begin to emerge quickly.

Office automation tools should fill needs clearly related to the goals of the organization. With these goals in mind and knowledge of OA tools available, strategists may begin to determine which ones the organization needs and their relative importance. For example, an organization operating from a single building with a large field sales force may not require teleconferencing but may need a terminal-based electronic mail system with portable terminals. A total system plan should be determined at this point even though some later stages may have to remain less detailed. Planners can save time and capital investment by affiliating with local chapters of professional societies concerned with office automation. In this way they can learn from counterparts in other organizations about various difficulties already experienced and overcome.

In some cases there may appear to be a conflict in priorities. Should the most widely needed tool be implemented first, or the one that is of greatest importance to upper management? On one hand, word processing might be most widely needed. On the other hand, audio teleconferencing might substantially decrease travel expenses and provide principals with early, positive proof of the value of the office automation effort.

The choice should be the tools that aid the principals, for they have the greatest potential for benefiting the entire organization. Choosing a fairly common tool will permit use of preexisting products. In this way it is also possible to avoid some of the costly errors previously encountered by others.

Audio teleconferencing is a reasonable choice if there are multiple remote locations and/or a great deal of travel by principals. The systems are relatively easy to plan and implement and quickly produce measurable benefits. However, those who regard business travel as a benefit rather than an inconvenience may resist teleconferencing.

Electronic calendars and appointment schedulers are complex by nature, are used primarily by secretaries, and do not directly affect the productivity of principals. Because they have little visibility to principals, they are not an effective starting point.

A freestanding records management system is unlikely to have much direct effect on the principals either. Even if successful, the tool is unlikely to generate much excitement or gain much visibility with them. Unless records management is of concern to management, such a system is a poor first choice.

A terminal-based electronic mail system directly affects the principals and is fast and simple to implement. It is a viable choice for a first tool.

Word processing is so widespread that it is often assumed to be the invariable starting point for office automation, but it does not directly involve or affect the productivity of most principals. Unless word processing has existed previously within the organization and its capabilities are already clearly understood, it can take time to plan and properly implement. Word processing is a good choice if it is used in conjunction with terminal-based electronic mail or if composing and revising documents is a meaningful portion of the activity of principals.

Whatever the choice, the first effort must be accomplished in a relatively short time, and it must be successful. Successful implementation will sustain high morale in the office automation group, generate positive interest among potential users, and reassure upper management that its decision to back the office automation effort was a good one.

Simplicity is the byword. Examine the hardware and software tools for ease of use. Can a device be activated with a single switch or are there several steps involved? Does a computer message system make any sense to uninitiated or intermittent users? Can the message be altered? Once information has been captured, can it be converted to other media with little or no manual intervention?

Plan for flexibility in size and configuration. Subunits in a user community may range in size from a single person to several large departments, and each subunit may need only certain tools.

Provide system users with a practical alternative to the medium of paper. At the same time, furnish the system with viable access to users who do not yet operate automated systems, including facilities for working with nonusers outside the immediate organization, such as vendors and customers.

Ensure that the most important kind of information is also the most accessible, that provision for its storage is adequate, and that outdated information is easily eliminated.

Typical Strategies

One strategy gaining widespread support is the Three Ps: Prototype, Pilot, and Production. It entails a progression from a prototype to a pilot installation and then to production use throughout the entire organization. This strategy maintains an inverse ratio of risk to expenditure: high risk at the outset is balanced by low investment; only when risk declines toward zero and system use rises toward production status is investment in tools permitted to rise in proportion to benefits. Five typical strategies employed in office automation are based on the Three Ps.

The horizontal strategy seems to have the greatest support. It implements one functional tool at a time until that tool has been put into production across the organization. A slight overlapping occurs with tools put into production in various stages of development to ensure a steady flow of implementation.

Vertical strategy implements the full range of tools in one department or group at a time. This strategy works well only if the system is not complex, because implementing too many tools in a short period can overload the comprehension of both the office automation department and the users.

The matrix strategy introduces one or two tools horizontally throughout an organization, then expands them vertically in selected departments on an as-needed basis. Provided that the tools installed horizontally meet a more or less universal need, the strategy has merit.

A shotgun strategy implements random tools in random departments, with little or no overall coordination. It is an erratic approach usually associated with organizations lacking a solid plan. It can also evolve within organizations in which some other strategy, poorly carried out, is making little or no progress. In such cases as these, potential users introduce their own OA tools and supersede the approved, central strategy.

A chorus-line strategy resembles the shotgun strategy and therefore must be carefully controlled. It, too, involves implementation of selected tools in selected departments on an as-needed basis, but in this case they have all been approved as part of a master plan to ensure ultimate compatibility and integration. The rationale is to put required tools at first only where they will do the most good. Because other departments may also want such tools, but have too low a priority for immediate assistance, the OA department may occasionally need to engage in some diplomacy.

Selecting a User Community

Once a strategy has been adopted, the OA department must select a user community for the prototype project. The purpose of the prototype is to discover and assess weaknesses before tools are installed in quantity, and to make the necessary adjustments before putting the tools into production use. The role of the user community is to identify problems and overcome them as soon as possible.

The office automation department itself is an excellent choice for the user community. The development of a unique combination of tools requires extensive testing, for although individual segments may be valid, the composite system is an unknown quantity. The testing process educates members of the group and increases their usefulness: anyone advising others on office automation should have hands-on experience with the recommended equipment. The first level of tools for a prototype is sometimes determined by trying several competing products. Possibly the prototype will develop only after a series of such trials. One way to limit both financial outlay and operational risk is to lease equipment under a short-term agreement. Prototype hardware should be purchased only as a last resort.

During the prototype stage it is essential to find out how someone with no previous data processing experience will react to a computerized tool. That question can be answered by asking a few potential end users to try the tools for an hour or two with the understanding that research conditions prevail. It is also worthwhile to invite various people to see the tools under test conditions. Certainly members of the steering committee and upper management will be curious to see what is happening. Management throughout the organization is also sure to express curiosity. The department should encourage the comments of these visitors and should place great value on the comments of nontechnical personnel. Any difficulties the nontechnical users have with concepts and tools are likely to be typical of most potential end users in the organization.

Office automation planning and development should be conducted as openly as possible; any activity perceived as secretive will foster speculation, rumor, and resentment. A modest public relations effort can be valuable. Some firms distribute pamphlets about their office automation efforts; others regularly place articles in corporate newspapers; still others conduct internal presentations about the office automation efforts, its goals, and the current status of projects—sometimes demonstrating the tools being tested. All such activity not only removes much of the ultimate end users' apprehension about the tools; it also whets their appetite for future use.

The Pilot Installation

While the prototype is being tested, the process of selecting a pilot user community should begin. To permit detailed study and analysis, this pilot group should not number more than a hundred. If communications tools are involved, the users should operate at a minimum of two locations, or at least on two separate floors. The pilot community should not at the time be deeply involved with data processing, for familiarity with those tools will distort perceptions and evaluations of terminal use for other purposes. The group should have a progressive management. Above all, individuals at the sites should need the tools.

Middle management's support of both the pilot and production phases is essential; the installation of a pilot project is best accomplished on a voluntary basis. Managers are understandably unwilling to reorganize their operations to accommodate office automation. Therefore, the most successful way to attract a pilot user community is to offer its management a choice of well-proven, beneficial tools that can be put to work with little or no change in the work habits of the group. Before approaching a potential pilot user department, the office automation department should focus on the department's specific needs and on something of interest to the local management: short, intermediate, or long-term benefits; economic benefits with hard-dollar returns; or value-added benefits, such as faster turnaround or improved accuracy.

A first step in securing the cooperation of the management of the targeted department is to show the product in action in the office automation department. There under normal circumstances progressive planning is under way, with some tools under consideration, others in test, and some in internal use. Exhibiting future plans and tools should help to convince the management of the proposed pilot group that there is a coherent and practical plan. Presentation to potential pilot management should be highly polished and should focus on how the tools will benefit them, not on technical aspects. Most users will have relatively nontechnical backgrounds, and technical discussion should be avoided altogether.

Another approach used with success is for the office automation department to offer to fund the pilot for a specified time, with the understanding that after the prescribed period the user department can either purchase the installed equipment and pay for service or withdraw.

When a pilot group has agreed to participate, the OA department must obtain equipment, prepare procedures, and both plan and implement training. It must also collect preinstallation statistics relevant to the pilot tools, such as number and sizes of documents; number of retypings and subsequent proofreadings; number of telephone calls made, received, resulting in no answers or "not ins"; and travel time and costs associated with face-to-face meetings.

When the tools are installed, office automation planners should maintain close liaison with the pilot group. Initially, they should take up residence at the pilot sites to give immediate support and to smooth any early difficulties or misunderstandings. The OA department personnel should seek constant feedback from their users and listen to what is meant rather than to what is said. If there is a problem, is it with the hardware? the procedure? the training?

Postimplementation Measurement

Postimplementation measurement should take place only after users are thoroughly at ease with the new tools, and the need for practice and the appeal of novelty have leveled off. A terminal-based electronic mail system should not be measured until at least two to three months after implementation. Word processing may require a six-month period for users to gain full competence, although a preliminary measurement can take place after as little as two months. The OA department personnel, based on their own use of the tools, can judge when the pilot users appear to have reached a level of competence and are ready for measurement.

After postimplementation measurement, the OA department can evaluate the impact of the tools and assess the need for changes, taking into account any technological advances that have occurred since the original planning of the tools. If the required adjustments are significant, the OA department may need to repeat the entire process to this point.

The Production System

After an acceptable pilot effort has been assessed, the OA department should submit a report on the results and a recommendation for subsequent action to the steering committee and upper management. Normally, there will be a decision to proceed to production implementation on a progressive basis.

At this point the policy makers must decide whether to rent, lease, or purchase hardware and whether to license, purchase, or write software. Using commercially available software will permit very rapid development of the tools; modifying such software will take a bit longer; writing custom software will take considerable time and should involve another cycle of prototype and pilot system installations, but it may offer more advantages in the long run.

Careful implementation of the prototype and pilot stages takes time, but it will result in relatively trouble-free implementation of production, particularly in enlisting the cooperation of departmental management. Salesmen say there is no sale so easy to make as a reference sale: the prospect is simply put in touch with a previous user, who always seems to have greater credibility than the vendor (in this case the office automation department). This is a very successful tactic to use with the first proposed production user department beyond the pilot department. Once that next department has become a user, the process can be repeated. In later stages of implementation, peer pressure exerts considerable influence. In the case of a U.S. government installation where the automation process is voluntary, some managers at first refused to take part. A short time later the nonusers found themselves without benefit of information disseminated through the terminal-based electronic mail system, while managers who were using the system had consistently better, more up-to-date information. Feeling some embarrassment during joint meetings at their lack of timely information, nonusers decided to enroll.[27]

NOTES

1. "Paper Files Cost Business a Bundle," *Information and Records Management*, August 1977, p. 23.

2. Wilmer O. Maedke, Mary F. Robek, and Gerald F. Brown, *Information and Records Management* (Beverly Hills: Glenco Press, 1974), p. 30.

3. Raymond R. Panko, "The Outlook for Computer Mail," *Telecommunications Policy*, June 1977.

4. Maedke, Robek, and Brown, *Information and Records Management*, pp. 13, 30.

5. Thomas J. Anderson and William R. Trotter, *Word Processing* (New York: AMACOM, 1974), p. 4.

6. Neil MacNeil and Harold W. Metz, *The Hoover Report: 1953–1955* (New York: Macmillan, 1956), pp. 89–90, 93.

7. Maedke, Robek, and Brown, *Information and Records Management*, p. 71; MacNeil and Metz, *Hoover Report*, p. 84.

8. Maedke, Robek, and Brown, *Information and Records Management*, p. 194.

9. Gilbert J. Konkel and Phyllis J. Peck, *The Word Processing Explosion* (Stamford, Conn.: Office Publications, 1976), p. 5.

10. John Connell, "The Office of the Future," *Journal of Systems Management*, February 1979, p. 6.

11. "Indirect Labor Productivity Not Much Better," *National Productivity Report*, December 15, 1979, p. 1.

12. Ibid., p. 2.

13. "Advice for Uncle Sam," *Datamation*, January 1981, p. 67.

14. Debra L. Haskell, "White-collar Productivity: Management's No. 1 Concern," *Modern Office Procedures*, September 1979, p. 46.

15. D. L. Holtzman and V. Rosenberg, "Understanding Shadow Functions: The Key to System Design and Evaluation" (Xerox workshop on evaluating the impact of office automation, Palo Alto, May 1976); James H. Bair, "Communication in the Office of the Future: Where the Real Payoff May Be," Proceedings of the International Computer Communications Conference, Kyoto, Japan, September 1978. (International Council on Computer Communications and SRI International, 1978).

16. Bair, "Communication in the Office of the Future."

17. Dal Berry, "Breaking Down Productivity," *Information Systems News*, June 2, 1980, p. 41.

18. "Suddenly a New Shortage of Secretaries," *Business Week*, August 8, 1977, p. 84.

19. "The Big Hunt for Secretaries," *Dun's Review*, May 1978, p. 89; Walter W. Macauley, "Secretaries Are an Endangered Species," *The Office*, May 1978.

20. John B. Miner, *The Human Constraint: The Coming Shortage of Managerial Talent* (Washington, D.C.: Bureau of National Affairs, 1974), pp. 3–4.

21. "Changes in the Work Force: How to Meet Them," *National Productivity Report*, February 15, 1979, p. 2.

22. Charles Cumpston, "Word Processing," *Administrative Management*, October 1979, p. 102; Willoughby Ann Walshe, "Administrative Support: The Go Between Principals and WP," *Word Processing Systems*, March 1980, p. 13; Victor Lederer, "It's More Than Faster Correspondence," *Administrative Management*, April 1978, p. 60.

23. F. Stanley Phillips, "An Update on Administrative Support Centers," *AMA Forum*, February 1978, p. 29.

24. Paul J. Nickels, "Adapting People to the Automated Office," *Modern Office Procedures*, September 1979, pp. 50–52.

25. Ann Dooley, "CRTs Radiation Not Harmful: NIOSH," *Computerworld* 14 (June 2, 1980): 2; "Data Processing Uncovering Health Dangers in VDTs," *Business Week*, June 30, 1980.

26. James H. Carlisle and Caroline Watteeuw, *Management Communication and Control* (Pennsauken, N.J.: Auerbach Publishers, 1980).

27. John C. Gilbert, "Can Today's MIS Manager Make the Transition?" *Datamation*, March 1978, pp. 141ff.

We have decided to call the entire field of
control and communication theory,
whether in the machine or in the animal,
by the name of Cybernetics, which we
form from the Greek (for) steersman.

Norbert Wiener
Cybernetics

3

A
COMMUNICATIONS
PRIMER

Communications, the transfer of information, is the basis of office automation. Advances in communications technology, combined with
rapidly evolving computer technology, have made possible much of the
progress in the field. For those with limited exposure to the subject,
this chapter introduces the fundamental terminology, principles, and
apparatus of electronic communications technology. It can be used alternatively as a reference. Readers with sufficient understanding of the
subject should move on to Chapter 4.

Electronic communications consists of telecommunications and data
communications. *Telecommunications* is the use of telephone, tele-
typewriting, telegraph, radio, or television facilities to transmit information, either directly or via computer. Data communications is the
transfer of data or information between computer-related devices. Office automation integrates the two.

TABLE 3.1   Some common baud rates.

Baud rate	Typical usage
45.45	U.S. government and Bell System 60 wpm
75	IBM Model 1050 (optional)
110	Teletype Corporation Models 33, 35 Teletypes
134.5	IBM models 2740, 2741, 1050 standard speed
150	Standard computer terminal
300	Standard computer terminal
600	Standard computer terminal
600	IBM system 1030
1200	Standard computer terminal
2400	Standard computer terminal
4800	Standard computer terminal
9600	Standard computer terminal

Source: Adapted from John E. McNamara, Technical Aspects of Data Communication (Bedford, Mass.: Digital Press: 1978), pp. 344, 345.

Units of Measure

Hertz and bandwidth define the volume of signals that can be transmitted through communication channels.

Hertz measures the speed of electromagnetic waves, which oscillate up and down. From the top center of one curve to the same point on the next curve represents one cycle. One wave passing by in one second, or one cycle per second, equals one hertz (Hz). Kilohertz (kHz, thousands of hertz), megahertz (mHz, millions of hertz), and gigahertz (gHz, billions of hertz) are the units most frequently encountered in office automation.

Bandwidth, expressed in hertz, defines the minimum and maximum volume of cycles that can be sent through a transmission channel in one second, and thus how much information can be transmitted in one second. In the transmission of electronic signals, bandwidth is critical. A voice-grade telephone circuit in North America has a bandwidth of 300 to 3,400 hertz, which is a narrowband channel. A VHF broadcast television signal requires a transmission capability of up to 300 megahertz (300 million cycles per second), which is considered a broadband channel. Trying to transmit that television signal through a standard telephone circuit is equivalent to trying to push a grand piano through a transom: it cannot be done because the electronic path is too narrow.

Another common unit of measure is the baud rate, the number of signaling elements transmitted per second. For devices using digital signals, the baud rate is usually expressed in terms of an approximate equivalent, bits per second. Thus, to say that a device can commu-

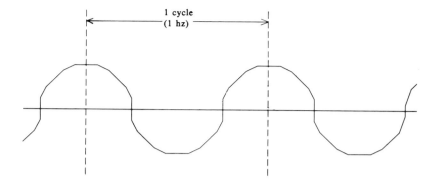

Electromagnetic waves. Computer-generated diagram produced by Tymshare, Inc., with AUGMENT software.

nicate at 300 baud usually means it can transmit or receive a maximum of 300 bits (roughly 30 characters) per second. (See Table 3.1.)

Analog and Digital Transmission

Communications signals are either analog or digital. An *analog* signal consists of continuous but variable electrical waves. *Digital* signals are discrete electronic units transmitted in extremely rapid succession, similar to ultrafast telegraphy. Telephone circuits and some specialized scientific equipment are analog; most computer and computer-related equipment is digital.

A device using digital signals can differentiate only between the presence ("on") and absence ("off") of electronic impulses; "on" equals the numeral one and "off" equals zero. A system using these two digits in various combinations to express any numeric quantity is known as binary arithmetic, and the two numerals are called *binary digits*. A *bit*, a contraction of binary digit, is the smallest element of data or information dealt with by digital apparatus. For convenience, bits are sometimes combined into larger units (usually groups of eight) called *bytes*.

Coding, the language of digital apparatus, represents alphanumeric characters, special characters (such as #, @, *), and equipment-control characters (such as carriage returns) in terms of bits. The common expressions "five-bit code," "five-unit code," or "five-level code" all indicate the number of bits required to represent each of the alphanumeric or other characters. The most widely used code is ASCII (American Standard Code for Information Interchange), a seven-bit code with 128 characters. The diversity of codes in use is one source of incompatibility, a principal handicap in office automation.

Protocols are technical customs or guidelines that govern the exchange of signal transmission and reception between equipment. Each protocol specifies the exact order in which signals will be transferred, what signal will indicate that the opposite device has completed its transfer, and so forth. Both *hardware* (equipment) and *software* (computer programs) are designed to handle specific protocols, and protocols are often named for the device with which they are associated. The IBM 3270-series terminals, for example, use 3270 protocol; teletypewriters (TTYs) use TTY protocol.

Only devices using the same protocols can communicate directly with one another. Devices using dissimilar protocols must transmit and receive through an intermediate interpretation device or program.

Modes of Transmission

The mode of transmission is the way in which the coded characters are assembled for the process of transmission and permits the receiving device to identify where the coding for each character begins and ends within the torrent of bits. The principal modes are asynchronous and synchronous. Bisynchronous is a variation of the synchronous mode used frequently in data communications.

In *asynchronous transmission* each character is transmitted separately. The character is preceded by a start bit, which tells the receiving device where the character coding begins, and is followed by a stop bit, which tells the receiving device where the character coding ends. This is the most common mode worldwide, especially for operation of interactive computer terminals and teletypewriters. Its principal advantage is accuracy. Its main drawback is slow transmission time, caused by the great number of start and stop bits.

In *synchronous transmission* characters are transmitted as groups, preceded and followed by control characters. The transmission and receiving intervals between each bit are precisely timed permitting grouping of bits into identifiable characters. Synchronous transmission occurs mainly between computers but is also used for human operation of buffered terminals, that is, terminals that can store information. Its chief advantage is speed, since fewer bits are needed to identify the beginning and end of the character coding. Its chief drawback is inaccuracy: when a receiver goes out of synchronization, losing track of where individual characters begin and end, correction of errors takes additional time.

One exotic mode, called *isochronous*, involves synchronous transmission of asynchronous format. The Comm-Stor II, a communications

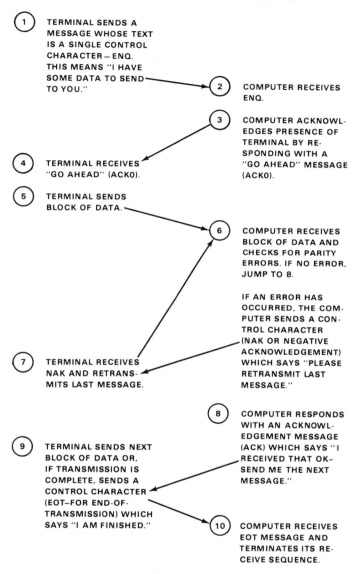

TERMINAL

COMPUTER

1. TERMINAL SENDS A MESSAGE WHOSE TEXT IS A SINGLE CONTROL CHARACTER – ENQ. THIS MEANS "I HAVE SOME DATA TO SEND TO YOU."

2. COMPUTER RECEIVES ENQ.

3. COMPUTER ACKNOWLEDGES PRESENCE OF TERMINAL BY RESPONDING WITH A "GO AHEAD" MESSAGE (ACK0).

4. TERMINAL RECEIVES "GO AHEAD" (ACK0).

5. TERMINAL SENDS BLOCK OF DATA.

6. COMPUTER RECEIVES BLOCK OF DATA AND CHECKS FOR PARITY ERRORS. IF NO ERROR, JUMP TO 8.

IF AN ERROR HAS OCCURRED, THE COMPUTER SENDS A CONTROL CHARACTER (NAK OR NEGATIVE ACKNOWLEDGEMENT) WHICH SAYS "PLEASE RETRANSMIT LAST MESSAGE."

7. TERMINAL RECEIVES NAK AND RETRANSMITS LAST MESSAGE.

8. COMPUTER RESPONDS WITH AN ACKNOWLEDGEMENT MESSAGE (ACK) WHICH SAYS "I RECEIVED THAT OK– SEND ME THE NEXT MESSAGE."

9. TERMINAL SENDS NEXT BLOCK OF DATA OR, IF TRANSMISSION IS COMPLETE, SENDS A CONTROL CHARACTER (EOT–FOR END-OF-TRANSMISSION) WHICH SAYS "I AM FINISHED."

10. COMPUTER RECEIVES EOT MESSAGE AND TERMINATES ITS RECEIVE SEQUENCE.

Data transmission using BISYNCH. From McNamara, *Technical Aspects of Data Communications.*

Modem (*left*) and acoustic coupler. Photos courtesy of Digital Equipment Corporation and Racal-Vadic.

storage unit offered by the American Telephone and Telegraph Company, uses this mode.

Acoustic Couplers and Modems

Digital transmission via an analog circuit requires the use of acoustic couplers or modems to resolve incompatibility.

An *acoustic coupler* is a small device with two openings that accommodate the earpiece and microphone ends of a telephone handset. The coupler converts outgoing electronic signals from the digital device into analog sounds and transmits them to the microphone of the telephone handset; they then are ready for transmission into the telephone line. At the earpiece end of the receiving telephone, the coupler reconverts the analog sounds into digital electronic signals and transmits them to the attached digital device. Acoustic couplers operate at speeds of either 300 or 1,200 baud. Most acoustic couplers link telephones to computer terminals and facsimile machines.

Acoustic couplers cost little to rent or purchase and permit use of any standard telephone for transmission and receiving. However, because the telephone is connected acoustically instead of being wired to the computer or facsimile device, loud background noises can sometimes penetrate the acoustical seal and cause transmission errors.

Modems (formed from "modulator" and "demodulator") directly convert signals from a computer or other digital device into analog form for transmission over analog links, and vice versa. They can operate at up to 9,600 baud over voice-grade telephone lines, but slower speeds are more common. Unlike acoustic couplers, modems are wired directly to both the digital devices and the transmission line, which limits portability but keeps room noises from interfering with transmission and reception. Some modems have only a dial-out capability; another

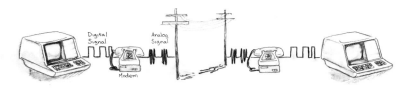

Conversion of digital to analog signals for transmission through standard telephone lines.

type, known as *auto-answer*, can be used for dialing out and can also automatically answer and connect calls to the local, parent device. Some modems of both types have telephones attached for normal call placing and receiving.

Wired Transmission

Transmission media are the electronic roadways along which signals are transferred. They range from telephone circuitry to laser beams and fiber optics (see Table 3.2).

One of the most common transmission methods is termed *hard-wired*, which means that two or more devices are connected directly by wiring. A *twisted pair* means that the connection uses two wires, sometimes in the same cord. A twisted pair handles narrowband transmissions. *Coaxial cable* also uses two wires, but one is a tube woven from very fine strands of metal; the second wire passes through the center along the length of the first. It is used for long-distance service by telephone companies and for both baseband and broadband transmission in local area networks (discussed below).

Direct distance dialing, or DDD, is the standard, voice-grade telephone service that provides direct dialing to other telephones without operator intervention. Such circuits accommodate narrowband analog transmission between 300 and 3,400 hertz, or a maximum of 10,000 bits per second. A user can obtain similar circuits with the same bandwidth on a dedicated basis but only for access between the devices to which the circuit is connected, such as between a terminal in one city and a computer in another. They are discussed further in Chapter 13. Telephone companies also provide broadband analog and digital circuits to accommodate special needs. Digital circuits for data transmission eliminate the need for acoustic couplers or modems.

Optical Fiber Transmission

Optical fiber systems consist of a transmitter, the glass fiber filaments along which data travel as high-speed pulses of light, and a receiver.

TABLE 3.2 Transmission media: tools, capabilities, applications, cost, and security.

Medium	Application	Narrowband	Broadband	Range	Cost	Security	Other factors
Hard-wiring	Telephones and narrowband local networks	X		Local	Low	Low	Simplicity
Coaxial cable	Long-distance telephone calls and networking		X	Unlimited with repeaters	Local: low Long distance: high	Moderate	Compactness and versatility
Microwave	Local area and long-distance networks		X	25 miles (more with relay stations)	Moderate	Moderate	Line-of-sight; assigned channel
Infrared	Local networks	X		Several hundred feet	Low to moderate	Moderate	Line-of-sight; affected by weather
Laser	Local and area networks		X	3–15 miles	Low to moderate	High	Line-of-sight
Satellite	Video Telephones High-speed fax Teletypewriter		X	7000–8000 terrestrial miles	High to very high	High with encoder	Line-of-sight; "echo"; affected by weather
Radio: Class A	Area voice communication (commercial)	X		10 miles	Low	Low	License; no data trans.; assigned channels
Class D	Area voice communication (citizens band)	X		10 miles	Low	None	License; no data trans.; 40 unassigned channels

Lighter, thinner, and stronger than copper wire, optical fibers carry a great deal more data. Further, they are impervious to electromagnetic interference and are highly secure: being optical in nature, they do not radiate electronic signals. Though their use in the United States has been limited mainly to the military, they are a component of some Japanese and European telephone installations and should have a growing use in telecommunications both here and abroad.

Microwave Transmission

Microwave transmission has become widely used for broadband communications and telephone service. Private microwave service is especially useful for organizations that need to link a number of locations within a limited area. Banks, for instance, often use it to connect suburban branch offices with city headquarters. Although private microwave service can provide dedicated communication at moderate cost, there are limitations to its use. First, in the United States microwave channels are assigned by the Federal Communications Commission, and in some cities few or no channels remain open. Second, unlike telephone wires and commercial radio signals, microwave transmission is *line-of-sight*; the signals, which pass through the atmosphere, must originate from a dish antenna, travel in a straight line free of material obstacles such as topographical features or tall buildings, and be received by another dish antenna. Third, the transmission range is limited to about 25 miles, after which the microwaves must be relayed (received, amplified, and retransmitted by another antenna).

Infrared Transmission

Infrared transmission is optical in nature, carried by beams of light invisible to the naked eye. It provides a compact and inexpensive means of line-of-sight, narrowband transmission among and between buildings within the same general area, for it is limited to distances of a few hundred feet. Though unaffected by most artificial light and weather conditions, very heavy snow or fog degrades its quality. Infrared is not subject to federal, state, or local licensing, since it operates outside the broadcast portion of the radio spectrum. It is moderately secure.

Laser Transmission

Communications *lasers* are generally very low powered and narrowly focused beams of light, invisible to the naked eye, that rely on sensitive receiving equipment. The equipment is marketed in both narrowband and broadband versions. The usual line-of-sight transmission range of 15 miles can be greater or less depending on the percentage of operating time acceptable to the user. Repeater (relay) stations can increase the total transmission distance. No licensing is required for laser communications which provide a high degree of inherent security.

Radio Transmission

Within the United States, the Federal Communications Commission has allocated certain radio frequencies for use by private businesses for direct voice communications. Word codes may be employed, but data transmission (or *telemetry* in radio parlance) is prohibited. Private citizens and business users may be licensed to operate either a Class A or Class D radio station, with a mobile or fixed location. The range of both classes is about 10 miles.

Users of Class A stations, such as taxicabs and delivery vehicles, operate only on a single, assigned frequency. Users of Class D stations, generally known as Citizens Band (CB) radio, operate on any of the 40 designated frequencies (channels) on a shared basis.

A mobile CB radio can be equipped with a special keypad and an unattended fixed (stationary) CB equipped with a matching device to make it possible for the user to dial into a telephone connected to the stationary radio. Once the circuit is completed, the person using the mobile CB radio can converse with the person answering the telephone call as if both were using a telephone. Owing to the special signaling requirements, the typical range between the mobile and base radio equipment is about three miles.

Security of such communications links is almost nonexistent. Even so, the equipment has many advantages and is widely used by taxi, repair, courier, and delivery services.

Satellite Transmission

A *satellite* is a form of relay station: it receives a signal from one earth station, amplifies it, and retransmits it to another earth station. Most communications satellites have multiple, independent reception and transmission devices known as *transponders*. In a commercial communications satellite, a single transponder is usually capable of handling a full-color, commercial television transmission, complete with audio. Transponders for data transmission may be even larger. Some firms that market satellite communications service own a satellite. Others lease a portion of a satellite and provide transmission facilities in smaller units to ultimate users. Some end users transmit only voice commu-

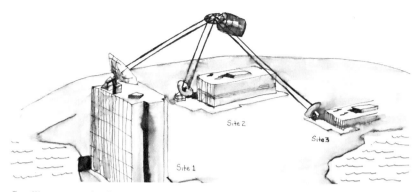

Satellite communications system connecting (1) company headquarters, (2) a manufacturing facility, and (3) a distribution center. Adapted from American Satellite Corporation.

nications during the working day and split their leased bandwidth (up to a full transponder) into many narrowband channels for that purpose. After office hours, these narrowband channels are electronically reorganized into fewer channels of wider bandwidth for high-speed data communications.

Several factors limit the use of satellite communications. Most communication satellites are placed in geosynchronous orbit above the equator, which means that their orbital speed is synchronized to keep them over the same point on the earth at all times. A satellite, then, is also a line-of-sight means of transmission. A second consideration is a signal delay caused by the extreme length of the transmission path between sender and receiver. This can cause an echo that is annoying to some individuals using voice communications, though the condition can be negated with electronic echo cancelers and suppressors. Other considerations are the weather sensitivity of high frequency transmission and electronic interference generally. Among the factors a prospective user must weigh is the relative importance of 20 to 40 hours of random reception difficulty per year.

Though some satellites can concentrate transmission signals to some degree, the area covered by those signals is still quite large, and anyone with the proper equipment can listen in. Security is usually provided by the user through coding and decoding equipment.

Directional Capability

All transmission links function in one of three ways:

- *Simplex:* transmission in one direction only. Wire service teletypewriters and stock tickers are examples.

- *Half duplex:* alternate transmission in both directions.
- *Full duplex:* simultaneous transmission in both directions.

Circuit Flexibility

User needs seldom tax the full capacity of a transmission system, resulting in inefficient utilization. On the other hand, a user sometimes needs limited amounts of both narrowband transmission and lower-range broadband for high-speed data transmission. Several devices subdivide wideband circuits into multiple narrowbands and link other circuits electronically to resemble wideband circuits.

Multiplexers, nicknamed "muxes," permit a single transmission link to perform as if it were several separate links. A *frequency-division multiplexer* (FDM) divides the actual bandwidth into smaller units of frequency and assigns each to a specific device. Each device sharing the circuit communicates on its individually assigned frequency as if it had its own dedicated circuit. Frequency-division multiplexing works best with low-speed devices. A *time-division multiplexer* (TDM) apportions very small segments of time in the bandwidth to each device, then polls each in sequence and permits it to communicate. The polling occurs so quickly that each device seems to have a separate circuit.

Concentrators operate synchronously and offer the functions of a multiplexer but can also store groups of characters, convert formats, check for errors, and perform other functions.

A *statistical multiplexer* is a hybrid of an FDM, TDM, and concentrator. Although a terminal or computer is intermittently inactive during interactive transmission, a TDM continues to offer it time regardless of need. An FDM likewise apportions a small portion of the bandwidth to each terminal regardless of need. But a statistical multiplexer will bypass a momentarily inactive terminal and give the bandwidth to an active one. If the volume of traffic from all the devices exceeds the capacity of the circuit, the statistical multiplexer will store the traffic until circuit time is available.

Some devices can combine two or more channels into a wider one by fragmenting data transmissions into segments of equal size and sending alternate segments down alternate physical links, then at the receiving end collate the signals before transferring them to the ultimate receiving device. A *biplexer*, for example, can link two 9.6-kilobaud circuits so that the devices communicating through the biplexer will view the circuit as 19.2 kilobauds in bandwidth.

Networks

Communications networks serve data transmission, voice transmission, or both. Communications common carriers provide transmission facilities and sometimes products and services. The telephone companies are the largest carriers, but there are others who own transmission networks or purchase bulk service for resale in smaller segments to the ultimate users. The primary service of these other carriers is data transmission, with voice a distant second.

If "intelligence" is added to a communications network, usually in the form of a computer for transmission switching or processing to provide compatibility between devices, the network becomes a *value-added network* (VAN).

To transmit between two points in a network of numerous transmission links requires selection of a combination of links to handle the job. Switched networks are those in which a specific route is temporarily established for the duration of each individual transmission. A telephone call from Raleigh, North Carolina, to Chicago may pass through intermediate switching centers at Lexington, Kentucky, and Columbus, Ohio, and these transmission links remain dedicated to that use throughout the call. Such circuits provide direct connection and are interactive, permitting two-way communication.

In *message-switching networks*, the transmission is intercepted at a switching point and stored in a computer. In some systems, the message is retransmitted to the next switching point as soon as a link is available; in others, the message remains stored until the intended recipient establishes connection with the computer.

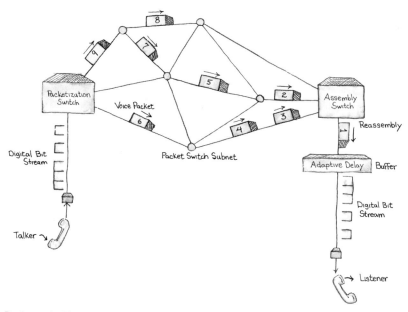

Packet-switching network.

Packet-switching networks, like statistical multiplexers, use all available transmission time by filling in the gaps between spurts of data or spoken words with parts of other transmissions. The computer at the switching center breaks up data it receives into groups of characters, or packets. To each packet are added a network address, a transmission identification, and an incremental sequence number. Each computerized switching center connects to at least two similar centers. Once a packet is assembled, the computer system searches for the shortest available network path to the destination and inserts the packet in the first gap on that path. Likewise, each successive packet takes any path that offers the first available gap, rather than following the same routing. At the final computer switchpoint, the system groups incoming packets according to identification, arranges them according to packet sequence number, and strips away all characters added by the packet-switching process. The data then move on to the ultimate recipient, usually a user's computer or terminal. The process is carried out with transparent speed. With digitized telephone service, it is possible to apply packet-switching to voice communications.

Networks can be configured in several ways. *Hub* or *Star networks*, the simplest to develop, pass all communications through a single switch or *node*. *Multidrop networks* connect all devices to a single, meandering set of links. These are inexpensive, full-time networks, but loss of service at any point will immediately deny access to those farther along the network. *Loop* or *ring networks* form an endless loop; they also are relatively inexpensive, and can provide an alternate route in case of loss of service at a given point. *Mesh networks* permit any two devices within the network to communicate directly. This type of configuration is very dependable, since it provides multiple routes into and out of each location.

Local Area Networks

A company that wishes to install its own local-area network (which seldom extend beyond the immediate premises) usually chooses between a private branch telephone exchange, such as those manufactured by Rolm, Northern Telecom, and Datapoint, and a baseband coaxial cable network, such as Ethernet by Xerox, Net/One by Ungermann-Bass, or Z-net by Zilog.

Private telephone-based systems variously described as PBXs (private branch exchanges), PABXs (private automated branch exchanges), EPABXs (electronic private automatic branch exchanges), or CBXs (computerized branch exchanges) are narrowband and either analog or digital in nature. They use twisted-pair telephone circuits as

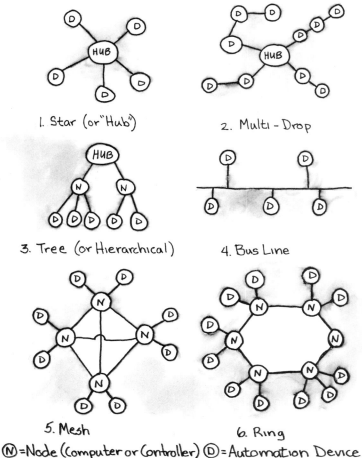

1. Star (or "Hub")

2. Multi-Drop

3. Tree (or Hierarchical)

4. Bus Line

5. Mesh

6. Ring

Ⓝ = Node (Computer or Controller) Ⓓ = Automation Device

Typical network configurations.

the transmission medium and are dependent on a single, central control unit.

In the baseband network, a single-channel coaxial cable links devices in a local digital network capable of transmission speeds up to 10 megabits (or about 500 pages) per second. Each device contains its own logic control or control is provided in an inexpensive ($400 and up) interface. Since the cable is passive, if one device fails, the others are unaffected and the network continues to operate.

Multichannel broadband coaxial cable networks such as DAX (Data Exchange) by Amdax, Advanced Local Area Network by Interactive Systems/3M, and Localnet by Network Resources Corporation, subdivide the total bandwidth into multiple subnetworks, each operating at specified frequencies. Only devices interfaced at similar frequencies

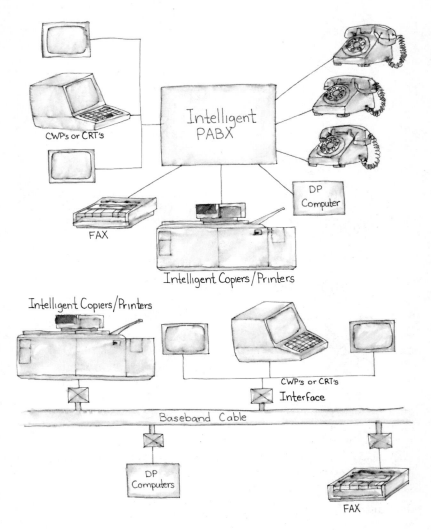

Types of local-area networks. Adapted, with permission, from International Resource Development, Inc.

can communicate with one another. The introduction of time-division modems will permit all devices on such networks to communicate in a manner similar to baseband networks. Broadband networks employ logical control devices at multiple points along the cable. The price of such control units must be averaged among the connected devices, along with their associated modems, making them less cost effective when small numbers of devices are networked.

Voice Apparatus

Telephone recorders or answering machines answer incoming calls when a person is absent or does not wish to be disturbed. Many types and several optional features are available. Some machines simply play back a recorded announcement and may be used for status reports, weather forecasts, and the like. Others permit the caller to leave a message. Another type asks a question, then records the caller's response, and repeats the process with subsequent questions. This recorder is useful for banking services, telephone orders and order inquiries, and reports from traveling sales representatives. Some telephone recorders can also be used for recording dictation. A useful option is remote access; a control unit smaller than a cigarette package permits the user to dial into the unit from distant locations, listen to messages, and dictate into the unit. The user holds the control unit near the telephone mouthpiece and by pressing buttons creates tones that control the recorder.

Call diverters have the same function as call forwarding in some private telephone systems. If a person is going to be temporarily at a location other than his office and still wants to receive calls coming to his office phone, he dials the temporary number into the memory unit of the diverter. When a call is received at the original location, the diverter automatically dials the temporary number and completes the connection. The caller is unaware of the transfer. A diverter requires two telephone lines: one for the incoming call and one for the outgoing one.

Automatic dialers are machines with memory devices that can record and then dial from 10 to 400 telephone numbers at the push of a button. Smaller units have a separate button beside each name on an index card, and when the button opposite a name is pressed, dial that number automatically. Larger units use other indexing techniques and a single "dial" button. Some units have an automatic redialing feature that will periodically try the number until the call goes through.

Conference calls among three or more telephone lines are made possible by two types of *bridge* connections. A dial-out bridge is most common; it is the type used by telephone company conference operators and is also available for installation on private telephone systems. Such bridges require that one person, usually the operator, place calls from one location to each of the participants.

A "meet me" or "dial in" bridge requires that a call be placed to the bridge from each telephone involved in the conference. The nickname comes from users who began to set up conference calls by saying "meet me at 10 o'clock." The use of an operator is optional with such bridges. Security is handled either by an operator, who can clear each incoming caller by means of a code word, or by limiting the distribution of the telephone number of the bridge. Another advantage is that each participant places and is separately billed for his own call. Bridging service can be rented from private vendors.

Other automated telephone devices used by the business community are hunt groups and keypads. *Hunt groups*, or rotary hunts, permit incoming calls to a given telephone number to be connected to the first open line among a group of telephones. Hunt groups are used in both voice and data communications.

Telephonic keypads, sets of 12 pushbuttons as on the Touch-Tone telephones, are also available as separate units from many vendors. Their most common use is to control a remotely accessed dictation system, but they can also be used to perform input and inquiries to a computer.

A device called Soft-Touch, offered by Buscom Systems, is an inexpensive replacement for the mouthpiece on certain rotary-dial telephone handsets which effectively converts them to keypad telephones. Ten digits and two control characters are positioned on the replacement mouthpiece, which still permits voice transmission. Use of such devices may be prohibited on handsets owned by telephone companies, and the local circuit must be capable of Touch-Tone operation. The primary office automation application is for remote data entry and computer control from temporary, remote locales.

Outside North America

In many countries telephone service is provided by nationalized communications systems operated by government agencies. Cumbersome communications bureaucracies can cause inconceivable delays in routine procedures. One communications planner advises American companies conducting business in some countries to lease a dedicated circuit on a continuous basis, even for occasional use, to avoid installation delays. Known as International Record Carriers, the communications companies that provide international services operate in a narrow and legally complex field. Consequently, some governmental communications agencies will deal only with them and not with end users. It is frequently better to retain services from such firms.

Communications Consultants

All but the simplest excursions into communications technology should be left to experts. Even large firms that have their own telecommunications and data communications departments seek outside assistance on specialized matters.

Vendors such as telephone companies, equipment manufacturing and sales organizations, and service vendors provide outside consulting, usually at no charge. The vendor's bias, of course, requires evaluation. Private business consultants or management consulting firms are other sources of assistance. Some consulting firms specialize in communications or particular aspects, such as data communications. Some large consulting firms offer communications consulting as one of many services.

Suit the action to the word; the word to
the action.

William Shakespeare
Hamlet

WORD
MANAGEMENT

Word management is to text what data processing is to numbers. Word
management is the electronic and/or mechanical capture, storage, manipulation, output, and ultimate disposition of text and sometimes of
graphic images. It can involve any combination of mechanical, electronic, micrographic, photographic, xerographic, electrostatic, communications, or other devices. Word management systems range from
simple to complex and small to large, with hardware and function
sometimes overlapping. Today, the primary end product is hard-copy
output (paper); the secondary end product is soft-copy output (display
on a CRT terminal resembling a television screen). The emphasis on
end products, however, is rapidly reversing.

Systems and Types

Today the most versatile and important tool for handling text is the
word processor. There are about a hundred brands of word processors
on the world market, offering dozens of features, functions, and options. Although they differ in detail, nearly all word processing systems
have a keyboard, a display unit, a computer, and one or more remov-

51

Electronic typewriters: *left*, with single-line display, daisy printing element, internal storage; *right*, with attributes of a word processor—large screen, removable storage, separate printer (not shown). Photos courtesy of Olivetti Corporation and Lanier Business Products.

able storage devices such as a disk or tape unit. These components permit the operator to create, modify, duplicate, file and refile, delete, and store text. Most word processing systems also include a printer for hard-copy output.

In terms of classification, word management devices with a single terminal are called standalone systems because they are self-contained; those with communications capabilities are sometimes referred to as intelligent terminals. Systems with multiple terminals attached to a single central processor are called shared-logic systems. The simplest word processors can begin their working lives as electronic typewriters and later be converted to word processors by the addition of removable storage media and sometimes a communications capacity. Standalone systems provided with CRT or video screens for electronic display of text, called display or soft-copy terminals, are more versatile; shared-logic systems are the most sophisticated. Many shared-logic systems are nothing more than timeshared data processing systems that run word processing as one of many concurrent jobs.

The simplest type of word management system is the repetitive mechanical typewriter, which plays out a form letter halting at designated points within the text to permit the operator to insert variable information such as names and addresses. Editing must be concurrent with original keystroke capture. Such devices are called blind terminals because they have no electronic display.

Electronic typewriters with small internal memories have a handful of manipulative functions, but those lacking removable storage media have limited applications. They are convenient for internal storage of

Microprocessor chips that fit on a finger tip provide internal storage and text editing functions for this IBM electronic typewriter. Photo courtesy of IBM Office Products Division.

brief clusters of text (such as product descriptions, frequently used names and addresses, and forms) and for making corrections during typing.

Text editing systems, the forebears of word processors, operate as jobs on timesharing computers. They use conventional data processing terminals and tend to be programmed to EDP-oriented commands. Most of them use line-editing techniques of simple design and data processing printers as output devices.

What are generically known as word processors are systems with removable storage devices such as magnetic tape or the popular floppy diskettes. For most organizations word processors are the conventional entry point to office automation because they are versatile turnkey devices whose use and cost are relatively simple to justify.

Word processors are designed to simplify the production of documents by eliminating repetitive typing and providing extensive text editing capabilities. Projects requiring days of manual typing can be initiated by a single operator in minutes, and the system can perform the balance of the task without further intervention. Because word processors provide for long-term storage of text after initial keying, they are most useful in the production of:

- Documents that are heavily revised
- Documents that are reissued after initial distribution
- Documents that contain forms or frequently used sections of text
- Lengthy documents of all kinds, for these usually require extensive editing.

Enormous production gains of 200 and 300 percent are possible when operators perform minimal keying in the revision of previously stored material.

Word processors capable of handling documents of more than 125 pages (the capacity of the floppy diskette) are sometimes called document processors. Most document processors are shared-logic systems and use large, hard-disk storage devices that permit on-line access to thousands of pages. Functionally, there is no difference between word and document processors. For purposes of discussion, the term "word processors" will include document processors. Photowordprocessors, hybrids that combine word processing and phototypesetting in a single unit, belong to a separate class.

The highest level of capability occurs in the multifunction text-management system that permits newspaper reporters to write their stories via display terminals. The system also permits editors to review and revise text. A common subsystem is used in classified advertising. When an ad is called in, the ad taker enters the billing information and the system runs an automatic credit check on the caller while the ad taker keys in the advertising text. The system computes the cost of the ad according to number of words, size of type specified, and the number of days it is to appear. Later it merges new ads with continuing ones while deleting those that have expired. Page makeup is performed under system control. All text and graphic sources can be manipulated from consoles containing video display terminals and high-resolution graphics screens. The graphic tube displays each alteration as it occurs. In minutes the image of the page is electronically displayed for final examination. With a single command, the system sends the image electronically to the platemaking operation. Similar systems are used by publishing houses.

Closely related to the systems used by newspapers and some publishing houses, page composition systems are advanced devices that permit the total composition of individual pages, up to and including text manipulation, electronic cropping, and placement of graphics and halftones within text. Their output requires no further preparation.

Components

CRT screen options include single- and multiple-line, partial-page, full-page, and twin-page displays; white characters on a black background, black characters on a white background, yellow characters on a green background, and two-tone amber. Some systems can display, as well as print, multiple sizes of characters, justified and proportionally spaced text. Some systems scroll text horizontally (to accommodate display of extra long lines) as well as vertically; some depict a full page in miniature so the operator can examine the overall composition.

Most word processors store material on magnetic media coated with metal oxide; others use paper. The most common magnetic devices are

A floppy diskette inserted in a disk drive.

the floppy diskette (a thin 8-inch platter that rotates within a paper envelope) and the minidiskette (5-1/4 inches in diameter). Other magnetic media include cards, tape cassettes, tape cartridges, and large hard disks like those used in data processing. The paper options include perforated paper tape and sheets of paper that can be optically scanned into a system. Table 4.1 lists the capacities of the various magnetic storage media.

Most word processors are connected to printers, which may be desktop or freestanding units. To print out a document or re-create one from an existing word processor file is nearly effortless. The operator selects a document from an electronic index and keys a print order into the system. Printers vary from model to model in speed of output and formation of characters; some produce two pages per second, but most are slower. Although word processors are not intended to be used as printing presses, they do make it possible for multiple addressees to get original documents instead of carbon copies.

Internal Operating Instructions and Capabilities

Operating systems, the internal instructions that control the functions of word processors, reside in hardware, firmware, or software.

Hardware operating systems are built in and offer few functions, but operators can quickly learn to operate them. Their drawback is that they can never be upgraded.

Firmware operating systems are ROMs (read-only memories) and PROMs (programmable read-only memories). Their somewhat limited repertoires can be upgraded by replacements from the manufacturer or dealer.

TABLE 4.1 Capacities of removable magnetic storage media.

Medium	Character capacity	Equivalent pages 8.5 × 11 in.
Magnetic card	5,000-10,000	1
Tape cassette	125,000-300,000	25-60
Tape cartridge	Varies with manufacturer	Varies
Minidiskette (5 in.)	60,000-80,000	15
Microdiskette	437,000	200-220
Diskette (8 in.; single sided; single density)	250,000	100-125
Diskette (8 in. double density)	500,000	225-250
Diskette (8 in. double density and double sided)	1,000,000	475-500
Hard disks	Varies with manufacturer (2,000,000- 50,000,000 +)	1,000-25,000

Figures stated are for single units; many word processors are able to support multiple units.

Software operating systems are programs stored on magnetic media, usually diskettes, and upgrading involves nothing more than purchasing new software. Because the hardware in such systems is usually a minicomputer in disguise, it is also possible to substitute data processing software for the word processing system. Some companies produce word processing operating system software with limited mathematical capabilities.

Many word processors with software operating systems can serve limited or extensive data processing needs, according to their configurations. Data processing software is available from many vendors and software houses. Two utilities commonly available, math utilities and sort utilities, allow simplifed computations and the sorting of small files, such as the alphabetizing of names. In addition, custom software can be written for specialized applications on many systems. With smaller, standalone word processors, the software governing word processing is replaced by data processing software.

All word processing systems can operate in foreground; that is, the unit controls are occupied with the work at hand. Foreground output, such as communications or printing, can waste operator time and sys-

Producing a Monthly Sales Report The system supervisor in a pharmaceutical wholesale company loads hybrid math/word processing software to generate the monthly sales reports for each salesman. Because the software operates unattended, the operator moves on to other tasks. The monthly sales results in each of four product categories have been communicated to the word processing center and recorded on a hard-disk file. The software system generates and prints individually addressed monthly sales letters, computing and entering at the appropriate places four separate commission subtotals by product line, product-line dollar amounts, total sales dollars, and total commissions. All computations are concurrent with the merging and printing process.

Updating a Simple Periodic Report The order processing department of a manufacturing firm distributes a weekly report consisting of a dated cover memo and a single attached chart of sales figures. When a new version is required, a word processing operator creates a new document file on the word processor system and calls an electronic file copy of a blank form from magnetic storage to the display screen. The operator presses a single key that moves the system directly to the location of the date on the first page and keys in the date. Page 1, the cover memo, is complete, for the text and distribution listing remain the same. The operator similarly alters the date on page 2. Pressing the key once more, the operator arrives at the first blank into which a dollar figure must be entered and keys in the amount. The amount is automatically aligned according to its decimal point. All preexisting vertical and horizontal rulings, which form the boxes, remain in place throughout the entry of amounts. The operator repeats the process of locating and entering all the new figures, and then, with two commands, electronically files the document and starts output printing on a letter-quality printer.

tem capabilities. Background operations are initiated by the operator but proceed to completion without further intervention; they do not occupy the controls and permit use of the keyboard and screen for other, concurrent purposes. Printing and sometimes communications are background operations.

The capabilities of word processors far exceed those of ordinary typewriters. Features like list processing, discussed below, enable knowledge workers to perform tasks that were impossible with traditional office equipment. Most word processors incorporate communications capabilities: users can dial from the word processor, using telephone lines or a private network, into "host" computers. Users can then transfer documents between the word processor and data processing or electronic messaging systems, or send documents to in-house or external typesetting systems or to microfilm conversion systems for efficient storage of large volumes of information.

Used effectively, word processors greatly reduce repetitiousness in information processing tasks. They optimize use of personnel by providing faster keyboarding and easier formatting and reformatting of complex layouts and by avoiding or reducing rekeying of portions of rough drafts into final documents. They also eliminate the need to print material until every portion is correct.

Applications

Nearly every document that can be produced on a typewriter can also be produced on a word processing system. However, so long as such systems are not universally available in offices, it is worthwhile to distinguish applications that can be typewritten as or more efficiently.

- One-time interoffice memos, letters, or other documents less than one page long and requiring no more than one revision
- Labels or envelopes for infrequently used addresses
- Charts or statistical documents requiring no revision
- Filling in infrequently used or single copies of preprinted forms

Documents that require more than one revision, whatever their length, should be considered word processing applications. These documents include:

- General documents (five pages or less)
    Letters and memos
    Reports
    Survey questionnaires
    Sales and legal documents
- Lengthy documents (more than five pages)
    Manuals
    Proposals
    Scientific documents
    Newsletters
    Reports
    Sales and legal documents
- Statistical documents
    Tables and charts
    Wide documents (80 + characters)
- List processing
    Standardized form letters and memos
    Tables and charts

Directories
Envelopes and labels
Distribution and mailing lists
Price lists
Mail and message logs
Forms
Engineering reports
- Libraries of often-used material ("boilerplate") and abbreviations
- Multicolumn text
  Continuous column text
  Side-by-side text
- Forms (preprinted or typed on system)
  Government reports
  Inventory lists
  Purchase orders
  Bills of materials
  Invoices.

Generally, documents of five pages or less form the majority of word processing applications. For correspondence that requires quality printing, the operator can use a letter-quality printer, a carbon ribbon, and a justified right margin. Correspondence of a repetitive nature is best generated through a list processing capability. Reports often go through several revision cycles and may require review by several people. Similarly, questionnaires usually require several stages of review, testing, and revision. Finally, most sales and legal documents consist largely of stock phrases or paragraphs reused many times, with a significantly smaller portion of text pertaining to individual customers or specific situations. Such documents may be kept in so-called library or boilerplate files for retrieval and customizing.

In the preparation of documents of five or more pages, retyping revisions is not cost effective. Technical and nontechnical manuals, for instance, usually require constant revision; proposals often pass through several reviews and revisions before final acceptance. Scientific documents that contain complex formulas requiring equations and special symbols are easy to construct with the special mathematics function and half-line spacing ruler available on many word processors. Word processing is particularly well suited to publication of a newsletter, which usually incorporates contributions from many sources and requires constant updating.

Statistical documents, with their special formatting requirements, are among the most difficult to create and edit. Frequent modifications are easy with a word processor; because it stores tab settings, entry locations, and other formatting specifications in its memory, it positions decimal points, justifies columns, and generally monitors all other en-

Word processing systems. Photos courtesy of (*top row, across both pages*) Xerox Corporation, IBM Corporation, NBI Inc., A.B. Dick Company; (*center row*) CPT Corporation, AM Jacquard; (*bottom row*) Philips Information Systems, Digital Equipment Corporation, Wang Laboratories.

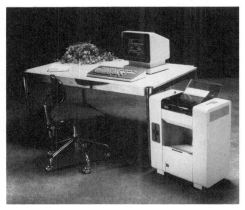

tries. With a few simple changes the system automatically reformats an entire chart or table, eliminating rekeying. With an appropriate printer, a word processor can produce documents of many widths.

List processing, a software package that can be added to a word processor, permits the generation of several different documents from a single base of information. It allows the user to specify the format and contents of a complete list or portions of a list. The word processing system merges the desired information into a single document and either prints out the result or stores it on a diskette for later editing and printing. List processing software currently available does not permit word processors to perform any other functions while it is operating. Form letters and memos are the most common list processing application. The list processing capability permits maintenance of form letters and lists separately, so that either may be periodically updated without extensive rekeying. A list used to produce letters and memos can also serve in the production of tables and charts; variety in formatting is unlimited.

Word processors permit rapid creation of such documents as proposals, legal documents, and sales contracts by storing frequently used words, phrases, and paragraphs in libraries and abbreviations files. An abbreviations file contains such material as company addresses, signature blocks, memo headings, and words that are difficult to spell. A library file contains so-called boilerplate material: often used paragraphs, sections of legal contracts or insurance policies, and formats for list processing records.

Publication formats that require multicolumn text are relatively easy to accommodate on a word processor; printing must occur on letter-

---

Directing a Letter to Selected Addresses A firm with several hundred customers learns of a change in shipping rates applicable to a specific class of products trucked into Ohio and Indiana. Letters are to be sent to those customers only. The word processing operator creates a single copy of the letter and stores it in the system. Calling up the selective merging function, the operator specifies the selection of names and addresses of only those customers who have previously purchased the particular product and who are also located in either Ohio or Indiana. The selective merging process automatically searches the customer information file for customers meeting both criteria. Finding a match, the system merges the name, address, and any personalized salutations that may appear in the file with the stored form letter, to be sent as output to the printer. The names and addresses of all other customers are ignored. Because the merging occurs without further intervention, the operator can perform other tasks during the process.

Creating a Format with Separate Fields for a List Sorting Procedure

In a customer list, creation of separate fields for city, state, zip code, company category, and region permits use of any one of these factors as the essential element in a "sort" routine.

Blank format

<name>
<address>
<city>
<state>
<zip>
<company category>
<region>
<>

<name>
<address>
<city>
<state>
<zip>
<company category>
<region>
<>

<name>
<address>
<city>
<state>
<zip>
<company category>
<region>
<>

<name>
<address>
<city>
<state>
<zip>
<company category>
<region>
<>

<name>
<address>
<city>
<state>
<zip>
<company category>
<region>
<>

Completed record

<name>Bailey and Younger
<address>3322 Montgomery Street
<city>San Francisco,
<state>CA
<zip>93001
<company category>legal
<region>Far West
<>

<name>Evan Manufacturing
<address>3380 Paramus Road
<city>Paramus,
<state>NJ
<zip>07410
<company category>manufacturing
<region>Middle Atlantic
<>

<name>Holmes and Moss
<address>3322 Maple Street
<city>Clifton,
<state>NJ
<zip>07734
<company category>manufacturing
<region>Middle Atlantic
<>

<name>Teen Knits Co.
<address>1450 Broadway
<city>New York,
<state>NY
<zip>10002
<company category>garment
<region>New York
<>

<name>Wordsworth Corp.
<address>134 Lake Drive
<city>Boston,
<state>MA
<zip>02134
<company category>manufacturing
<region>New England
<>

quality printers equipped with special pin-feed tractors (sprocket-type paper feeders). The user specifies the number of columns and the spacing between them, then types the text into the system as one continuous column. At the end of one column, the printer runs the paper back to the top of the page and prints the next column.

A user can easily create a blank form on a word processor and store it on a diskette for reuse. An interface with a phototypesetting system will produce high-quality forms in any typeface.

Because of their sophisticated storage and retrieval capabilities, word processors are well suited to administrative applications. They are useful for maintaining lists or records shared by several users in an of-

---

Merging Document Fragments At 8:30 a.m. the customer relations department of a data processing firm finds that a lengthy proposal, now in draft form as 60 handwritten pages, must be presented the next day—two weeks early. By 9:00 a.m. the word processing supervisor has assigned 6 handwritten pages to each of 10 word processing operators. By 9:55 a.m. all the material has been keyed, and at 10:00 a.m. the draft printing is complete. At 10:10 a.m. one of the authors picks up the draft, now 30 typewritten pages. By 11:00 a.m. the author has proofread, edited, and returned the text to the word processing center. The 10 operators edit the sections they keyed earlier. At 11:25 a.m. the lead operator assumes control of all 10 parts, instructing the word processing system to consider them a single document for printing purposes. At 12:10 p.m. the printing is complete, and by 1:00 p.m. the finished version of the proposal is waiting for the customer relations staff. Only a proofreading of altered sections is needed. By 1:30 p.m. the proposal is ready for duplicating and binding. Elapsed time from handwritten draft to final copy: five hours.

Assembling and Communicating a Contract An attorney in Cleveland dictates a contract comprising 26 standard sections and 9 special sections. Each standard section is dictated as "insert lease section 21; insert lease section 45." The 9 special sections are dictated verbatim. The legal secretary, using a word processor, begins the transcription. Each standard section, keyed in by "lease 21," "lease 46," etc., is electronically copied into the current document from a boilerplate library stored within the system. A draft-quality proof is printed for review by the attorney.

Once the draft is approved, the secretary dials the San Francisco word processing center of the firm. The operator in San Francisco is at lunch, but the word processor has automatic answering capability and records the document. At 1:00 p.m. San Francisco time, the word processing operator there has the 14 pages printed out and delivered to the local manager. An original copy of a 14-page lease, ready for signature, has been assembled and delivered across country in less than four hours.

---

fice or department: mail logs, lists of incoming mail, its recipient, and its final destination; signature logs, continuing records of expense requests and vouchers and the dates they were made and approved; message logs of telephone calls, retained electronically in the word processor instead of on slips of paper; addresses of users with exclusive access to a terminal; and conference room calendars, updatable by several users with access to a single, mutually accessible floppy diskette.

Word processors equipped with communications capabilities—the ability to establish direct connections to other computers or to peripheral devices—possess immense versatility. There is increasing recognition of the need for electronic transmission of text, and some vendors privately report that 90 percent of their word processors are now sold with communications options.

Communicating word processors can transmit documents between geographically separate locations when normal delivery of interoffice or regular mail is unavailable or would take too long. To communicate, the two word processing systems must have compatible modems and must be operating with the same communications protocol. On some word processors the operator can set line speed, coding, and mode of transmission; others have a single, preset group of parameters. Unless

---

A Star-Type Word Processing Network A wholesaler of auto parts stocks specialized, high-priced parts only at a single store but has five branch stores in two adjoining states. They guarantee availability of special parts in any store in 24 hours. The wholesaler uses a single shared-logic word processor located at the central location, with a standalone word processor at each of the branches. One terminal at the central location is operated for conventional purposes; the second terminal is loaded with the word processing vendor's automatic transmit-and-receive communications package and is connected to an auto-answer modem.

Branch 4 takes an order for an antique auto tire at 9:20 a.m. The branch secretary enters the order in her system and at 11:00 a.m., the deadline for afternoon delivery, dials the home office word processor, which automatically answers and identifies itself. The branch secretary keys in an assigned password, and the second word processor accepts the order into the home office system files. The secretary then accesses the branch 4 messages document to see if there are any messages for the store. Messages are transmitted onto the branch 4 diskette for subsequent printout.

At 12:30 p.m. the home office word processing operator enters commands to print the incoming orders; the commands are stored in sequence and immediately start a printer located in the warehouse foreman's office and loaded with continuous interstore stock transfer forms. The order forms are printed under control of a merge package, with the original information placed in the proper locations on the forms. By 2:00 p.m. the ordered items are being loaded on trucks for delivery to the branch stores.

---

transmission is in an automatic mode, the operators of the two systems must communicate verbally to synchronize and verify transmissions.

A word processor can be used as an electronic mail terminal. The most cost-efficient means of document or message creation is off-line, before establishing connection with the communicating computer. This reduces the connection time between the systems and in some processors keeps the entire range of editing capabilities available. The user may then transmit the message or document to the electronic mail system by means of the appropriate communications protocol. After composing and sending a message, the user may store it on a diskette, edit it, and reissue it as necessary.

With the communications option, a word processing user may access computer data bases, transmit to and receive information from a host computer, or write and edit programs off line for later transmission to and completion on the host computer.

Several highly specialized hybrid word processor/message systems are able to perform numerous word processing input, storage, and editing functions and to communicate by line printer, by direct communication with telex and TWX networks, or through a facsimile unit or a computer-based electronic mail system (CBMS). These systems are discussed in detail in Chapter 5.

Optical Character Recognition (OCR)

Initial keying of lengthy documents often takes as much as 50 percent of total production time. Using a word processor for such a task monopolizes expensive equipment whose primary function is editing. Initial keying of draft text may be more cost efficient on a standard electric typewriter equipped with an optical character recognition (OCR) font. An OCR unit can then scan the typed copy, convert the typed characters to machine code, and automatically transfer the coded matter to a magnetic storage media for subsequent editing and printing. Smaller OCR units for use in word processing, called page readers, are attached either directly to word processors or to specialized devices that accommodate the magnetic recording media. Most are very reliable and accurate; some will misinterpret only one character of every 140,000 scanned.

Many page readers have a reserved character to handle corrections during typing. Typing this character once, twice, or three times in succession will cause the page reader to ignore the previous character, the previous word, or the entire line from that point back to the left margin. The gaps on the input sheets are eliminated during the scanning process. An optional means of deletion is to draw an ink line through one or more characters. OCR scanners recognize certain colors and disregard others. Page readers treat lined-out characters or words as though they never existed, and the adjacent text sections are joined.

One OCR unit can scan and transfer over 200 pages per hour, equivalent to the typing workload of more than 30 secretaries. Thus, optical character readers provide a solution to periods of high-volume production and to competition for word processing resources. Moreover, keying can take place within the user department, where formatting requirements and the spelling of special terms are known at firsthand, reducing the costs of production. File contents can be transferred between incompatible equipment by printing it out of one system in a scannable font and scanning it into the other.

Formerly, OCR units required input in unusual, highly stylized type fonts. Today they can scan a range of familiar typefaces, and text can be printed out in any of a wide variety of type styles.

Both phototypesetting and text editing use electronic methods for creating and printing high-quality documents. Using a floppy diskette as an input device to a phototypesetter eliminates duplicate keying and saves both time and money. Phototypesetting provides better image quality, a variety of styles and sizes of type, and text compression. A phototypesetter easily becomes part of an integrated system when a document is typed on a typewriter, read by an OCR device, edited on a word processor, and finally output to a phototypesetting device.

Providing an interface between word processors and a micrographics conversion system reduces output of paper and provides an efficient means of storing vast amounts of information. Micrographics, described in detail in Chapter 8, is a means of miniaturizing documents. Computerized technology incorporates manual or electronic transfers of magnetic media to a computer output microfilm camera, which can image pages directly or transfer them to microfiche or microfilm. Four ounces of microfiche is equivalent to 60 pounds of printed material. Information stored on microfiche can easily be viewed with the aid of a microfiche reader. Reader-printers are also available. They allow users not only to view documents but also to reconvert information to paper form on demand.

How Word Processors Function

Word processed documents are accessed by means of an index. Magnetic cards are an exception, since they record approximately a single page per card and are visually labeled and physically filed. Other magnetic media, such as diskettes and tape cassettes, contain multiple documents and have an internal, magnetically stored index, sometimes manually updated by the word processing operator, sometimes automatically maintained by the operating system. Manually stored indexes are susceptible to operator oversight, whereas automatic ones let the system do the work. Some provide additional information, such as the dates a document was created and last revised and the hours and minutes spent on the latest revision and cumulative time since the document's creation.

A word processor, like a typewriter, is adjusted to the job at hand by setting margin positions and tab stops. More sophisticated word processors contain both margin and tab controls on what is called a ruler. Rulers govern left and right margins and tab stops in between. Controls can sometimes be set for single to triple spacing, in half-line increments. Right margins can be set for ragged line ends or for right justification (all rightmost characters vertically aligned). Top and bottom margins can be set by specifying the number of lines in the text, in the margins themselves, or both.

Word processors have tabs for both flush-left and flush-right text. Decimal tabs vertically align decimal points regardless of the nature of the numbers. Another type of tab provides for automatic centering, either in the middle of the line or off-center, over a column of text. A word-wrap tab provides automatic return and indentation and also functions as a flush-left tab, particularly helpful for lists within text. Dot leader tabs automatically insert a series of points between the end of an entry and the next tab to assist in visual alignment.

Headers and footers, repetitive material that appears at the top and bottom of each page within a document, are entered once in the document with automatic commands. The headers and footers appear only once on the recording medium, but will print at the top of each page. They can also be made to appear only on selected pages. Automatic sequential page numbering is usually positioned within a header or footer.

A number of rulers can be embedded in a single document to permit formatting variation. An extract from another source, for example, can be set off within the main text by an embedded ruler with a shorter line length. Most word processors can store multiple rulers for recall on demand, any of which may be modified and stored for reuse.

The most powerful function of word processors is their tremendous editing capability, that is, the ease with which they can alter and manipulate text for document output. Freeing word processors to optimize their editing capability is motivation for relieving them from original keystroke capture, providing background printing, and installing output alternatives. The text entry features discussed in this section demonstrate the diversity of the editing functions of word processors.

The feature called *wraparound* is a tremendous advantage in both editing and original keying. It eliminates the need to press the return key as on a typewriter: it creates line breaks and new lines automat-

Word processor keyboard, highlighting special function keys.

ically. When a word extends beyond the right margin, the system moves the entire word to begin a new line. The operator keys text continuously within paragraphs without regard for carriage returns. Similarly, if words are added later during editing, the soft return previously inserted by the wraparound feature moves text from line to line throughout the paragraph; when words are deleted, the soft return closes the gap.

In addition to conventional hyphenation, some word processors provide wrappable and invisible hyphenation. Conventional hyphenation is always visible. Wrappable hyphenation, also visible, is inserted when a word or group of words is particularly lengthy. If part of a multiword group containing wrappable hyphens extends beyond the right margin, the wraparound software finds the rightmost wrappable hyphen still within the margin, inserts a soft return, and wraps the remaining characters to the following line.

Invisible hyphenation, used between syllables of a word that is not normally hyphenated, may or may not be displayed on the terminal. It displays or prints only if the word extends beyond the right margin during printout. If editing causes the formerly split word to move back inside the margin, the hyphen disappears from view and will not print.

Word processors possess the important capability of deleting single characters, whole words, or entire documents in forward or reverse direction. Some systems delete through command keys, some through keyed-in commands, and some through a combination. Some systems permit automated restoration of unintentional deletions.

A cut-and-paste function removes a section of text from its existing position and temporarily stores it in a reserved storage area. Once the operator specifies its new position, the system electronically copies the stored passage into the document. In some systems the cutting and pasting functions are separate.

Search functions electronically locate the occurrences of a character string within a document. For example, the number 14.3 appears in a draft copy as 143. The word processing operator accesses the document, activates the search, and in response to the search prompt enters 143. The system locates 143 and halts. The operator can activate a continuation of the search to locate all occurrences of that same character string or may enter a different one. If the feature is available, "global search and replace" repetitively substitutes one word or phrase for another throughout a document without operator intervention.

Word processors can insert preexisting material ranging up to entire documents into other documents without destroying the original.

When material is added, deleted, or moved during editing, page numbers sometimes require alteration. In some systems pagination is semiautomatic; other systems repaginate with no operator intervention.

Word processors can perform superscripting and subscripting, but the printing of such characters depends on the capabilities of the printer and the operating software. If the printer is unidirectional, some operating systems permit half-line advancing, and the operator has to key in the superscripts on one line, the basic characters on a second line, and subscripts on a third. If the tractor is bidirectional, the operator enters material on a single line, and the printer raises and lowers the paper to accommodate placement of the special characters.

When pressed concurrently with any alphanumeric or special text character, a repeat key will insert a character continuously or perform a function repetitively until one or both keys are released.

Grammatical controls perform a secondary action on existing text of

---

Inserting Text in a Multipage Document   Three paragraphs are to be inserted on page 3 of a 21-page document. The operator invokes the system's automatic search capability, which stops at the insertion point. The operator keys in the three paragraphs, files the document electronically, and enters a print command that instructs the system to ignore pages 1 and 2, because they need not be reprinted. The system reorganizes the text into proper page lengths, starts numbering pages from 3, and revises successive page numbers as the printing takes place. None of the preexisting material has to be rekeyed for the revision.

---

intermixed characters, such as underscoring, boldfacing, or changing all characters to uppercase or lowercase; some word processors also support reversal of the actions. Object keys can be invoked to stipulate any length section of text for boldfacing, underscoring, etc. Natural-language keyboards and commands are becoming more widespread as prices and the size of logic, memory, and recording media decrease. For example, an operator may press keys labeled BACKUP and PARAGRAPH to back up one paragraph.

When it is necessary to perform a series of editing actions repeatedly, such as reversing the order of two lines in a long list of names and addresses, *soft keys* can perform the task unattended. The word processing operator instructs the system to retain magnetically a specified sequence of entry and editing functions. The operator may specify the number of repetitions of the function sequence to be performed without operator intervention. Such sequences can be stored for later use.

Dictionaries in word processing systems contain no definitions. They are magnetic files of correct spellings and hyphenations. Normally they contain a few thousand of the most common words and room for several thousand more. Users can enter terms suitable to their use, such as legal words and phrases, scientific terminology, or frequently recurring names of individuals.

Automatic proofreaders compare each word of text in a given document with the contents of the internal dictionary. The system flags any

Daisy-wheel printing element. Photo courtesy of Digital Equipment Corporation.

term that is incorrectly spelled or that cannot be located in the dictionary. Automatic proofreaders operate on a word-by-word basis and have no grammatical ability. If, for example, the word "read" is transcribed as "red," the automatic proofreader will be unable to judge that it is out of context and will not flag the error.

Printers

Many word processing systems are used mainly as high-speed typing devices for producing hard copy with either draft-quality or letter-quality printers. Draft-quality printers are generally faster than letter-quality printers of the impact type. Impact printers print by means of physical pressure; nonimpact printers produce images by such means as electricity, heat, or squirts of ink. A low-speed printer with a capacity of 15 characters per second will take over two to three minutes to print an ordinary page of about 2,000 characters. A printer with a speed of 45 characters per second will take about 60 seconds; a printer capable of 180 characters per second will take about 15 seconds.

Most impact printers can generate either carbon or carbonless copies. Nonimpact printers are incapable of printing multiple copies (such as a multipart form) in a single operation, but offer high-speed, multifont printing, and graphic printing. All nonimpact printers and two types of impact printers offer plotting capabilities. Table 4.2 lists the types of impact printers and their capabilities.

Daisy (or petal) wheel printers and thimble printers have similar characteristics. Some are bidirectional; by printing alternate lines from right to left, they save time in returning the mechanism to the left margin. They also bypass blank portions of lines at high speed, rather than advancing across them space by space. Daisy wheel printers are marketed as conventional carriage, wide-carriage, and twin-head units; the latter can print two different documents simultaneously. Some vendors offer a two-color ribbon for daisy wheel printers, whose software shifts it for multicolor output in a single print run.

Nonimpact printers are gaining preference because of their multifont and graphics capabilities. Table 4.3 lists the types of nonimpact printers.

Intelligent copiers can mix vertically and horizontally oriented pages in the same word processing document in a single print run.

Ink-jet printers are increasingly popular because of their versatility and because the U.S. Postal Service considers them printers, allowing their output to be mailed at less than first-class postal rates. Applicon and PrintaColor Corporation manufacture interesting off-line color ink-jet printer/plotters. Using three primary colors, magenta, yellow, and cyan, the systems create multicolor images of alphanumeric characters

TABLE 4.2 Types of impact printers.

	Dot matrix	Horizontal drum	Chain and train	Single element	Vertical drum	Daisy wheel	Thimble
Draft quality	X	X	X		X		
Letter quality	X			X		X	X
Multifont	Variety in software	One per drum	One per chain	One per element inter-changeable	Inter-changeable element	One per unit; variety available	One per unit; variety available
Speed	Up to 500 lpm*	Up to 2000 lpm	Up to 2300 lpm	9–15 lpm	9–15 lpm	30–60 lpm	30–60 lpm
Cost	Low	High	High	Low	Low	Low	Low
Plotting	X					X	X
Use in WP	Frequent	Rare	Rare	Frequent	Rare	Frequent	Frequent

*lpm: lines per minute.

TABLE 4.3 Types of nonimpact printers.

	Conventional electrostatic	Electrographic	Thermal	Intelligent copiers	Ink jet
Draft quality	X	X	X		X
Letter quality				X	X
Multifont	X			X	X
Plotting	X	X	X	X	X
Speed	300–20,000 lpm	34 lpm	30–90 lpm	Up to 14,000 lpm	Up to 45,000 lpm
Cost	Low	Low	Low	Moderate to high	Moderate
Use in WP	Rare	Rare	Rare	Frequent	Frequent

*lpm: lines per minute.

in a variety of sizes, as well as computer-generated graphics. Output can be either on paper stock or on acetate for direct use as overhead transparencies. Color ink-jet printing will come into word processing as output devices for recently announced color word processing systems.

Some word processing software systems will support two or more printers of similar or different types concurrently. Independent vendors and some manufacturers also offer a switchbox that permits manual routing of output signals to either of two printers: a high-speed draft printer can be used on the first pass, and a letter-quality printer can be reserved for the final version.

Many word processed documents are destined for reproduction on an offset or other printing press. A wide choice of type styles, sizes, and proportionally spaced fonts is available for letter-quality impact printers. Some systems also support multifont printing, either by halts during a single print sequence to allow the type style to be changed or by means of two separate printing runs.

With "poor man's typesetting," a user can now produce printed material with a word processor. Poor man's typesetting produces camera-ready copy from which a printing plate is produced. For offset printing of up to 1,000 copies, a letter-quality impact printer can enter information directly on the surface of a paper printing plate without significantly affecting image quality.

Phototypesetting and Photocomposing

In-house phototypesetting and photocomposition are increasingly attractive adjuncts to word processing, for they bring the management of text directly to the printing press. Phototypesetters can output text in various sizes and typefaces; type set in conventional sizes can reduce the final number of pages to two-thirds or half. The phototypesetter output, graphics, and photographs (halftones) usually are manually made up into final page form for conversion to a printing plate.

Text prepared on word processors can be phototypeset through translation programs on magnetic media, thus avoiding rekeying the material. A word processing operator inserts brief character codes in the text that instruct the phototypesetting system as to typeface, size, and format. A highly specialized hybrid of a word processor and a phototypesetter is called a photowordprocessor. Because of its cost, it should be used only in selected applications and definitely not for routine, on-line keystroke capture.

Some typesetting service vendors and printers now have various models of communicating word processors in their facilities to receive text directly from customers without the delays inherent in physical transfer of diskettes or other media.

Determining Need

The purchase of a word processor is an investment requiring careful consideration. What problems are a word processor expected to solve? Who will use it and how often? A thorough understanding of available word processing systems and the capabilities of each will help prospective end users make an intelligent choice. Some overall characteristics that require evaluation are:

- Simplicity of operator training
- Efficiency and ease of use (user friendliness)
- Expandability
- Storage capacity
- Functional capabilities/options (word processing, math, sort, forms and records management)
- File-sharing capabilities
- Space requirements
- Compatibility with other devices/systems
- Availability and type of communications
- Price.

For a small department or organization requiring only one person to operate the word processor, a standalone system is probably adequate. If, however, a user community plans to increase staff size within a year or two, an expandable system may be a worthwhile investment. The more sophisticated systems provide greater storage capacities for document filing, and their storage disks permit multiuser access to specified files. A department that stores lengthy documents for long periods or requires that several users share files should consider purchasing one of these. A central servicing organization or a large department may operate a shared-logic system, with hard-wired or dial-up terminals dispersed through a building, a complex, or even across a wide geographic area.

Among specific features and options to be considered are:

- Type of display
    limited ("thin window")
    partial page
    full page
    color of characters and background
- Storage media
    hard disk
    diskette
    dual diskette
    minidiskette

cassette

magnetic card

- Operating speed(s)
- Size of buffer memory
- Compatibility with other office automation components
- Communications capability (Check limitations this may put on other capabilities.)
- Arithmetic capability
- Sort capability
- List processing capability
- Data processing capability
- Graphic functions (horizontal, vertical lines)
- Mathematical functions (for equations, engineering documentation).

Service Bureaus and Timesharing Services

Word processing service bureaus can be useful whether or not there is word processing on the premises. Most bureaus provide dial-up dictation, magnetic keystroke capture, and output. They are useful both to small firms that cannot justify purchasing their own equipment and to firms with occasional production peaks.

Another type of service bureau, which handles only magnetic media conversion, is of great value when an organization is acquiring equipment with incompatible media. The conversion of media and formats permits continuity of use of preexisting files on new equipment without the need to rekey.

A firm can also institute access to word processing through a timesharing service. The vendor installs terminals at the customer site; the shared-logic processor, magnetic media, printers, and other output devices are at the vendor site. Justification must take into account transmission line charges, since keystroke capture is performed remotely; turnaround time, since printing is done off-site; and the level of security provided.

Equipment and Media Maintenance

A word processor is not merely a typewriter with video screen; it is a computer. It therefore requires both an appropriate environment and proper maintenance in order to function well. Physical space and electrical power are obvious necessities; electronic equipment also requires maintenance of appropriate temperature and humidity levels.

Under proper storage conditions, document media can be maintained for years. In heavy, daily use a diskette generally has an average life of six months, though many serve much longer.

The useful life of magnetic media will be enhanced if they are given reasonable care and stored in accordance with the environmental specifications provided by vendors. Magnetic media are susceptible to low temperatures and should be permitted five to ten minutes to return to specified operating temperatures after being exposed to low temperatures during wintertime transport. Cold media often give falsified read errors; when returned to proper temperatures, they read correctly.

Magnetic media should be stored at a distance from magnetic force fields, such as magnetic copy holders, transformers, and high-voltage equipment, and from sources of static electricity, all of which can cause erasure, or wipeout. Carpeting under word processors should be the antistatic or grounded variety used for data processing. At a minimum there should be antistatic mats under the equipment. Using vacuum cleaners that emit electromagnetic force fields can also wipe out magnetic media left in underslung diskette and disk drive units. Static buildup on the clothing of an operator can be transferred to the word processor by touch, resulting in a wipeout or a system crash (a system failure that results in the need to restart the system and that may cause information loss).

Staffing Considerations

Secretaries and clerk typists usually operate dedicated word processing systems within established departments. In larger companies, word processing centers and smaller administrative support units are usually located at convenient points throughout a building. Some of the firms foster staff stability, and therefore higher productivity, by using part-time operators and handicapped individuals. Homemakers and college students working part-time tend to remain with an organization because part-time jobs with convenient hours and reasonable pay scales are hard to obtain. Since part-time employees usually receive fewer fringe benefits, the employer's payroll expenses are lower. Among handicapped workers, blind people are good at transcribing machine dictation, for they are not distracted by motion in the area in which they work. Deaf operators have a similar advantage in keying visual input, in that they are not distracted by noises. The deaf are also impervious to the effect of audio-induced speed averaging, the tendency among a group of neighboring keyboard operators to pace themselves unconsciously to the tempo of key clicks of adjacent equipment until all are working at one average speed. The provision of sound-masking devices (which generate humming sounds) or music systems can counteract this phenomenon.

International Considerations

Not all brands of word processors are available in all nations. To communicate internationally, organizations can use a conversion service bureau, a mutually compatible, customized intermediate device or electronic mail system, or OCR page readers.

Printers are available with many optional type fonts for a variety of natural languages, including Japanese and Chinese. Unfortunately, there are no fully automatic systems for translation between natural languages, although some software systems come very close. These operate from dictionaries, relying on human translators or translator/operators for grammatical refinements.

5

ELECTRONIC
MAIL SYSTEMS

Conventional mail systems are said to date from the Persian Empire.
Though not as old, electronic mail systems date from 1837, when Samuel F. B. Morse first demonstrated the telegraph. An electronic mail
system (EMS) is an electronic point-to-point conveyor of audio,
data/text, graphic, or hybrid modes of information. An EMS can be
anything from two telephones to the most advanced computerized message system.

Electronic mail systems serve many purposes, depending on the type
selected. Some of the more important purposes are:

- Faster delivery of information
- Reduced photocopying volume and expense
- Reduced paperwork volume and mailing expenses
- Geographic independence
- Time-zone transparency
- Elimination of unnecessary interruptions
- Improved access to personnel.

Electronic mail systems are either computerized or non-
computerized. Important among the computerized systems are the ter-

minal-based ones organized into networks of various sizes. Most non-computerized electronic mail systems such as facsimile units of various kinds are simple, turnkey systems that require little effort to install. Though often of value in conventional applications, these systems have only interim worth in office automation unless they can be electronically integrated.

Communication in an EMS is either synchronous or nonsynchronous. People involved in synchronous communication must be available at the same absolute time, such as during a telephone call. A nonsynchronous system frees its users from this time constraint; sender and recipient(s) may be involved at different times.

Electronic mail systems output soft copy or hard copy. Soft copy is preferred for its ease of manipulation and reduction in paper handling, but many applications will continue to require hard copy for some time to come.

Computer-Based Message Systems (CBMS)

One of the most important elements in office automation is the computer-based message system. These systems are electronic substitutes for paper correspondence functions such as typing, photocopying, envelope addressing, filing, retrieving, etc. The name was originally a generic term but has come to specify computerized, terminal-based, user-to-user electronic mail systems. Given that 90 percent of all paper business documents consist of internal correspondence and 90 percent of that involves only alphanumeric characters, there is great need for improved efficiency in generating and communicating intraorganizational messages: 81 percent of all business documents are textual and/or numeric in nature, and both originate and remain within the same organization.[1] There is another powerful incentive for using computer-based message systems, at least as a partial replacement for telephone discussions: independent studies have shown that 72–74 percent of all telephone calls do not reach the intended recipient on the first try.[2]

Of all the electronic mail systems, CBMSs best meet the need for improved communication efficiency. Unlike electronic message switches that force the delivery of a message through a hard-copy output terminal, CBMSs retain messages in computerized files and permit users to receive messages on their terminals at their convenience and from any location. In the individual user's work place, CBMS equipment usually consists of a CRT screen and a keyboard. These frequently are communicating word processors. Most CBMSs produce hard copy only on demand, usually on a printer shared with other users. A CBMS operates more cost efficiently with soft copy; hard copy increases the cost of supplies and of labor to manipulate and transfer documents.

CBMSs provide many advantages:

- Improved coordination of group activities
  Rapid transmission of messages to individuals or groups
  Rapid, paperless forwarding of messages
- Shortened messages and reading times
- Automatic records of messages
- Nonsynchronous communications
  Around-the-clock messaging
  Time-zone and geographic transparency
  Remote access
- Reduction of paperwork and paper handling
- Reduction in volume of photocopying
- Reduction in postage cost
- Reduction in expensive office space used for files
- Reduction in labor and transport when moving offices
- Efficient automated file searching and retrieval
- Elimination of misplaced or lost documents
- Delivery impervious to weather conditions and holidays
- Powerful manipulative options from primary operation in electronic and magnetic media
- Improvement of time management
  Elimination of no-contact telephone calls (telephone tag)
  Reduction of managerial interruptions.

In a year-long CBMS pilot involving 800 users, telephone calls decreased by almost 25 percent and interoffice memos by 15·percent, even though less than 2 percent of the corporate population took part.[3] In 1975 Stanford Research Institute studied six message systems and found that costs for messages averaging 50 words ranged from 50 cents to $1.50; today, commercial CBMS service for messages averaging 150 words costs roughly 70 cents, which of course includes a profit margin. In a private study conducted by the author in 1978–79, message text averaged 100 to 170 words. The effectiveness of computer-based message systems may be limited by the inability or unwillingness of principals to perform their own keying. In such cases secretaries or clerical personnel key the material sent and received. This approach generates more paperwork, for it requires production of hard copies, and results in the usual percentage of mislaid incoming messages. Principals who do not key also limit their ability to communicate while away from the office. However, less complicated system designs and proper terminal selection may encourage wider use (see Chapter 12).

Computer-based message systems have single or multinode configurations. Decisions about which to use depend on the capacity of the hardware/software relative to the user community to be supported, how much and how often they will use the system, and the geographic dispersion pattern of the users. The trend is toward a PBX system or local area networks linked by private cable (see Chapter 3). The costs of dial-up or private network service must be weighed against the costs of an additional node that can perform prescheduled batch transfers of messages at high baud rates.

Limited observations by the author reveal that in a community of 600 users, ranging from inactive to very active (about two hours per day), a system with 40 access lines will have between 35 and 40 users on line at any given time during normal office hours. Incorporation of a detailed user statistics program within a CBMS is desirable, at least at the outset. Some detailed programs pinpoint the count of individual accesses and duration of use for each function by user.

CBMS Functions

A basic CBMS performs three functions: (1) creation, (2) storage, and (3) receipt. Message creation involves the input, editing, and transmission of text. The storage function maintains files for the originator and the recipient. Receipt is reading and disposing of the messages.

A typical CBMS may offer a command mode of operation, a menu mode, or both. In a command mode, the user receives limited prompts, perhaps only a decimal point at the left margin of the display screen, an angle bracket (>), the word COMMAND, or the cursor simply returns to a predetermined position on the screen. In a menu mode, a numbered list of options is displayed to the user; by entering the corresponding number, the user either directly accesses the function or brings a submenu to the screen.

If the CBMS is running as one of many tasks on a timeshared system, the user will need to specify the CBMS by name when dialing in. If a system offers a choice between menu and command modes, the user makes the choice at this point. Dedicated CBMSs customarily begin by asking for the user's name. Some systems employ a user identification name, a unique combination of alphanumeric characters used for both log-on and message addressing; friendlier systems accept actual surnames and sometimes given names. Next comes a request for the user's unique password, which provides a degree of security.

Usually the system then greets the user with a welcome and typical announcements referred to as system mail. Friendly systems provide a brief explanatory introduction to new users at their first log-on, such as "Welcome to the XKJ Electronic Message System. Please note that the system will be down from 1800 hours on Friday, 11/16 until 0600 hours on Monday, 11/19 to permit installation of additional dial-up lines. On-line assistance is available by typing in HELP at the left margin at any time." The explicit welcome and use of the word "typing" instead of "keying" are meant to convey friendly and familiar notes to those unaccustomed to dealing with computerized systems.

At this point the system will probably display the user's message status: the number of unread and unsent messages. Unread messages are the new electronic mail received; unsent messages may be partial messages or complete ones not yet sent.

At the completion of a session, the user must log off. In a command mode, the user keys in L(OGOFF), Q(UIT), F(INISHED), or some such signal. With a menu type system the user keys in the number corresponding to "LOGOFF." New users unaware of the final step often simply hang up the telephone or let the terminal stand idle; a well-designed system will support such a log-off.

Sometimes a user steps away from a terminal forgetting that he or she is logged on. That ties up a port on the system, and, if traffic is heavy, can shut other users out. An automatic log-off solves the problem. In that case, the system clocks periods of inactivity for each user; after a stipulated number of minutes, automatic log-off occurs.

Some designs display a system message just before log-off, reminding the user of any unsent or unread messages, including any received while the user was on line. The user may opt to deal with pending messages or just complete the log-off.

In a typical CBMS, the word WRITE, COMPOSE, or a shortened version (W, WR, C, COM) invokes the creation of a message. Most systems recognize all users at log-on and automatically complete the FROM line. For users who delegate the writing to their secretaries or others, some systems also prompt for FROM. The sender is then prompted for TO and enters the name of the recipient(s). A system that operates with user name codes usually has an on-line directory; when the sender keys in the surname of a recipient, the system displays the corresponding user name code, which the sender must then key in. A sender may direct messages to as many addressees as desired.

For user efficiency, a CBMS generally supports both individual and group addressing ("Branch Managers," "Biology Department"). The names of individual users in each group address are stored by the system. Thereafter messages can be sent to all these individuals by entering only the group name as the addressee, eliminating the need to enter each separate name.

Most CBMSs also support individual or group functional addresses such as "Carpenters," "Travel," or "EDP Manager." This form of address permits a person temporarily responsible for the function named to log on under that name and send or receive a message. This capability is especially helpful during vacation periods or when there are several working shifts. Group functional addressing tends to decrease response time, since more group members are likely to see the message.

```
                    THU 29 OCT 1981 10:48 AM

You have 3 UNREAD memos
You have 0 UNSENT memos
You have 8 TICKLERS

*** E M S ROUTINES ***

1. CALENDAR KEEPER
2. MEMO HANDLER
3. DOCUMENT HANDLER
4. UTILITIES

ENTER ROUTINE DESIRED > 2
```
Step 1

```
*** MEMO ROUTINES ***

1. WRITE MEMO
2. READ MEMO
3. FILE AND MEMO MANAGER
4. MEMO SEARCH
5. DIRECTORIES

ENTER ROUTINE DESIRED > 1
```
Step 2

```
TO >  Mary Good, Tom Shade
cc>   Grace Glade
SUBJECT > PROJECT REPORT DUE DATES

* Text: type <CR> "." <CR> to finish

Please note that monthly project reports
for Q2 are due Oct. 25, Nov. 20, Dec. 23.


SELECT OPTIONS? <Y>
```
Step 3

```
*** OPTIONS ***

1. EDIT
2. SEND
3. FORWARD
4. DELETE
5. PRINT
6. READ AGAIN

ENTER ROUTINE DESIRED > 2

  - memo sent
```
Step 4

```
*** OPTIONS ***

1. FILE
2. FORWARD
3. DELETE
4. PRINT
5. READ AGAIN

ENTER ROUTINE DESIRED > 1
   into file(s) REPORTS
   - filed
```
Step 5

```
TO:  MARY GOOD
CONCERNING: PROJECT REPORTS
FILE: UNSENT

*** OPTIONS ***

1. EDIT
2. SEND
3. FORWARD
4. DELETE
5. PRINT
6. READ AGAIN

ENTER ROUTINE DESIRED > 4

Delete - Are you sure?  <Y> YES

  - Done
```
Alternate Step

A typical electronic mail menu sequence. Step 1, selecting a function from the main EMS menu. Step 2, choosing a function from the memo-handling menu. Step 3, writing a short memo. Step 4, sending the memo. Step 5, filing the memo. Note that the system inhibits filing of the unsent message by not offering this option until the memo has been distributed. Alternate procedure: deleting the memo instead of sending it.

Subscriber lists may also include inanimate users. Reservations and confirmations for conference rooms ("Room C"), vehicles ("Shuttle Van"), or slide projectors can all be handled directly through a CBMS.

A well-designed CBMS can route messages to those who are not users of the system, either by interconnection to a public teletypewriter network or by a hard-copy printout.

CBMSs usually have one or more directories: alphabetic subscriber listings (names only, which the user may command to be displayed beginning at any letter of the alphabet); group addresses (no individual names); members within a specified group address; and a detailed individual listing, sometimes including surname, given name, department name, mail stop, telephone number/extension, group addresses to which the individual belongs, and sometimes other details. Most systems also prompt for CC, courtesy copies, to any number of individual or group addresses. Blind copies can exist in CBMSs but are ethically questionable.

The SUBJECT can be from a few characters maximum up to a one-line maximum. Systems with automatic search capabilities also prompt for keywords to assist in subsequent automated retrieval by topic.

In older or less sophisticated systems, the command SEND invokes message creation. Some designs then prompt as above; others prompt only for TO, permitting a number of names to be entered in succession in a single field. The balance of the conventional message header (SUBJECT, RE:, etc.), is actually part of the message and must be manually entered text. In more sophisticated systems, the next prompt may read WHEN FINISHED ENTERING TEXT, TYPE A CARRIAGE RETURN, A PERIOD, AND ANOTHER CARRIAGE RETURN, or something similar. Next comes a prompt such as TEXT or MESSAGE, whereupon the sender keys in the message body.

Keying in a period against the left margin, an illogical grammatical occurrence, is a common means of message text termination and is usually combined with pressing the return key or entering a word such as END or FINISHED. Programmable function (PF) keys can also be used for that purpose.

After entering the text, the user normally can choose to read (review), edit, or delete. Some systems allow the user to delete characters only during composition and do not permit editing once a line has been bypassed. More advanced designs allow the user to edit or add to both header and text prior to transmission. Since pressing DELETE cannot erase printed text from a message being sent from a hard-copy terminal, the user checks the result by causing the CBMS to reprint the corrected version.

Because much of the time spent in message creation involves thinking rather than interacting with the computer, it is more efficient to write and edit long messages off line, on smart or intelligent terminals such as communicating word processors. This frees the CBMS ports only for actual input and output as well as reduces communications time and expense.

An odd fact which has emerged from experience with CMBSs is that users tend to consider such messaging as relatively informal. Minor typographical errors—and even some that are not very minor—are generally acceptable, as long as they do not obscure the meaning.

Once message creation or editing is complete, most systems automatically insert the message in a PENDING or UNSENT file, where it awaits further action. An immediate SEND command will cause most systems to ignore other messages in the UNSENT file and transmit the message just created. Messages can also remain in such files for future delivery.

Some systems permit the sender to specify a time for the transmission of the message; some support priority mail, in which messages go to the top of the recipients' message queues; others support return-receipt mail, in which the system automatically notifies the sender when the message is read.

Certain systems permit the sender to specify both a hard and a soft copy for the recipient—a convenience when the message is lengthy and will be provided to persons not using the system. The hard copy is usually generated on printing terminals with auto-answering modems located in the recipient's general area.

Once the user has entered the SEND command and any options, the CBMS automatically enters the name of the sender along with the date, and usually the local time of day, and confirms the action to the user to indicate completion. Some systems permit the user to retrieve and alter the message until one or more addressees have actually read it. Most systems, however, do not permit retrieval once the message has reached the recipient's message queue.

CBMSs customarily maintain both system files and user-defined files, discussed in detail in Chapter 6. System files usually are of four types: UNSENT, SENT, UNREAD, and READ. When the user sends or reads a message, the CBMS automatically refiles it in chronological order. Users may not delete any of these files.

User files in a CBMS are similar to conventional paper files: users may create files with natural-language names. File names generally are limited to a maximum 78 characters.

The usual filing command is FILE or F. To store a message in a file named "Terminals," the user keys in FILE IN TERMINALS or just FILE TERMINALS. To cross-file, the user keys in the name of each file, separated by a reserved character such as a comma or a slash symbol. To refile material, the user simply keys in the numbers of the messages and the file name.

Some CBMS systems require users to establish new files prior to filing; others permit instantaneous file creation. If a user attempts to store material in a nonexistent file, the system will display a message that no such file exists and will ask whether the user wishes to create one. A YES or Y will command it to do so. This is a form of user protection. Otherwise one could accidentally create multiple files with similar names ("staellite" instead of "satellite").

Good CBMS design provides for automatic file directory maintenance in alphabetical order; a command such as LIST FILES or DISPLAY FILES causes the directory to be displayed or printed. A command such as LIST or DISPLAY, followed by the name of a specific file, will call the contents of that file to the display screen.

Users can create new files in some systems by invoking a maintenance command such as CHANGE FILENAME, which asks first the existing file name and then the new one. Another way is to create the new file first. The user displays the index of the original file, enters the command FILE ALL IN [new file name], and deletes the old file.

To safeguard against accidental destruction of file contents, users usually may not delete any other than their own files so long as the file has message contents. Consider a user who has created a file called "Fax" which contains three messages, and another called "Facsimile," with no contents. If the user were to note the duplication and mistakenly specify deletion of Fax, the system would respond with YOU MAY NOT DELETE A FILE WHICH CONTAINS MESSAGES or something similar.

To safeguard against accidental deletion of messages, a DELETE command may invoke a response that gives the user a second chance to review the action. Another approach is to place the message immediately in a special system-maintained DELETED file, sometimes referred to as an "electronic wastebasket." If the deletion was in error, the user may access the DELETED file and refile the message from there. Only by deleting the DELETED file is the message actually eliminated from the user's files.

Filing anything implies a reason to retrieve it later. Good CBMS design frees the user from the drudgery and frustration of locating messages. Automated search and retrieval functions, discussed in Chapter 6, permit users to search their files in numerous ways: by author, by date or inclusive dates (from/to), or by key words in subject lines or text. Searches in subject lines are based on key words or phrases, and the phrasing of the subject is secondary to how many applicable words or terms are entered in the field. This relieves the user from having to recall where anything may be located, as long as it pertains to the subject. The most sophisticated automated retrieval designs called bibliographic searches can search the full message text for single or multiple key words or phrases.

Most file purges are handled by conversion to COM-generated microfiche (see Chapter 6).

Generally the user accesses his or her index of unread messages with a command such as LIST UNREAD, SCAN UNREAD, or DISPLAY UNREAD. A typical index shows the assigned sequence number of each message in the UNREAD file. By invoking the READ command, the user reads the messages in the order of the UNREAD file sequence. If the user enters READ 1, 3 or any other sequence, the system displays the messages in that specified order.

Reading on hard-copy terminals is continuous to the end of the message; reading on most soft-copy terminals is based on the screen size. A standard display screen has 24 lines and displays complete messages up to that length; for a longer message the screen displays 22 lines, followed by a blank line and a line of instructions, such as PRESS ENTER KEY FOR MORE or PRESS RETURN FOR MORE; B TO SEE PRIOR PAGE; E FOR END. The user should be able to terminate the printout or display at any point.

After reading each message, the user generally may choose to answer, forward, reread, file, print, or delete it.

The ANSWER command typically prompts with INCLUDE ALL CC'S IN ANSWER?, which allows either a private response to the originator or inclusion of all original addresses. Usually CBMS software automatically reverses the original TO and FROM fields, relieving the user from rekeying headings. Next, some systems permit entry of a new subject and move the original subject to a new field called RE:, which subsequently appears below the subject line; others use the original subject preceded by RE:. With the next prompt, TEXT, the process parallels the message creation commands.

Forwarding a message to other than the original addressees is the electronic equivalent of photocopying messages and addressing envelopes. When the user invokes the FORWARD function, the process is the same as in message creation permitting a "cover memo" message to

---

Forwarding with a Computer-Based Message System A marketing manager wants to communicate to the staff a message from a district manager announcing the award of a bid to their firm. After reading the message on his terminal, he enters a FORWARD command. The system displays the prompt TO and the manager enters MARKETING STAFF. At the next prompt, TEXT, the manager keys in "Thought you should see this." The number 3 beside the word "SEND" appears on a menu of options. The manager keys in "3," presses RETURN, and the system answers with the screened response MESSAGE SENT. The members of the marketing staff now have both the marketing manager's comment and the full text of the district manager's message in their respective electronic mailboxes.

---

be entered. When the user sends the message, the system electronically attaches the message(s) to be forwarded.

With a text/graphic CBMS the user can generate graphic images such as flow charts, organizational charts, floor plans, pie charts, and line graphs, combine the images with text, and transmit the resulting text/graphic document. Such systems require graphic terminals with high resolutions (usually 1,024 by 1,024 pixels), and transmission times are somewhat longer. Output can be either via another soft-copy graphics terminal, a hard-copy printer/plotter, or an intelligent copier.

A text/audio CBMS permits optional audio retrieval of messages via a voice-response unit. A Touch-Tone telephone or a tone-generating device provides access; the CBMS computer must be equipped to interpret the tone signals. All system responses to the user are given in natural language: the computer "speaks" its responses. Being able to listen to one's electronic messages from a telephone handset offers an outstanding advantage to a user who is traveling or otherwise temporarily out of reach of a terminal.

A particular type of voice-response unit uses special firmware to convert the digitally encoded CBMS responses into phonemes. From these the voice-synthesizer unit generates an audio version of each phoneme to the user over the telephone. Such devices are more fully explained in Chapter 10.

Other Computerized Text Systems

In addition to CBMSs, computerized electronic mail systems include teletypewriters, communicating word processors/teletypewriters, and store-and-forward destination-oriented systems.

Teletypewriter systems are included in computerized electronic mail systems because transmissions between devices are channeled through message-switching computers that operate over telephone or telegraph channels. Most common are Telex (international) and Western Union International's TWX (North America only); there are also private point-to-point and multipoint services.

Teletypewriter systems have been in use for a long time, and both public and private versions are commonplace in large organizations. It is estimated that there are altogether more than 150,000 TWX and Telex teletypewriters worldwide. These devices provide rapid communication at modest costs. Through interconnection to other types of computerized message systems, they make computerized systems more effective and cost efficient in a shorter time. Communicating word processors are discussed in Chapter 4.

Two hybrid devices incorporating word processing capabilities qualify as electronic mail systems: word processors with a teletypewriter exchange-communications option and teletypewriters with limited word processing functions. Such devices can receive messages from original keystroke capture, OCR devices, and other word processors or computers, and store the text magnetically, usually on diskettes. Once the text is in the system it may be edited as on any other word processor. The systems can then interconnect with teletypewriter networks and transmit the text directly from the magnetic medium, simulating a teletypewriter. This capability permits communication flow from system to system, with limited human intervention.

Message-switching systems use a computer to accept, sort, and reroute messages that are ultimately to be converted to hard copy. There are both private and public systems, including the Mailgram service operated jointly by the U.S. Postal Service and Western Union. Messages are routed to a message-switching computer, where they are filed according to destination code. When the file contains a given number of characters or messages, or when a specified period of time has passed, transmission begins. Connection is made to the destination (sometimes via an intermediate message-switching computer), where the message is output in hard copy. For private systems the destination is a message center, a mailroom, or a department. Mailgrams go to selected post offices where the hard copy is inserted in envelopes and delivered by carriers to local addresses.

Private systems are modest in cost, but because they are destination- rather than individual-oriented, delays can occur if the hard copy is output in a message center or mailroom from which it must be manually delivered or if the recipient is temporarily away from that location.

Noncomputerized Graphics Systems: Conventional Facsimile (Fax)

Facsimile, or fax, is the most prevalent of the noncomputerized graphic systems. Fax is a kind of long-distance photocopying: a hard copy sent from one point is duplicated at a remote location. So long as sending and receiving units are compatible, an image can be transmitted, even internationally. Two factors contribute to the popularity of fax units. One is ease of use, and the other is the need for copying signatures, which fax devices can duplicate cheaply and easily.

Compatibility has been a serious problem; intense competition has produced a bewildering array of dissimilar, often incompatible devices. In the 1970s the Comite Consultatif Internationale de Telegraphie et Telephonie (CCITT), a United Nations international standards body, worked with manufacturers to establish compatibility standards. Although progress toward meeting those standards has been rapid, the diversity of models is still confusing for system planners and end users.

Resolution and transmission speed are of great importance in facsimile devices. Fax systems scan and remotely recreate images in terms of

Desktop and console facsimile units. Photo courtesy of Xerox Corporation.

vertical lines per inch (lpi) and horizontally as pixels per inch (ppi). Each pixel represents a single picture element or point in the overall image. Fax machines may employ at least seven separate types of scanning technology, but all utilize an inherent light source (recently, a laser) and recognition of reflected light patterns. The CCITT standard for scanners in digital fax units is 1,728 pixels along a horizontal standard line of 8.46 inches (about 215 mm). For general business use, resolutions of 196 ppi by 100 lpi are usually sufficient. Units with a resolution of 190 ppi by 130 lpi will transmit readable 8-point type; with 200 ppi by 200 lpi, 6-point type; and with 200 ppi by 300 lpi, 4-point type.

Most units for business use have only black-and-white capability, which is sufficient for general applications. For fine work, such as drawings with delicate detailing or photographs, higher resolutions and gray-scale capability are needed. The higher the resolution and the transmission speed, the greater the cost. Transmission speeds of general-purpose business fax units using ordinary narrowband media range from 20 seconds to 12 minutes per letter-size page. Special units that operate at 2 seconds per page require wideband transmission paths. Some fax units provide a choice of speeds. The operator selects the highest speed consistent with legibility or image in relation to ultimate use, since faster transmission takes less telephone time and thus reduces costs. For smaller documents some fax devices scan and transmit only the exact image size, and transmission time is proportional to the size of the document sent. At a setting of 2 minutes, for example, a half page is transmitted in 1 minute, a time savings of 50 percent over a full page.

The CCITT-recommended international standard for paper size is 210 by 297 mm (8 1/4 by 11 3/4 inches), close enough to letter-size paper to present few problems. For smaller or larger page sizes, such as forms, legal documents, or engineering drawings, there are devices using a 500-foot roll of 8 1/2-inch-wide paper that produce cut-to-length output.

Alden Electronic and Impulse Recording Company manufactures an array of special-purpose fax equipment in addition to conventional business units. For special applications such as remote signature verification at branch banks, they manufacture a fax with a 5-inch paper width. Another device accepts 35-mm micrographic aperture cards as input and can remotely output hard copy. Another unit can scan engineering drawings in a variety of sizes up to C-size in multiple, 18-inch-wide passes.

Facsimile devices use either transmitters and compatible receivers or transceivers (both transmitter and receiver in a single device). Some transceivers are half duplex: they can alternately send and receive; others are full duplex and can both send and receive simultaneously.

Fax options include unattended sending; unattended receiving (for other than normal working hours); portability (for use by sales personnel or at off-site meetings); compatibility with other, preexisting fax units; and entering (scrambler) features for security.

Table 5.1 shows a range of five hypothetical models and their capabilities. The simplest units for low-volume, synchronous general busi-

TABLE 5.1 Various fax model capabilities.

	Model A	Model B	Model C	Model D	Model E
Number of pages sent and received monthly					
1-20 (convenience; no OA integration; trial use)	X				
21-30 (3-4 specific documented types; OA integration)		X			
50 or more (daily, dedicated department use)			X	X	X

TABLE 5.1 (cont.)

	Model A	Model B	Model C	Model D	Model E
Number of receiving locations					
1	X	X	X	X	X
4		X	X	X	X
4 or more			X	X	X
Size of originals (in inches)					
5 1/2 × 8 1/2	X	X	X	X	X
8 1/2 × 11	X	X	X	X	X
8 1/2 × 14			X	X	X
11 × 17			X		X
Computer printouts		X		X	
Types of originals					
Typed memos	X	X	X	X	X
Handwritten memos		X	X	X	X
Ledgers (pencil entries) and financial reports		X	X	X	
Invoices (originals/copies)		X	X	X	X
Copies—carbon/carbonless		X	X	X	X
Checks		X	X	X	X
Drawings (ink/pencil) and graphics with text		X	X	X	X
Photos		X	X	X	X
Magazine articles	X	X	X	X	X
Computer printouts (bursted or continuous)			X		X
Reduced originals			X	X	X
Resolution					
Information quality	X	X	X	X	X
Source quality		X	X	X	X
Interface with present user					
4-6 minutes	X	X	X	X	X
2-3 minutes		X	X	X	X
Transmission					
Less than 500 miles	X				
More than 500 miles and attended		X			
More than 500 miles and unattended			X	X	X
More than 500 miles, unattended and international			X	X	X

TABLE 5.1 (cont.)

	Model A	Model B	Model C	Model D	Model E
Machine requirements					
Unattended or automatic send only					X
Unattended or automatic receive only				X	
Automatic loading			X		X
Semiautomatic loading	X				
Unattended send and receive			X		
Attended or manually operated	X	X			
Multiple send			X		X
Multiple receive			X	X	
Full duplex			X		
Confidentiality			X		

ness use cost about $70 per month to rent; $1800 to purchase. The more sophisticated model for general business use, with high-volume, long-distance, nonsynchronous transmission capabilities, cost about $600 per month to rent, $16,000 to purchase.

Special-purpose fax equipment, such as high-speed/high-resolution units used to transmit fully composed pages of *The Wall Street Journal* to remote printing plants via satellite, and color fax systems, may cost up to $300,000 per device.

In addition to conventional fax devices, other noncomputerized graphic systems useful in business communications include electronic blackboards, slow-scan and semimotion TV, and full-motion closed-circuit TV. These systems are often used as visual aids in teleconferencing and are discussed in Chapter 9.

Computerized Fax Systems

Nonsynchronous computer-based graphics systems share the benefits discussed above for nonsynchronous communications. Prominent among them are computerized fax systems that transmit either text or graphics as graphic images; alphanumeric material is graphically portrayed, rather than encoded, and it cannot be edited.

Hard-copy store-and-forward facsimile systems consist of either analog or digital units used with a keyboard input device. The keyboard is

Alaskan Weather No Match for Fax System The U.S. Postal Service claims deliveries despite rain or snow or gloom of night, but this doesn't always include mail to or from King Cove Village, the last outpost in Alaska before the Aleutian Islands. Air mail can take up to seven days. Telegrams and radio experience constant delays. Under extreme weather conditions, even satellite service is sometimes unreliable.

Peter Pan Seafoods, Inc., a leading producer of seafoods from the North Pacific, maintains a network of plants and buying stations from Bristol Bay, Alaska, to northern California. Fast processing and rapid communications are essential to the company's operations.

Long distances and violent weather make ordinary communications difficult. In 1979 the company's managers heard about another firm's facsimile system, saw a demonstration, and decided to install a system of their own.

Two Panafax units with automatic document feeders were installed at the King Cove plant manager's office and at Seattle headquarters. They are in use 24 hours a day, seven days a week, with a considerable amount of unattended service.

The solid-state machines include miniature microprocessors to control logic functions. They transmit documents with superior clarity because 2056 photocells scan for sending and 2056 printing elements aid at the receiving end.

An electronic-handshake capability allows the sending machine to automatically and electronically query the receiving unit regarding transmitting speeds, mode selection, line quality, paper supply, etc. It adjusts automatically for the most compatible transmitting conditions. The system also steps down the speed to ensure good copy even during noisy line transmission. Controls on the unit's data modem help overcome line problems when they occur. Because traditional fax paper tends to deteriorate in the dry Alaskan air, the manufacturer developed a 0° humidity paper. Copies require no retyping and can be filed indefinitely.

A dedicated line was installed to carry messages and further cut the cost of fast facsimile transmission. The machines handle communications such as daily catch information; production reports; shipping documents; purchasing requisitions, covering equipment and supplies for fishing operations, plant maintenance, the cafeteria, the store and infirmary; payroll information and administrative documents.

Although the fax units save money over other methods of routine communication, that's really not the important factor. In the past, a fish-processing operation could be shut down for quite some time because of the need to have a small gear replaced. With the facsimile units, complete, detailed specifications can get to Seattle and to a supplier in hours.

Also, prompt information on a good catch can generate additional sales and help respond more rapidly to customer needs. As a result of its experience with Panafax machines, Peter Pan is planning to establish a worldwide facsimile network.

Source: Abridged, with permission, from an article by Jack L. Lind, Vice President, Peter Pan Seafoods, *The Office,* May 1981, pp. 30, 62.

used for addressing, and the fax unit receives the body of the message, the scanned page. Input from an analog fax passes through an analog-to-digital converter; input from digital fax units requires no conversion. The computer treats the input, usually an ASCII encoded bit-stream (a continuous sequence of bits), like any other encoded message, for the computer is not required to differentiate between words and graphics.

Because uncompressed fax encoding of a single letter-size page would involve about 2 million bits, most digital fax units incorporate some type of compression to eliminate white space, reducing the encoding to about 200,000–300,000 bits per letter-size page. Because the storage of graphic images requires more file storage capacity than a text system, this type of system is most useful for graphic transmissions. Once the hard-copy document has been produced at the receiving end, the user should delete the image from the system to conserve file space.

Glass fax systems are extended versions of store-and-forward fax systems, except that graphic documents may be stored within users' files for subsequent redisplay. Though the systems can also utilize hard copy, display is primarily on special, high-resolution terminal screens. A hard-copy option eliminates the document multiplication required with conventional, hard-copy fax systems. Compression techniques reduce the storage capacity required, but glass fax devices should be used only for graphic images and should be purged of images as soon as possible.

Some combination text/graphic systems make use of fax devices. These systems commingle encoded textual data or information with graphic images. Their primary application is for editing and for placing graphics close to related text.

Merged text/fax systems overlay text within individual faxed images by means of a keyboard terminal used with the fax transmitter. Output is via a hard-copy fax receiver. The primary use is for the labeling and transmission of weather maps.

A hybrid text/fax system, such as the Compression Labs CLI-441, inputs text through a keyboard terminal and produces hard-copy output through a remotely located fax receiver or transceiver. Specialized software converts encoded characters into graphic format, which the fax output unit then reproduces. The Panafax MV-3000 Transverter series fax has similar capabilities.

In the late 1970s Compuscan, Burroughs, IBM, and Stewart-Warner developed hybrid OCR/fax as a type of store-and-forward system. Document pages containing both scannable typed characters and graphic images are scanned directly into the system. The scanner attempts to read in OCR mode, converting character images to computer code. Whenever the system encounters an image that is not a recognizable alphanumeric character, the scanning software switches to fax mode for just those portions and digitizes the image graphically, then automatically returns to OCR mode. In the transmission of a letter, such a device scans the text but switches to fax mode for the letterhead logo and personal signature.

The result of this hybrid system is a highly compact, digitally encoded record. In addition to saving file space, such hybrids also dramatically reduce transmission times and costs. A 300-word letter with logo and signature yields the following record sizes when scanned by different types of fax systems:

- Uncompressed fax: 2,000,000 bits
- Compressed fax: 300,000 bits
- Hybrid OCR/fax: 37,000 bits.

Videotex Systems

Videotex is the generic name for a type of electronic publishing system sometimes integrated with other functional tools. Videotex systems use keyboards or more often hand-held control units about pocket-calculator size, ordinary TV sets, and telephone lines in two-way communications between the publishing service and the receiver. Most systems currently are oriented toward home consumers, who eventually will be able to shop, bank, and perhaps read the newspaper through their television sets. The American Telephone and Telegraph Company has already set standards for U.S. systems using its lines for transmission and has announced its intention to market videotex equipment and services by the mid-eighties. Its standards are compatible with the Canadian government's Telidon system and with the Columbia Broadcasting System's modification of the French Antiope system.

Though promoted for use in the home, videotex systems also have great appeal for commercial applications because of their simplicity of

 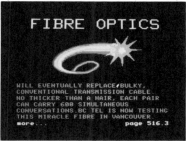

Videotex images from the Telidon system. Courtesy of Telidon Program Office, Government of Canada, Department of Communications.

operation and their ability to handle text, graphic images, and continuous-tone photographs. The Telidon system, for instance, compresses graphics by defining and storing lines in terms of starting and ending points and degree of curvature, instead of storing each of the individual and overlapping points along the line, as in standard graphics encoding. Both file space and transmission time are dramatically lower and operating efficiency is significantly improved. The combining of videotex with the marketing of data banks holds much promise for the future.

Audio Systems

Audio systems also contribute to the automated office: telephones, Picturephones, telephone answering systems, and filed audio systems are all noncomputerized. Voice filing systems can also be computerized.

The underrated electronic marvel, the telephone, is a tool we often abuse by improper and excessive use, and it in turn abuses us by demanding to be answered. Research indicates that telephone shadow functions (activities making no direct contribution to accomplishment of a task) are the cause of half an hour of wasted managerial time per day—6 percent of normal working hours, or three weeks per year.[4] Computerized devices put telephones to more efficient use.

The Picturephone, a combination of telephone and miniature interactive television, permits two people to see each other while they talk. Only a few such installations exist, and service is limited to the premises of the user only; no network transmission service is available. AT&T's Long Lines Department has now implemented the Picturephone Meeting Service, a transcontinental video teleconferencing service discussed in Chapter 9.

Telephone answering systems, especially in smaller (single-person) offices, play a limited but significant role in office automation. By

---

A Simple Audio Mail System For two international commodity traders, success or failure frequently hinges on information that affects their market in a matter of minutes. They use a simple audio electronic mail system: a single, remotely accessed, hybrid telephone answering/dictation machine.

The first trader learns of a shortage in a particular commodity, goes to a telephone, calls the number of the device, and leaves a message. A short time later his partner completes a purchase of 12 tons of the same product and decides to call in for messages. After placing a pocket-size tone unit near the telephone receiver, the trader presses a button that creates a tone. The telephone answering machine responds by playing back the message recorded minutes before. Knowing of the shortage, the second trader immediately returns to the firm and doubles the previous purchase.

---

eliminating interruptions from telephone calls, such systems bring the workday under greater executive control; one or more well-publicized units can relieve a department staff from answering calls for simple information, such as office closings in inclement weather, the operating status of timeshared computers, or upcoming company events. Telephone answering machines are discussed in more detail in Chapter 3.

The only computerized audio mail systems are voice filing systems, which convert audio input to digitized form for computer storage. Storage capacity is relatively high, the equivalent of about 60 pages of text per minute. A Touch-Tone telephone serves as the input/output terminal with the pushbuttons acting as the control keys. Voice input passes through an analog-to-digital converter and can be filed in a mainframe computer. Stored messages are individually retrievable and can be forwarded. Audio quality closely resembles the original.

The features of audio mail systems vary from manufacturer to manufacturer but sometimes include full dial-up dictation capabilities, the ability to forward messages to a third party, facilities similar to those of telephone answering machines for callers who are not system users, and the ability to hold postdated messages and reminders for future delivery. Some systems have preset limits for message lengths; others offer adjustable or even unlimited lengths. The users of most systems must dial in to determine whether new messages have been received, but at least one manufacturer provides a visual-signal device which attaches to the side of a telephone. Manufacturers of audio systems include Voice & Data Systems, ECS Telecommunications, Wang Laboratories, IBM, and Delphi Communications, an Exxon subsidiary.

NOTES

1. Robert J. Potter, "Electronic Mail," *Science*, March 19, 1977, pp. 1160–1161; Robert A. Shiff, "Processing Information, Not Paper," *IMPACT: Information Technology*, July 1978, p. 5.

2. Thomas Marill, "Why the Telephone Is on Its Way Out and Electronic Mail Is on Its Way In," *Datamation*, August 1979, pp. 185–188; David A. Potter, "Software Objectives for the Administrative Network," paper presented to conference on "Information Networks in Tomorrow's Office," Hollywood, Florida, November 10, 1977.

3. Vin McLellan, "Electronic Mail: Buzzing DEC on its EMS," *Datamation*, August 1979, P. 68.

4. James H. Bair, "Communication in the Office of the Future: Where the Real Payoff May Be," Proceedings of the International Computer Communications Conference, Kyoto, Japan, September 1978, p. 735.

Let all things be done decently and in order.
I Corinthians 14:40

6

ELECTRONIC
FILING AND RETRIEVAL

Electronic filing (sometimes called electronic file cabinets) is an important component of all office automation systems. A rapid and accurate means of accessing information, electronic filing and retrieval is the technically enhanced storage and recall of data or information. Word processors, computer-based message systems, electronic calendars and tickler files, micrographic units, and integrated office automation systems must all file (store) and retrieve (access) files of data or information. There are also electronic filing systems for facsimile, photographic, and micrographic images, and for video signals.

Because retrieval is inherent in filing (after all, if there is no need to retrieve data or information, there is no need to file it in the first place), electronic filing includes both automatic file searching and retrieval tools. The system can be either closed loop, in which both the means of location and the information have been electronically encoded, or it can be open loop, in which the means of location is electronic but the information is not. A user may enter one or more specifications in a computerized system and gain direct access to the information or, in a semiautomated system, be given the source and location of the off-line information.

The purpose of electronic filing is to promote the straightforward management of information regardless of the recording medium. Therefore, it follows conventional file systems precepts. Simple, natural-language access is essential. The faster and more accurate the retrieval, the lower the labor expenditure; the better the file management, the lower its cost.

Some 35 percent of all filed papers are never retrieved; 90 to 95 percent are never accessed after the first year. Moreover, office studies show that 1 to 5 percent of all documents are misfiled, and that the average cost of a misfiled document is between $50 and $75. In other words, every document placed in a conventional paperwork file costs 9 cents a year in misfiling costs, arising primarily from the labor involved in searching for misfiled material. The average firm has 500,000 filed documents in 20,000 file folders and spends $29,000 annually to retain them, based on an estimated cost of a little more than $7 per filing

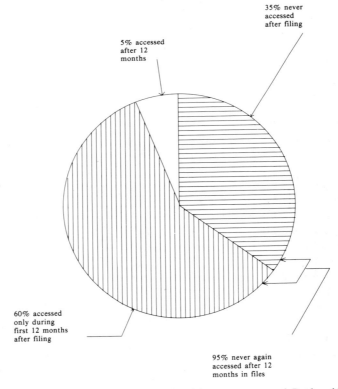

35% never
accessed
after filing

5% accessed
after 12
months

60% accessed
only during
first 12 months
after filing

95% never again
accessed after 12
months in files

Computer-generated diagram showing percent of documents accessed. Produced by Tymshare, Inc., with AUGMENT software.

inch. Adding the misfiling expense of $45,000 per year to the annual maintenance cost yields a yearly expense of $74,000, or 15 cents per page, for the 500,000 documents.[1] Some 61 percent of that amount is for misfiling.

Electronic filing and retrieval has many advantages. The most obvious are:

- Faster access to information
- Reduction in misfiling
- Reduction in amount of office floor space
- Storage efficiency through shared access
- Portability of files
- Time transparency for access
- Geographic transparency for access
- Limited dependence on human knowledge of filing techniques.

The only limitations of electronic filing and retrieval are that the user must have access to a terminal, and that, unless a user is already on-line, it takes a few seconds to dial up a computer system and log on.

Use in Word Management

The design of word management systems is nearly as diverse as the number of firms that manufacture them; but generally, word processors support only the separate filing of individual documents. As pointed out in Chapter 4, some require the operator to create and maintain a manual index; others automatically create and update the document indexes on magnetic media. Automated indexes generally maintain production statistics, such as size of documents, dates created, last date edited, and cumulative time spent working on the document. Document naming conventions vary from several numeric characters to full-line alphanumeric titles. The more freedom afforded the operator, the better.

Use in Computer-Based Message Systems

In most computer-based message systems, the text of every message appears only once regardless of the number of people to whom it is addressed or subsequently forwarded. The message itself does not appear in the personal files of the originator; instead, one master file maintains all messages. All that exists in the personal files of the originator and all subsequent recipients is a citation containing the names of the originator and recipient(s), the date and time of the message (for clarity, usually in a 24-hour clock also specifying the local time standard), the subject, and a unique identification of each message. The citation field may also contain provision for other information. The single occurrence of text within a single computer system results in exceptional file efficiency.

CBMSs also customarily provide automated directory maintenance. Such systems keep up to date, in alphabetic order, the names of all system-generated and user-generated files, the number of messages within each file, and sometimes the size or length of each message.

Computer-based message systems, as discussed in Chapter 5, support two classes of files: system and user. The system files, usually including IN-BOX or UNREAD, READ, UNSENT, SENT, and DELETED, are under the control of the CBMS software, and the user can control their activity only indirectly. For instance, the system automatically files an incoming message citation under UNREAD and, after the recipient has read the message, transfers it to the READ file in either chronological or reverse chronological order. Similarly, when a user creates a message, the citation appears in her or his file, but the text is in the master file. Once the originator issues the SEND command, the system automatically refiles the citation under SENT, again in chronological or reverse chronological order. Most CBMSs prohibit users from filing unread and unsent messages and from directing that other messages be placed in the system-generated files. However, users can file, perform multiple cross-filing, and refile messages from the READ, SENT, and DELETED files into their own files. Most systems guard against accidental deletion of valuable information.

User-generated files are under user control. Within the space provided for the file name field, a user may select any name for a file. Some systems limit a user to 15 characters in a single string, with no spaces; others permit spacing between words and allow 65 or more characters. In addition, a CBMS should provide the user with an index of the contents of every file. The index to a specific file should include at least the name of the originator, the date of the message, the subject, and sequential document numbers for each message within each file. This procedure gives the user a relatively fast means of accessing messages in his or her file.

Filing and Retrieving in a CBMS

After reading an incoming message, perhaps about a business competitor's new product, a user of a CBMS might issue a natural-language file command, FILE IN COMPETITIVE INFORMATION. The system responds, YOU DO NOT HAVE A FILE NAMED COMPETITIVE INFORMATION. CREATE IT? The user enters Y

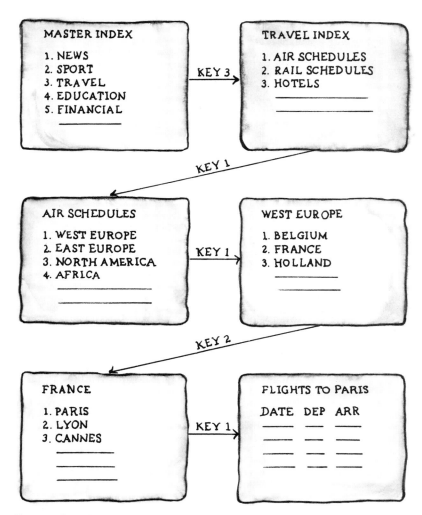

Tree-search method of retrieving filed information.

(for yes) and the system responds with OK! (slight pause) COMPETITIVE INFORMATION—FILED. If the user later wants to access the document but is not sure of its number, he may command LIST COMPETITIVE INFORMATION; the system will then display an index of the contents of the file.

Automated files generally provide multiple parametric search capabilities: to and from the user, author's name, specific date or inclusive dates, key word(s), and message number. The first specifications allow a user to see only messages sent, only messages received, or both on a specific topic. The author's-name parameter can support both the insertion of one or more specific names and the command ALL (for all

Subject Search The director of quality control in a hardware manufacturing firm needs to locate every message sent and received about bolts during the first quarter of the year. He invokes the automated search and retrieval function of the computer-based message system and enters the dates 1/1–3/31 (the system assumes the user means the current year) and the key word BOLT. A few moments later a message appears on the screen: 386 MEMOS SEARCHED. THERE ARE 17 MEMOS DEALING WITH "BOLT." THEY ARE STORED IN THE FILE NAMED "SEARCH 3." WOULD YOU CARE TO SEE AN INDEX?

the authors) or a default with the same effect. Date selection can encompass specific dates, all messages before or after a specific date, and all messages between two dates. In most cases, the software assumes that unless otherwise specified the current year is being requested.

To conserve file space and discourage users from filing unnecessary information, at least one commercially available system allocates a specific amount of file space to each user. Also to conserve storage space, given that users retrieve only 5 to 10 percent of all filed material after one year, it is advisable to convert most files to off-line status after that period. To prevent the purging of active files dealing with long-term matters, such as standing committees and long-term projects, systems usually place the purging utility under the control of each user. The utility searches for messages at least one year old and displays an index for review. The user can then selectively forward copies of such messages (or even perform mass transfers of entire files, such as those dealing with closed projects) by subject and in chronological order to a computer output microfilm (COM) facility, retaining the material in specially flagged files. When the microfiche copies arrive, the user should be able to delete the flagged files en masse.

Internal and Commercial Data Banks

The growth of electronic filing and retrieval systems parallels that of electronic data banks—vast libraries of information stored in central computers. Both systems have expanded with the rapid increase in computer capacity and accompanying decrease in computer costs. Managers and professionals are relying more and more on access to both internal and external data bases for long-term decision support and daily operational information.

Internal data bases may cover all manner of materials, from ordinary customer lists and financial data to complex statistical information. The data must be filed in such a way that access to it is easy and quick.

External data banks are a growing feature of the information revolution. They are maintained by vendor companies who collect, package, and electronically distribute information. The vending firms usually draw their data from provider companies such as Standard and Poor's, Value Line, New York Times Information Service, and so on. They then index the information, file or store it, and make it accessible on line to their customers. The information vended generally falls into three categories: statistical, bibliographic, and computational. The computational, or "value-added," data banks, such as Data Resources of Lexington, Massachusetts, construct their own mathematical or econometric models which subscribers may manipulate on line for an added fee.

Among large vendors are Lockheed's Dialog Information System, Mead Data Control, and System Development Corporation. They and many others maintain data banks covering such areas as agriculture, demographics, economics, education, energy, engineering, environment, finances, foundations, government, industry, international affairs, law, patents, social science, and science.[2]

Computer-Aided Retrieval (CAR) of Micrographics

The principles of filing, search, and retrieval operate in computer-aided retrieval of micrographics (see Chapter 8).

Computer-aided retrieval (CAR) systems require initial establishment of a data base of container (reel, cassette, cartridge, or fiche) numbers, key words, and individual microfilm frame numbers. Some microfiche retrieval devices operate by physical address; that is, they move to a specific slot holding a single fiche with a unique identifier. Some rotary and microfiche cameras assist in the identification process by imprinting the documents with unique numbers during filming. Some microfiche cameras also generate magnetic computer tape indexes concurrently with filming. These magnetic tape indexes serve to update on-line files for future CAR use. Other CAR systems use binary-coded, comblike metal strips attached to the bottom of each fiche. The removal of teeth in various combinations provides unique identification encoding.

Dialing a Data Bank An actual data base search, using the Dialog Information Service, involves the steps on the following pages. To begin, you dial the service on the modem connected to your terminal. You are seeking information about the effects of stress on executives. The data base's on-line index tells you that File 15 covers articles on business and management. (Continued on next page.)

Adapted, with permission, from Dialog Information Service, Inc., a subsidiary of the Lockheed Corporation.

Dialing a Data Bank (continued)

What you say to DIALOG
and how it responds

What you see on
your office terminal

```
? Begin 15
File 15:ABI/INFORM71-80/MARCH
(Copr. Data Courier Inc.)
?    Set    Items           Description.
```

Q. I'd like to search File 15, please.

A. What would you like me to find for
   you?

```
? SELECT STRESS OR TENSION
          997            STRESS
          259            TENSION
   1     1178            STRESS OR TENSION
```

Q. Do you have any articles that include
   the word *stress* or the word *tension*?

A. Yes. I have 997 that refer to *stress*
   and 259 that include a reference to
   tension for a total of 1,178 documents that mention either or both
   terms.

```
? SELECT EXECUTIVES OR MANAGERS
   OR ADMINISTRATORS
         5349            EXECUTIVES
        10253            MANAGERS
          648            ADMINISTRATORS
   2    14962            EXECUTIVES OR MANAGERS
                         OR ADMINISTRATORS
```

Q. How many articles do you have that
   mention *executives* or *managers* or
   administrators?

A. I have the following references:
   executives—5,349;
   managers—10,253;
   administrators—648, for a total of
   14,962.

```
? COMBINE 1 AND 2
   3      311           1 AND 2
```

Q. How many of those articles or
   documents contain the terms *stress*
   or *tension* AND ALSO the terms
   executives or *managers* or
   administrators?

A. Only 311.

Dialing a Data Bank (concluded)

*What you say to DIALOG
and how it responds*

*What you see on
your office terminal*

```
? SELECT S3 AND PY = 1980
              2347          PY = 1980
      4    7                3 AND PY = 1980
```

Q. I'm interested only in *recent* articles.
How many of those 311 were published during 1980?

A. Seven.

Q. I'd like the following information
about the first of those: record number, title, journal title, date, pages,
and an abstract if available.

A. Title of the article is "Learning to
Handle Stress—A Matter of Time and
Training." It's by Dennis R. Briscoe
and appeared in *Supervisory Management*, volume 25, number 2, on
pages 35 to 38 of the February 1980
issue. Please see the 150-word
abstract.

```
? TYPE 4/7/1
  4/7/1
  80005291
  Learning to Handle Stress-a Matter of
    Time and Training
    Briscoe, Dennis R.
    Supervisory Mgmt   v25n2      35-38   Feb 1980

Management jobs are becoming increasingly stressful.
Considering the nature of managerial work today,
people can survive only by learning to avoid the
situations they find stressful or by adjusting . . . . . . . . . . . . .
```

Q. For the remaining six articles please
give me only the basic information,
no abstracts.

A. Here is the list of articles with basic
publication facts.

```
? TYPE 4/3/2-7
  4/3/2
    80005280
    Managing Yourself
    Kleiner, Brian H.
    Management World  v9n2   17-18,36  Feb 1980
  4/3/3
  80004717
  Managerial/Organizational Stress: Identification
  of Factors and Symptoms
  Appelbaum, Steven H.
  Health Care Mgmt Review   v5n1   7-16   Winter 1980

  . . . . . . . . . . . . . . . . . . . . . . . . . . . . . . . . . . .
```

Q. Thank you, I'm finished. Please log
me out and give me a record on this
search and its cost.

A. This search, made April 25, 1980,
was completed at 3:15:44 p.m. Your
identification number is 3268. Computer time cost $3.30. Time to con-
duct the search was 0.044 hours. It
was made in File 15 using six
descriptive terms. Communications
(TELENET) cost $.22. The total
estimated cost was $3.52.

```
? LOGOFF
  25apr80 15:15:44 User3268
  $3.30      0.044 Hrs File 15 6 Descriptors
  $ .22      Telenet
  $3.52      Estimated Total Cost
```

A Semiautomated Micrographic Retrieval System   An inventory clerk institutes a search for all material related to master purchase order number 15,001. The computerized search software responds with MICROFICHE #AP07798, FRAME J6, PURCHASE ORDER # 15,001, PO # 15,001. Turning to his microfiche tub, the user selects fiche number AP07798, inserts it in a viewer, moves the indexing pointer to coordinates J6, and views the microphotograph of the document.

CAR provides end users with either partial or total retrieval assistance. In an open-loop system, the computer automatically searches data bases and generates lists of pointers to the locations of specific film images. The user must then select and manually insert the microfilm in the retrieval device and locate the specified frame with mechanical assistance. Such systems must be independently acquired and are not integrated with the retrieval units. Those who have a computer-based message system with an automated retrieval or key-word search feature can use it as part of an open-loop CAR system. Though not as efficient as a system designed specifically for open-loop CAR, it is superior to a manual system in speed and accuracy.

Standalone semiautomatic retrieval units provide limited assistance through incorporated data bases. A typical device is the 3M system that uses a 16mm cartridge. The user accesses the data base, which is on diskettes, via a CRT terminal. When the screen displays the pointers, the operator selects and inserts the correct cartridge in the viewer, which then locates and displays the desired frame.

In a closed-loop system, the computer not only searches the data base and identifies the location of each micrographic image, but also retrieves the container, moves to the correct frame, and displays the image to the user. Thus closed-loop local retrieval devices control the entire search, retrieval, and local projection process. There must be one retrieval device and one full set of microfilm per workstation. Such systems offer rapid and accurate retrieval, but distribution of updated copies of microfilm is slow, and each workstation must have both a CRT and a storage/projection unit.

The most sophisticated micrographic retrieval systems are those that are closed-loop and provide soft-copy images on high-resolution CRT display terminals. The computer, which has a single copy of any microfilm file, looks up the address of each frame of information, calls the image to a scanning station similar to a facsimile device, converts the graphic image to a digitized one, stores that image, and immediately returns the cartridge or microfiche to its storage address for access by other users. If more than one image meets the search criteria, the computer repeats the process, scanning subsequent frames and queuing

Shared-Access Automated Retrieval The international vice-president of a major bank needs immediate information about a particular aspect of international banking laws. Turning to a soft-copy micrographics terminal on his credenza, he requests a subject search and enters PROMISSORY NOTE and NORWAY. In less than 2 seconds, an index of documents pertaining to the requested combination of key words appears on the screen. Since the fifth document appears to be the one needed, he enters the number 5, and in less than 1/2 second the micrographic document image appears on the CRT screen providing the needed reference. Total time: less than 40 seconds.

them for sequential viewing on the user's display screen. Such systems ensure that everyone is working from the most current information.

Each closed-loop soft-copy system presently available has additional features that merit consideration. The Automated Records Management System (ARMS), manufactured by Teknekron, Inc., operates with both microfiche and digitized hard-copy files. Each ARMS carousel can handle 350,000 letter-size pages, and because the system is modular there is theoretically no limit to the number of carousels that may be configured into the system. Access time for the initial page retrieval is about 5.0 seconds, 0.4 second for subsequent queued pages. A CCD (charge-coupled device) camera scans at a resolution of 200 lines per inch. One ARMS option links a word processor to the system and stores word processing output as bar codes, like those found on many grocery product packages, on microfiche. Another option scans hard copy into the computerized files in digitized form for retrieval in the same manner as the microfiche and optionally outputs hard copies of screened images. The system can also search its microfiche files for related information. This feature is particularly helpful in purging the system's internal micrographic files. Access to the ARMS files is through either local or remote terminals.

Planning Research Corporation designs and builds the versatile integrated Telefiche system. Telefiche can be configured to file, retrieve, or communicate any combination of carousel-mounted 16mm microfilm and microfiche or digitized hard copy, all accessible by an automated search of key words. Both local and remote output can be either soft or hard copy. The user terminal has two soft-copy display screens; one displays alphanumeric text for searches while the other displays graphic images scanned from the micrographic or digitized hard-copy input files. The graphic screen also has an instantaneous zoom feature for viewing fine detail. The operator can generate a hard copy of any screened image with a locally incorporated printer or transmit the image for hard-copy output at a remote site. This feature is generically referred to as microfacsimile (microfax). Several hundred terminals, either hard-wired or dial-up, can operate in the system.

Holofile Industries, Ltd., a subsidiary of Holofile Technology, Inc., manufactures holofiche retrieval devices and the page composers to create them. Holofile retrieval devices provide interfaces for shared-access retrieval in both soft and hard copy from local and remote workstations. A special keypad and display terminal, standard CRT, or plasma-panel terminal can accomplish soft-copy retrieval. Since holofiche are recorded in binary code rather than photographic images, magnetic tapes, diskettes, disks, plotters, and printers can also be used for retrieval.

Use in Electronic Calendars and Tickler Files

Both electronic calendars and tickler files present somewhat different filing and retrieval requirements. Chapter 7 discusses provisions for access in detail.

NOTES

1. See "Paper Files Cost Business a Bundle," *Information and Records Management*, August 1977, p. 23; Frank Greenwood, "Your New Job in Information Management Resource," *Journal of Systems Management*, April 1979.

2. See Walter Kiechel III, "Everything You Always Wanted to Know May Soon Be On-line," *Fortune*, May 5, 1980, pp. 226ff.; Denise R. Guillet, "On-line Databanks," *Administrative Management*, July 1980, pp. 44ff.; Donna S. Stein, "Data Banks: How to Know Everything," *Output*, June 1980, pp. 36ff.

One of these days is none of these days.

English proverb

7

ELECTRONIC
CALENDARS
AND REMINDERS

Appointment calendars and ticklers (reminders) are time management tools. Appointment calendars allocate specific time segments for activities on a given day; ticklers provide reminders of daily tasks that do not require specific allotments of time.

The usefulness of all time management tools depends upon their users' remembering to look at them. Nonautomated calendars are generally paper pads or books kept on office desks. Nonautomated tickler files are sometimes file folders, sequentially dated from January 1 through December 31, or notes on slips of paper taped or tacked to visible surfaces.

Electronic calendars and tickler files reside in a terminal, a far more prominent visual reminder to consult the calendar. In this respect electronic calendars and tickler files are computerized versions of their paper counterparts, but they also have many other uses.

Their primary purpose is to optimize time management. Electronic calendars do this by providing a single, centralized, remotely accessible source for scheduling appointments for a variety of users and thus minimize or eliminate scheduling conflicts and oversights. Electronic tickler files provide ready access to both personal and organizational reminders.

Studies show that upper-level managers spend 60 percent of the working day in scheduled meetings and another 10 percent in unscheduled ones.[1] Other managers and professionals devote about 40 percent of their working hours to meetings.[2] Missing a meeting wastes the time of all participants and requires either the scheduling of yet another meeting or a private briefing by someone who did attend. Electronic calendars, by making it possible to keep one complete, up-to-date appointment schedule, including time to get to the meeting, reduce the likelihood of missed meetings and late arrivals.

Principals are not the only ones who experience stress about meetings. Secretaries find scheduling meetings one of the most distasteful aspects of their job, involving many frustrations. Calling the offices of other requested attendees results in busy signals, no answer, or unavailability of someone who can confirm the appointment. Moreover, scheduling a meeting for several people almost always entails overcoming conflicts in other participants' schedules: the first few people may be available at the requested time, but someone farther down the list may not be. If that person is essential to the success of the meeting, the entire process must begin again, based on that person's schedule. In one study, an average meeting involving six people, including the initiator, took 60 to 75 minutes to schedule.[3] An electronic calendar and appointment scheduler can schedule such a meeting in 2 to 3 minutes.

The advantages of electronic calendars include:

· Existence of a single, uniform copy
· Efficient scheduling of meetings
· More efficient use of support personnel time
· Portability
· Time-zone transparency
· Geographic transparency.

Calendar and Tickler File Designs

One design maintains electronic calendars and tickler files separately. The tickler file works with the terminal-oriented electronic mail system, reminding the user at log-on and log-off that tickler file items are pending. The user treats the ticklers like messages and may display either the index or the entire text of the ticklers.

Another design integrates calendar and tickler files. The calendar displays the reminders at the bottom of the terminal screen. For extensive lists, users are provided instructions for display. (Hard-copy terminals print additional tickler items sequentially as a single document.)

Both calendars and ticklers perform filing in chronological order by date; in addition, calendars file according to sequential time segments within a date. Therefore, a user specifies personal calendar retrieval by date and also may view her or his personal calendar by week and by month, beginning at any date or day of the week.

Electronic calendars and electronic tickler files usually follow either a prompt-and-response or a direct-writing format. The former alternately asks the user for each entry in sequence and accepts the keyed-in answers. The latter displays a calendar or tickler file with only headings and line captions for a specific date and the user keys in appropriate entries at the designated positions.

Early electronic calendars tended to schedule on a basis of 15- or 30-minute time intervals, and the trend is now to even shorter intervals. Calendars should support meetings for any desired time span, say from 10:40 to 10:50 a.m.

Access to electronic calendars and ticklers requires inquiry into computer files, so users must have access to terminals. There is a movement to increase portability by supporting voice-response calendars via dial-up telephone. The tone handset or tone-generator would cause the computer to convert the calendar entries to audio mode through a voice-response unit, making it possible for a user away from the office to check calendar and tickler entries.

Virtually any discussion of calendars involves the issue of access for scheduling and other purposes. Most people feel that, as with paper calendars, only the "owner" and her or his secretary should be permitted to schedule on and view the owner's calendar. To make it easier to schedule meetings, however, most electronic calendars permit the user to establish and alter a listing of so-called privileged users who may schedule a calendar; each user is automatically entitled to control his or her own calendar scheduling. Automatic appointment schedulers will schedule a meeting on the calendars of only the initiator and privileged users. Other participants' calendars contain only a notice that the initiator has reserved a specified time segment.

Some electronic calendar systems permit access to the individual calendars of other users. These systems should incorporate a screening program that determines whether the person making the inquiry is a privileged user. To nonprivileged users the calendar can respond with an equivalent of UNAVAILABLE.

Scheduling Your Own Calendar You decide to reserve the entire after-noon of the last Friday of the month to draft the monthly status report. You dial the computer and access your calendar. You are asked for, and enter, the date you want to schedule on your calendar. To the next prompt, START TIME?, you respond "1" (the calendar is programmed to know that "1" is p.m. rather than a.m.). Next comes the prompt, HOW MANY HALF-HOUR TIME SLOTS? Since you want to reserve the time between 1:00 and 5:00, containing eight half-hour time slots, you enter "8." The next prompts are SUBJECT? (to which you respond "reserved"), LOCATION? (which you leave blank), and WITH? (for the names of other attendees; left blank by you in this case). The calendar system then confirms what you have entered.

Scheduling Functions

In creating and maintaining separate files for each date on which indi-vidual users have activities, an electronic calendar serves the same function as its paper counterpart; but to make scheduling easier the calendar itself must have a built-in calendar to distinguish weekends and holidays from working days and provide system users with mes-sages to that effect. Because some meetings may occur on weekends, however, the system design should permit users to schedule on any day or date.

Like their paper counterparts, electronic calendars and their ap-pointment schedulers contain specific dates and space for notations of the time, place, subject, and anticipated attendees at a meeting. They also provide functions that eliminate many of the difficulties involved in scheduling a meeting with many people.

For instance, an automatic scheduler first asks for a series of individ-ual or group names, then requests the meeting date. When the user has entered the names for the requested date and time, the scheduler can advise the user whether the meeting can be scheduled as requested or of a lack of available time periods on that date. Another design permits senior supervisory initiators to override previously scheduled appoint-ments on the calendars of their subordinates. Electronic calendars and schedulers linked to terminal-based electronic mail systems can auto-matically notify users whenever someone has either scheduled or re-served time on their calendars.

Cancellations and reschedulings of appointments or meetings are common occurrences. Users can easily effect mass cancellation and rescheduling on an electronic calendar.

Electronic calendars can schedule not only for individuals but also for groups, rooms, and equipment. Calendars can support group ad-dresses just as electronic mail systems do. Entry of a group name

```
Secretary's CALENDAR
1981----------------------------------------------------------------
|MON 8/3    |TUE 8/4    |WED 8/5       |THUR 8/6     |FRI 8/7
|           |           |11:45 L       |             |
|           |           |1:00 Bob Reid |MOLLY - CAR  |
|           |           |              |             |1:00 Pat Blake
|           |4:00 Brown |6:00 Oliver   |             |MITCH - VAC
◇1981------------------------------------------------------------
|MON 8/10   |TUE 8/11   |WED 8/12       |THUR 8/13    |FRI 8/14
|MITCH-VAC  |           |2:30 SHERI TANNER |          |
|           |           |Lisa George   |2:00 EMS-NETWK|
|MJ DRB     |           |              |DEB's        |
|           |           |5:00 Pat-Home |             |


Executive's Calendar
◇1981----------------------------------------------------------------
MONDAY 7/13   |TUESDAY 7/14 |WEDNESDAY 7/15|THURSDAY 7/16|FRIDAY 7/17
              |             |              |             |8:30 ROBERTS
8:30 COMM PROD|             |WWWWWWWWWWWWWWWWWWWWWWWWW    |9:00 FPS MR
Marker staff  |9:00 Lignos  |   S. Library |             |
              |sys.arch. grp|              |             |12:00 ZK
              |10:00 Bill R. |             |             |1:00 OF I
              |             |              |             |
              |3:00 T decision|            |(EAS)        |4:00 Cutler
              |             |              |6:30         |
4:00 Museum -MR|            |Woods         |Chez Jacques |
◇1981------------------------------------------------------------
MONDAY 7/20   |TUESDAY 7/21 |WEDNESDAY 7/22|THURSDAY 7/23|FRIDAY 7/24
8:30 Ulf Staff-MR|          |              |             |8:15 GRAPHICS (15 min)
              |9:30 TJ rap  |              |             |
              |             |JJJJJJJJJJJJJ |JJJJJJJJJJJJJJJ|9:00 TJ* +LP
              |Prod MKT. &  |              |             |BOD
              |10:30 Harvey |              |             |10:00 WILLIAMS
              |Mfg.Eng. intface|PEG J      |PEG J        |11:00 Pierce
              |11:55 Dewey-quick|           |            |
              |12:00 Hanson re|Fitz Inn     |             |12:15 Shade
2:00 BJ + LP  |1:00 PHIL    |              |             |
              |2:00 Gorman--11 org|        |             |4:00 Ollie
              |3:00 Savour et al|          |             |re RPG - here


CONFERENCE ROOM SCHEDULE
---------------------------------------------------------------------------
|MONDAY 8/17             |TUESDAY 8/18    |WEDNESDAY 8/19     |THURSDAY 8/20       |FRIDAY 8/21
|8-1:30 Gladys X3957|8:30-5 KATHY KING   |                   |8-12---STRATEGIC PLANNING|9:00 to 12:00
|                   |568-1431 X2054      |                   |Will - X4851        |Artificial Intell. demo
|                   |                    |1-3---PIERCE REVIEWS|12-5-PEG           |Debbie X4858
|                   |                    |ANDREA, X1396      |                    |ELECTROHOME
◇
|MONDAY 8/24        |TUESDAY 8/25        |WEDNESDAY 8/26     |THURSDAY 8/27       |FRIDAY 8/28
|                   |                    |                   |8-11---ENG. COM.    |
|10-12 MOLLY X9050  |                    |9:30-11 MILDRED X5671|                  |9-10:30 ROSALIE X2403
|                   |1-5 DAVE Pate X3-6688|                  |                    |10:30-12 MARILYN
|                   |                    |2-3:30 ANN X6409   |12-5 EF&A           |X4006
◇
|MONDAY 8/31        |TUESDAY 9/1         |WEDNESDAY 9/2      |THURSDAY 9/3        |FRIDAY 9/4
|                   |                    |                   |                    |9-5 SHEPERD X5957
|                   |8:30-12 MARY X2936  |                   |8:30-10 D. Brown X2193|
|                   |                    |9:30-11 MILDRED X5671|                  |(CUSTOMER VISIT)
|                   |1:15-5 MEYER STAFF X2906|               |12-5---ENG STAFF    |
◇
```

Electronic calendar printouts. *Top to bottom*, secretary's calendar, executive's calendar, and conference room calendar. The "J"s and "W"s on the executive's calendar indicate special types of meetings nicknamed "Jungle" and "Woods."

causes the system to access first the listing for that name and then the individual calendar of each person in the group.

A calendar's automatic appointment scheduler can also maintain the equivalent of an appointment book for a conference room: a room can be a "user." When the name of the room is entered among the names of the attendees, the automatic scheduler searches the calendar of the conference room as well as those of the proposed attendees for concurrently open time. Another design incorporates information about room seating capacity, location, and equipment and lets the system select and schedule the appropriate room according to requirements.

Calendars can similarly schedule use of vehicles, audiovisual equip-

Setting Up Appointments You call a staff meeting of seven people, including yourself. Your secretary accesses the calendar, invokes the appointment scheduler, and enters the requested date, starting time, and meeting duration. The scheduler then prompts with NAME and the secretary enters a name. The scheduler and secretary repeat this procedure six times; at the eighth name prompt the secretary enters nothing, the system responds with JUST A MOMENT—CHECKING AVAILABILITY, then displays a confirmation: (YOUR NAME): SCHEDULED. Beside other names are the words TIME RESERVED, since only the individual users or their secretaries can confirm scheduling on their calendars.

---

ment, films, videotapes, and other services not necessarily related to meetings.

The appointment-scheduling software can also take into consideration the required travel time of attendees by scanning for the time and location of each person's immediately previous appointment. This feature assumes great importance when scheduling involves international meetings. For meetings nearby, an alarm function in a calendar can also be of value. Most terminals have either a bell or a buzzer. At some interval before a specific event, the bell or buzzer sounds momentarily, drawing the user's attention to the screen, which displays a reminder of the event and its time.

When scheduling involves participants from diverse time zones, an automatic scheduler can inform the initiator of their respective local times. It can also convert the numerical orientation of dates to accord with customs elsewhere. For example, 11/3 may mean November 3 to the initiator, but in other nations it might mean March 11.

When transborder calendar scheduling is not interactive because of limitations in transmission facilities, an electronic calendar can use batch-mode appointment scheduling. Such a system identifies the user nodes of the proposed participants and transmits the message to those nodes. At the time of entering the appointment requests, the system should display a message that the requests are pending subject to confirmation. Once responses come from the remote nodes, a system that is integrated with an EMS can generate a message of confirmation to the initiator, placing it in the electronic in-box.

Two design features can help users after a meeting. One permits appending extended remarks, such as the minutes of a meeting, to the records of specific meetings contained within an electronic calendar. The other, closely associated, incorporates an automated search capability in a personal calendar; by entering one or more key words the user can obtain a chronological history of a particular working group, committee, task force, or project. These two features help reconstruct valuable information.

Tickler File Attributes

Tickler files can support not only individuals but also groups, by addressing reminders to group names or group addresses and projects. Tickler entries remain in the electronic files until the specified date, when they move to the user's files for viewing. The files provide space for messages as well as dates. Tickler functions tied to CBMSs follow the conventional message concept and provide space for both subject and message.

Like an electronic calendar, a tickler file has its own calendar so that its software can differentiate a working day from a weekend or holiday and notify a user entering an item of a conflict. Output conflict is not so important; the tickler message will simply remain in the viewing file until the user deletes it: a tickler item that appears on Saturday will still be there on Monday morning.

Ticklers serve individual and group needs by providing advance notice of recurrent activities such as periodic reports, thus allowing users time to prepare the updated material. Such entries are termed permanent ticklers, but users may alter or delete them at any time. A well-organized tickler system supports virtually any calendar relationship: every Monday, the third Wednesday of each month, every December 15, the first and third Thursdays of each month, and so forth. Deletion of a particular permanent tickler message deletes only the current re-

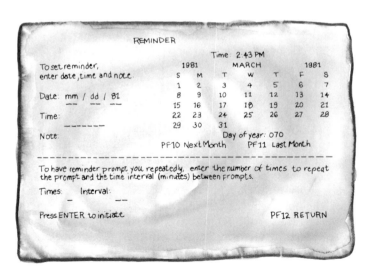

At a preselected time, the reminder function of IBM's Professional Office System displays a message and sounds a tone. Reprinted by permission from "IBM Professional Office System General Information Manual," © 1981 by International Business Machines Corporation.

minder; the overall file entry remains until permanent deletion occurs. A tickler system may also furnish the user with a means of assigning a priority value, say from one to five, to an entry, so that items of highest priority appear at the top of the list.

Tickler files can also provide notices for equipment reservations or loans, and reminders for required services, reordering, or reviewing or renewing contracts.

Also like electronic calendars, electronic tickler files must create and maintain separate files for each date on which there is tickler activity for individual users. Unlike calendars, however, tickler files may contain more than one date. In addition to the "delivery date" when the item is first to appear, it can also contain the input date. An electronic reminder of project milestones may also contain a due date and completion date for the sake of a project record.

Project control ticklers link individuals' names with task assignments and deadlines and send reminders of milestone dates to those responsible for completing the assignments. The individuals responsible should set the intervals for such reminders, because some people require more advance notice than others. On the milestone date, the tickler sends the responsible project management a list of what is due and from whom. If the deadline has been met, a simple instruction changes the file notation from "due" to "complete" and enters the current date. If the event is incomplete on the due date, the project management still sees the tickler item on that date but need take no action. If the tickler system software finds that an event is overdue, it automatically reminds the responsible party. From then until the project manager deletes the item, both the project management and the person responsible receive a daily tickler item concerning the overdue action.

Purging Systems

Like other electronic files, calendars without some means of purging eventually overflow capacity. The most efficient solution is conversion to microfiche in the same way that terminal-oriented CBMSs are purged. The calendar can periodically notify the user that its files should be cleared, and the user decides which calendar dates can be deleted and which should be converted to COM (computer output microfilm). Until the user receives the microforms, the system can flag those files and suspend them. Afterward the user can effect a mass deletion of the flagged files.

Few tickler items except project histories are worth retaining. Once a project is complete, a system-generated reminder notifies the project management and offers the option of conversion to microforms or total deletion of file contents.

NOTES

1. Henry Mintzberg, *The Nature of Managerial Work* (New York: Harper and Row, 1973), p. 39.

2. James H. Bair, "Communications in the Office of the Future: Where the Real Payoff May Be," Proceedings of the International Computer Communications Conference, Kyoto, Japan, September 1978 (International Council on Computer Communications and SRI International, 1978), p. 735.

3. Study conducted by author, 1977.

Less is more.

Robert Browning
"Andrea Del Sarto"

8

MICROGRAPHICS IN
OFFICE AUTOMATION

Micrographics is the capture, retrieval, and display of miniaturized, high-resolution photographic images containing either textual or graphic information. Occasionally the image exists on paper, but more often it is on film.

Micrographics dates from 1839, but until recently most people knew about microphotography only through tales of spies and saboteurs who communicated with their superiors by using microdots, photographic images the size of a period that could contain a page of information. Micrographics is now a valuable part of office automation. It provides for quick and inexpensive duplication of images for group distribution, for easy viewing by projection or computerized display, and for recreation of hard copies of microforms.

Micrographics also offers compact maintenance of active files and archival storage. With its array of film types, techniques, and retrieval options, micrographics affords the end user many benefits:

- Economy of document and file creation
- Economy of duplication (a 208-page fiche costs 5 cents to duplicate; 208 computer-printed pages would cost $5–$10.)
- Rapidity of duplication (5,000–6,000 pages per minute)

- Economy of distribution (less weight and bulk than paper)
- Reduction in filing costs by 50–80 percent
- Reduction in misfiling from 3–5 percent to 1 percent[1]
- Compact storage (90–98 percent space reductions)
- File integrity (difficult to misplace a single document)
- Speed of retrieval
- Economy of retrieval (all files at workstation)
- Proximity to users of voluminous information in compact form
- Portability
- Protection of vital records and disaster recovery (master copies of microfilm are usually stored in fire-resistant cabinets or vaults)
- Computer freed for other uses by rapidity of COM output
- Backup of on-line files in the event of down time.

The limitations are few. Except in jacket cards, microfilm provides no space for annotation; like other electronic systems, it requires access to a viewer or terminal; frequent updating of information requires an appropriate microform and system; and roll film can be accessed only serially.

International use of micrographics entails two possible difficulties: incompatibility of film types and reduction ratios when distributing copies, and taxation of imported microfiche.

Types of Microforms

There are three basic film types: silver, diazo, and vesicular. Silver film, like standard photographic film, is developed and made permanent by chemical fixation and has gray-to-black images, although the micrographic images can be either negative or positive. Diazo microfilm is developed in a bath of ammonia fumes and has bluish images. Vesicular film, developed by heat, tends to have pale gray images. Full-color film types are also available.

In office automation, 16mm and 105mm microfilm are the standard sizes. The 16mm film, about the size of the film in a pocket camera, comes on reels, in cartridges or cassettes, and in jackets. Reels in the viewing device accommodate 100-foot spools; such a spool may contain up to 2,800 page images; film thinner than the standard 5.5 mils can double the capacity. Cartridges provide a protective case for the spool, again with the take-up reel on the viewer; a cassette has a self-contained take-up reel. Cartridges and cassettes make loading and unloading faster. All three types of roll film provide sequential imaging and access, but random access can be provided through random filming and indexing.

Jackets are plastic sheets sandwiched together to form horizontal channels into which the 16mm film is inserted. Jacket cards are diecut cardboard forms that contain a miniature jacket. Both jackets and jacket cards permit easy updating by the exchange or addition of micrographic frames. The cardboard cover of a jacket card provides a place for an identifying mark or notation and is filed as a conventional document. Both jackets and jacket cards are random-access files.

Aperture cards are 35mm versions of jacket cards, containing only one frame. Their primary use is for engineering drawings. They have the same dimensions as a data processing tab card and are often encoded not only by printing but also by keypunching, which permits mechanical sorting into sequential order or location according to category. Hybrid jacket cards incorporate a 35mm film image beside 12 16mm frames and thus permit simultaneous viewing of an engineering drawing and its associated documentation.

The standard size film for microfiche, usually referred to as "fiche" (pronounced "feesh"), is 105mm. The film is normally cut into 6-inch lengths to form the customary microfiche sheet of 4 by 6 inches (known as "A6" size), though one device uses the film in uncut, roll form. The number of frames per microfiche depends on the reduction ratio at which the documents are filmed. Fiche are randomly accessed.

Reduction Ratios

The reduction ratio states the size of the original document (or CRT image) relative to the size of the final microphotographic image and is the same both horizontally and vertically. A reduction ratio of $24\times$ means that the microphotographic image is 1/24th the dimensional size of the original, both horizontally and vertically. The most common reduction ratios are $24\times$, $42\times$, and $48\times$. The industry standard for 16mm roll film and the standard of the National Micrographics Association is $24\times$. The U.S. government standard for microfiche is $48\times$.[2]

Ultrafiche is microfiche with a reduction ratio of $90\times$ or more. A standard microfiche sheet at a $90\times$ reduction contains the equivalent of more than 1,000 ordinary 8 1/2 by 11-inch pages.[3] Holofiche can contain up to 20,000 pages in a 4 by 6-inch ultrafiche. In the provision of storage capacity, holofiche are reputed to cost 1 percent as much as magnetic tape. Holofiche offers advantages for systems requiring rapid access to great quantities of information. Recorded in binary code, it permits direct reconvertibility to magnetic format for manipulation as computerized data or output. It is possible to deface, puncture, or even burn a portion of holofiche and still view the missing images. Creating a master costs approximately 50 cents; like any other microfiche, duplication costs only 5 cents.

Source document microfilming is the filming of a hard-copy source; computer output microfilming (COM) is the direct filming of computerized information without resorting to an immediate conversion to hard copy. The two processes require different kinds of tools.

Depending on both the original and ultimate mediums, five types of cameras are used in microfilming. The capture of hard-copy documents for roll, cartridge, cassette, or jackets requires either a rotary or a planetary camera. A rotary camera uses motorized rollers to transport each document into and out of the unit; some can photograph both sides of a document. Planetary cameras, usually oriented above a work surface or table, use manual or semiautomated systems. The first entails hand placement and removal of each document. A semiautomatic system involves manual insertion of each document in a mechanical feeder, which positions it for microphotographing and then automatically ejects it into a stacker.

Photographing hard-copy documents for production of microfiche requires a step-and-repeat camera, mounted above a flatbed table containing the documents. The camera mechanism successively aligns each small segment of 105mm film.

A specialized step-and-repeat camera uses a specialized film to create updatable microfiche. This system permits exposure and development of one or more frames at one or more times on the same piece of film. It also permits voiding of preexisting frames. Thus, related documents acquired at various times can be placed on the same piece of film without rephotographing the entire microfiche or juggling individual film frames. Updatable microfiche have a $24\times$ reduction and can contain 60 legal-size or 98 letter-size documents.

The more sophisticated source document cameras, such as the Docu-Mate II, manufactured by Terminal Data Corporation, have great versatility. A single unit can use 16mm, 35mm, 70mm, 82.5mm, and 105mm film; provide programmable titling on microfiche; handle reduction ratios from $20\times$ to $48\times$; film both sides of a document without operator intervention; and capture up to 5,000 source documents per hour.

Computer output microfilm (COM) cameras convert computer-generated material, usually a reel of magnetic tape, to microfiche. Typically, a high-resolution CRT displays the characters in the file, and an internal step-and-repeat camera photographs each "page" of information as it appears on the screen. Less commonly, COM cameras generate 16mm film.

COM cameras can capture 10,000–30,000 lines of up to 132 characters, or more than 500 pages, per minute. Holofiche page composers, a special type of COM device, can photograph up to 100,000 lines, or

DocuMate source document camera. Photo courtesy of Terminal Data Corporation.

1,800 pages, per minute. When compared with the usual 1,200- or 2,000-line-per-minute printers in many data centers, the advantages of COM cameras are obvious: faster output, freeing of off-line equipment, and reduced bulk and weight for transport.

Other types of COM imaging systems operate with unconventional processes. Both electron-beam recorders (EBRs) and laser-beam recorders (LBRs) image directly onto dry, silver film. Fiber optic systems use light-emitting diodes to pass light through bundles of fiber optic strands that face the film. Fiber optic systems cost only a fraction as much as other types of COM systems.

Xerox Corporation now offers a microfiche attachment for its Model 9700 intelligent copier, a highly specialized printer. With the microfiche attachment and other options, images can be transferred to the 9700 via magnetic media or electronic communications for conversion directly to fiche format.

Page composers, COM devices used as one means of generating holofiche, use either on-line or off-line electronic data files as their information source and capture information with laser beams.

COM cameras, unlike most other micrographic apparatus, are relatively expensive, in the $75,000 to $250,000 range, according to type and options. Only the generation of 90,000–100,000 frames a month justifies the cost of owning a COM camera system. Often, however, reduced turnaround time or portability of files can justify use of COM devices.

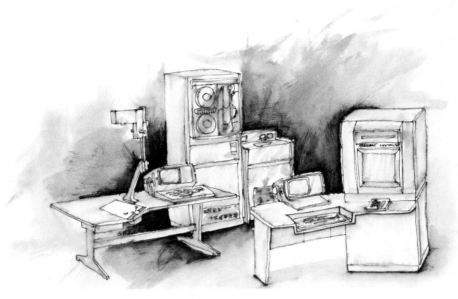

Microfilm information management system providing random data entry (*left*), storage (*center*), and automated retrieval (*right*). Based on Ragen Information Systems' System 95.

Smaller organizations or departments within large organizations that want to use micrographics with little investment can turn to numerous micrographic service bureaus worldwide. Most offer a variety of roll filming and COM services; some offer step-and-repeat filming for source documents and duplication services; and some provide on-site filming of critical or proprietary documents, affording maximum security to the user.

Conventional Retrieval

Conventional microfilm retrieval systems have external indexes for locating specific frames on rolls, cassettes, cartridges, and fiche. The nature of the records filmed usually dictates the scheme used: for source documents filmed in chronological order, it is customary to label reels, cassettes, and cartridges by inclusive dates; filmed purchase order files often use inclusive, sequential purchase order numbers. To locate specific frames, some indexing systems and viewers rely on a type of distance indicator that passes film through at high speed until the footage approaches the desired point. Others index by line codes, marks placed at various intervals on a scale between frames and parallel to the length of film; the lines appear at the edge of the screen opposite a numbered scale, indicating the approximate position in the reel, cassette, or car-

Large Reports A large, multinational firm has to mail multiple copies of a monthly report containing an equivalent of 2,600 pages of standard-size paper. By converting the data on computerized files to microfiche, each containing 208 photographic frames (at 42×) of standard-size pages of computer printout, the firm reduces the entire report to 13 sheets of microfiche that can be mailed in a small envelope.

tridge. Another means of locating images in reel-type micrographic files is blip coding, in which small marks are placed along the edge of the film during exposure; viewers equipped with a blip feature count the number of blips, corresponding to the number of frames, as the microfilm passes. Jackets and jacket cards have typed or hand-printed headers that can be color-coded or notched.

The top edge of a microfiche header usually includes large alphanumeric images stating the title and/or date of the documents included on the fiche. Other means of identifying fiche are striped, color-coded headers, such as blue for financial and green for sales reports. Fiche usually have self-contained indexes in the lower right corner of the frame. These indexes may identify individual document frames by purchase order number, alphabetically by name, or by any other convenient means. Grid coordinates specify the frame reference: horizontal rows have letters, columns have numbers. The upper left frame is usually identified as A1. Many users of microfiche become so proficient that they almost entirely avoid accessing indexes. Once familiar with specific reports and listings, they can quickly locate the specific frame of information.

In an automated office, where there may be millions of micrographic images, computer-aided retrieval (CAR), discussed in detail in Chapter 6, provides rapid access to specific frames.

Cost justification of CAR systems depends on the volume of information and the number of lookups per day, usually a minimum of 700–2,000 new frames and 35–200 lookups.[4] Manpower displacement at lower volumes of retrieval can also justify the cost of CAR. Hardware and software as a turnkey package presently ranges in cost from $26,000 to well over $100,000.

Viewers and Projectors

Manufacturers offer micrographic viewers for every need and circumstance. Tabletop viewers come both with and without built-in hardcopy printers. Many roll, cassette, and cartridge viewers are now motorized to accelerate the retrieval process. Some microfiche models have

Tabletop microfiche readers. The PRO model (*below*) is a projecting viewer suitable for group use. Photos courtesy of Realist, Inc. (*above left*), Micron Corporation (*above right*), and Northwest Microfilm, Inc.

a glass-topped bed that users can move forward, backward, and from side to side to position the correct frame beneath the lens; some of these have two or three carriers with relatively small capacities for up to 600 frames; another type has a wide screen and displays two frames side by side to permit viewing both a diagram and related data. Microfiche viewers have a pointer affixed to the carrier, and a matrix table containing the full set of image coordinates. With the pointer placed at a particular set of coordinates, the viewer projects the corresponding image on the screen. The cost of a tabletop viewer without a hard-copy printer starts at $160, depending on make and options.

One viewer, the Strobe/Search 100, holds a 500-foot roll of uncut 105mm microfiche film (1,000 fiche) mounted on a motorized mechanism that permits high-speed forward and reverse movement. During a file search, as each fiche draws opposite the optical assembly, a strobe light flashes to illuminate the header information and projects it on a screen. The action continues with successive headers and resembles

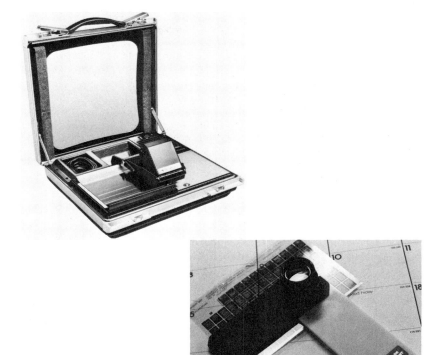

Portable microfiche readers. Photo of briefcase model courtesy of Bell and Howell; photo of Taylor Merchant pocket-size model courtesy of John King.

that of a motion picture projector. As the number approaches the required information, the operator decreases the speed with a knob, stops at the correct fiche, and can index the unit to the specific frame. At 42×, the viewer holds more than 200,000 fiche pages. The unit is essentially a serial file, but it ensures file integrity since the magazine remains within the viewer and there are no loose fiche; there is no loading and unloading time as with cut fiche; and one-hand operation frees the user to take notes or perform other activities.

A less bulky device, a lap viewer, is slightly larger than a standard textbook. There are also portable viewers in attache cases. Some have projection screens inside the lids, and some have screens that attach to the top of the case along with the projection heads. Since the projection heads take little room within the portable cases, these viewers provide portable storage for hundreds of thousands of microfiche pages. Portable viewers range in cost from $130, depending on capacity.

Carrying a File Room in an Attache Case A computer service technician, recently transferred to Canberra, Australia, arrives at a customer site and discovers a malfunctioning tape drive that he is unfamiliar with. He goes to the parking lot, returns from his car with a small attache case and a deck of microfiche, and opens the case, revealing a portable microfiche projector, complete with a screen. Inserting one of the microfiche, the technician locates the information needed to repair the tape drive. In a small tray in the car are hundreds of similar microfiche containing a full set of technical facts related to every product manufactured by his firm.

An even smaller device, the pocket viewer, is little more than a lens, a handle, and a clamping device to hold the fiche in place for viewing. Most are smaller than a flashlight. Some use a battery-powered bulb to illuminate the microfiche frame: some rely entirely on ambient light. All are quite inexpensive and make it possible to carry a rather large microfiche file in a coat pocket or purse, right along with the viewer. Prices for pocket viewers start at $10.

Microfiche projectors are useful when several people must view one micrographic image. A unit manufactured by Northwest Microfilm, Inc., has interchangeable lenses and indexing grids that permit projection of microfiche at 24×, 42×, or 48×. The unit can also project on any nearby light-colored surface. Projecting viewers are not a replacement for slide projectors. Projecting viewers cost under $300.

Viewers that are integrated with computerized microfiche retrieval systems are discussed in detail in Chapter 6.

Microfacsimile

Microfacsimile is a hybrid of facsimile and micrographics that digitizes and transmits microfilm input and outputs facsimile hard copy. Alden Electronic and Impulse Recorder Equipment Company, Inc.; Planning Research Corporation; Rapicom, Inc.; and Ragen Information Systems offer microfacsimile products.

The Rapicom standalone units scan and transmit a single frame of microfiche at a time. Output is via Rapicom fax devices on standard letter-size paper. The Alden standalone unit, intended for technical applications, accommodates 35mm aperture cards for input. Output can be on either standard-size paper or 18-inch-wide paper for engineering drawings. The usefulness of such freestanding systems is decreasing rapidly with the advent of on-line retrieval systems. Planning Research Corporation and Ragen Information Systems incorporate microfacsimile as part of systems with more extensive capabilities.

Micropublishing

Micropublishing, the publication of documents on microfilm instead of on paper, is now a well established part of micrographics. Large and small public and private libraries have microfilm departments housing extensive collections of back issues of newspapers and other periodicals. A number of business firms, governmental agencies, and professional societies offer thousands of books, reports, proceedings, and telephone directories of major cities on microfilm media. The private sector is turning to micropublishing for the production of catalogs, parts lists, instruction manuals, internal telephone directories, and other documents. The low cost and high speed of publication eliminates the lag time involved in hard-copy production: a computer can update a manual, convert it to fiche, and duplicate it in quantity overnight. Even with increased frequency of publication, savings can be considerable: creating a duplicate fiche containing 208 pages of information costs about 5 cents.

Current Directions

Concurrent filming and data base capture will become more important as office use of on-line micrographic data bases becomes more prevalent. There will also probably be more product offerings that, like the ARMS and the Telefiche systems, integrate the retrieval of micrographic and alphanumeric, graphic, and facsimile data bases.

Soft-copy retrieval is becoming a popular means of limiting the volume of paper and of microfilm created and maintained. The maintenance of a single data base reduces duplication costs and eliminates distribution time lag and retention of outdated documents or microfilm files. Soft copy ensures that everyone is working with the same, most current information.

Computer input microfilm (CIM), close relative of COM, exists in a few installations and is intended mainly as a cost-efficient alternative to on-line magnetic files when information is semiactive. A micrographic frame is scanned for conversion to digitized code and further manipulation by a computer. Users cannot alter the microfiche files.

Other hybrid micrographics systems have received preliminary publicity but have not materialized in the marketplace. Microvonics, for instance, deals with erasable and reimagable microfilm as distinct from updatable microfilm. Microvonics would make it possible to update an on-line microfiche data base by "erasing" selected frames and reimaging them, even via a communications link. Another desirable application could be a facsimile combination with fiche input and fiche output, which would offer rapid, remote creation of micrographic files.

NOTES

1. Industry consensus.
2. Frederick W. Miller, "Looking at Microforms," *Infosystems*, November 1978, p. 59.
3. Wilmer O. Maedke, Mary F. Robek, and Gerald F. Brown, *Information and Records Management* (Beverly Hills, Calif.: Glencoe Press, 1974), p. 372; Miller, "Looking at Microforms," p. 59.
4. Robert D. Atkins, "Teaming up Micrographics and Computers to Help the Information Manager," *The Information Manager*, September/October 1979, p. 36.

In the space age, man will be able to go
around the world in two hours—one hour
for flying and the other to get to the
airport.

Neil McElroy
Look, February 18, 1958

9

TELECONFERENCING

Teleconferences are meetings among people at physically distant locations by means of telecommunications. Teleconferencing may consist
of a conventional long-distance telephone call or a complex electronic
integration of audio, visual, and computer elements. Although a teleconference implies physical separation of participants, there is often a
group gathered at one or all locations: the teleconference becomes a
mixture of face-to-face, local group interaction and remote interaction.
In addition teleconferencing is often a substitute for no meeting at all
or for a delayed meeting when time or a budget is limited. It can also
be a source of additional information before or after a face-to-face
meeting.

A survey conducted by International Data Corporation indicates
that $30 million was spent on teleconferencing in the United States in
1978, with $10 million of that amount for hardware. By 1985, the U.S.
market for teleconferencing equipment and service is projected to be
$220 million, to be achieved largely through increasing use of commu-
nications services.[1]

Administrative conferences are perhaps the most common type of
business teleconference. They may involve exchanges of administrative
and technical information, staff meetings, announcements of new products, press conferences, and other business-oriented uses.

Other important categories of teleconferencing are telemedicine, the

137

conduct of medical diagnoses and treatment with the patient at one location and the physician or a specialist or a team of specialists at another, and teleteaching, the use of teleconferencing in education. The University of Wisconsin–Extension operates the largest teleteaching network in the world, with more than 200 locations throughout the state. Each year more than 30,000 students participate in courses from town halls, libraries, and other remote locations. Intrastate costs for operation of this system are about 30 cents per student hour.[2] Businesses also use teleteaching for specialized instruction or training.

Teleservicing—the diagnosis, service scheduling, and servicing of equipment at long distance—is the technological equivalent of telemedicine and is likely to parallel technological growth. Eastern Airlines operates perhaps the second largest audio teleconferencing network in the world for both administrative use and to schedule aircraft maintenance. Eastern's maintenance personnel across the United States use the system to determine the availability of hangar space, spare parts, and so on.

Only about 30 percent of business meetings require face-to-face contact, yet 40 percent of all U.S. air travel is for business purposes; that travel consumes 250,000 barrels of jet fuel daily. U.S. business travel by automobile consumes 400,000 barrels of gasoline per day. Replacing only 20 percent of U.S. business travel with teleconferencing could save 33 million barrels of fuel per year. Federal energy studies indicate that use of teleconferencing could reduce the country's annual petroleum consumption as much as 5 percent.[3] In fact, petroleum shortages and costs may prove the most significant motive force for implementing teleconferencing.

In addition to fuel conservation, other reasons for using teleconferencing include the following:

- Improved productivity
- More effective use of time
- Reduced labor costs
- Reduced travel cost
- Ability to attend several meetings at diverse locations in a single day
- Quicker solution of problems
- Short reaction time.

Not all types of teleconferencing are suited to all business meeting activities, though they serve with varying effectiveness for sessions involving brainstorming, exchanging information, and disseminating instructions. About one-third of business meetings involve conflict situations, bargaining, and interpersonal interactions and therefore are more successful when conducted face-to-face.[4]

Attention spans, as in face-to-face meetings, have limits in teleconferences. Two hours without a break is the approximate limit for problem solving; teleteaching should not exceed three hours.[5]

Types of Teleconferencing: Audio, Video, Computer

Audio and video teleconferencing are synchronous; that is, all participants, regardless of geographic locale, must take part at the same absolute time. Graphically enhanced audio teleconferencing (discussed below), which sometimes uses computer terminals, is also synchronous. Computer teleconferencing is nonsynchronous: participants need not all be present at any given time.

Audio is the simplest, least expensive, and most pervasive kind of teleconferencing. It may involve only audio transmission or may also incorporate graphics (transparencies, slow-scan TV, or semimotion TV). See Table 9.1 for a cost comparison of face-to-face and teleconferenced meetings.

Video teleconferencing uses the familiar commercial type of television with audio; participants can both see every movement as it occurs and hear all speakers; it can be in black-and-white or color.

TABLE 9.1 Comparative costs per participant of face-to-face vs teleconferenced meetings. Conference participants were from Boston, MA, and Phoenix, AZ.

Conventional Meeting
Round trip, tourist air fare	$832.00
Hotel/motel	70.00
Meals	46.00
Lost time (4 hours; other half of working day)	120.00
Car rental	25.00
Total	$1,093.00

Teleconferenced Meeting
Teleconferencing service and equipment (2 lines)	5.00
Depreciation (2 purchased, high-quality audio terminals)	10.24
Tie line use (240 min. × $0.36/min. via leased line)	86.40
Total	$101.64

Source: Teleconferencing consulting assignment conducted by the author early in 1979.

Computer teleconferencing is closely related to electronic mail systems but provides more built-in assistance to the conferees. Participants in a computer teleconference use terminals to read the comments of others, key in their own comments, and vote.

Various federal, state, and local laws affect the recording of teleconferences. In the United States, federal law prohibits recording a teleconference without the prior knowledge of all participants. Many conference rooms use backlit signs to indicate that recording is taking place. Planners and operators should consult with an attorney about requirements in each location involved.

Audio Teleconferencing

Research shows that at least 50 percent of meetings among three or more people are as effective if conducted with audio teleconferencing as they are face-to-face.[6] One study which analyzed more than 6,000

Types of Face-to-Face Meetings That Convert Successfully to Teleconferencing

Announcements	Medical diagnoses
Brainstorming sessions	Negotiation
Briefings	Press conferences
Budget reviews	Problem solving
Contract negotiations	Product introductions
Coordination	Production forecasts
Employment interviews	Quick approvals
Engineering changes	Resolving minor conflicts
Failure analysis	Reviews / updates
Goal setting	Staff meetings
Interactive information	Teaching
exchange	Technical exchanges
Interim discussion	Trip planning
and understanding	Trip reports

Types of Meetings Not Normally Suited to Audio and Video Teleconferencing

Annual personnel reviews
Bargaining (emotionally charged, as opposed to negotiation)
Disciplinary actions
First meetings between individuals
Personnel matters
Persuasion
Resolving conflicts involving human feelings

---

meetings and dozens of other such studies, which cover a broad range of public and private organizations in several different nations, revealed similar findings.[7]

In some cases the absence of the visual dimension is a positive factor. Market testing of the Picturephone, for example, revealed that people sometimes do not wish to be seen.[8] Lack of the visual medium also confers transactional advantages. Face-to-face meetings are frequently controlled by a dominant participant who monopolizes the discussion; audio teleconferences by their nature exert a degree of control over dominant individuals, permitting broader participation. In negotiation and bargaining, when objectivity and comprehension are of first importance, visual elements can be distracting and disrupt concentration. Furthermore, participants in a meeting with a controversial topic are more likely to change their opinion in teleconferences than in face-to-face meetings.[9] Finally, it is not only easier to be objective in an audio-only mode; it is also less expensive: audio teleconferences tend to be shorter than any other form of group meeting.

The kinds of face-to-face meetings that convert successfully to audio teleconferences include information exchange, directives, brainstorming and other forms of creative thinking, proposal presentations, resolution of minor conflicts, cooperative problem solving, and decision making.[10] A more detailed list appears in the accompanying tabulation.

Arranging and Conducting an Audio Teleconference

The process of arranging and conducting the audio teleconference is simple:

1. Arrange the meeting; reserve teleconferencing rooms.
2. Issue an agenda (option: distribute graphics).
3. Place the conference call.
4. Hold the teleconference.

Usually the chairperson arranges the teleconference and appoints a local coordinator at each remote location to make arrangements for equipment and to maintain order at that location. A written agenda distributed in advance is desirable. The chairperson sends agendas and any nonelectronic graphic materials to coordinators for distribution or projection.

The chairperson and all coordinators arrive at their respective meeting rooms about five minutes before the teleconference, and the chairperson places the conference call. In rotation, the chairperson and each coordinator then ask the respective participants to introduce themselves. Ideally, all participants should have met face-to-face on at least one occasion; if some have not, it is good practice to have all participants state their title, responsibility, or background.

Once the teleconference is under way, it is up to the chairperson and the coordinators to follow the schedule on the agenda. When the meeting involves projected graphics, a predesignated individual operates the overhead transparency or slide projector. Each person presenting graphics announces when to turn the page or change the image. The only equipment essential to audio teleconferencing is a telephone handset. A conventional telephone, though adequate for brief, infrequent teleconferencing, is inconvenient to hold to one's ear during long or frequent meetings and provides generally inferior audio quality. Experienced planners and consultants cite audio quality as the single most important element of this type of teleconferencing. Most audio teleconferencing takes place on specialized telephones called audio terminals, equipped both with a built-in device that modulates the volume of the speaker's voice (the outgoing sounds) and with a control knob to adjust the volume of incoming sounds.

Types of terminals vary from a single portable unit to permanent installations with separate, built-in components. Portable audio terminals are about the size of a portable typewriter and plug into telephone jacks. They are practical when the cost of a permanent terminal is not justifiable or when a user requires a temporary installation outside the organization. A few private manufacturers sell catalog models for about $500 up; most telephone companies rent them for about $11–$20 per month, depending on locale. Those that are frequently moved should have a carrying case with a padded lining to protect the termi-

Portable teleconferencing equipment permitting simultaneous two-way conversation over standard telephone circuits. Photo courtesy of Darome, Inc.

nal. Larger models, suitable for use by large groups in auditoriums, are also available for rental from telephone companies for as short a time as a day; they can be supplied with up to 8 microphones and 4 large loudspeakers per terminal. Few people are aware of their availability, and rental costs vary. Telephone company representatives will obtain details and prices for users who are interested. Table 9.2 compares the cost and capacities of audio teleconferencing equipment.

Permanent installations in rooms dedicated to audio teleconferencing have one or more permanently attached or built-in components, such as microphone cables installed in electrical conduits within the floors and loudspeakers bolted to walls. Excellent terminals are available from private manufacturers and their dealers for $500 and up. Custom-built units vary widely in price according to sophistication and number of microphones and loudspeakers. One high-quality custom unit supporting 16 microphones and 4 column speakers, associated mixers, automatic volume controls, and amplifiers can cost $16,000 per room. Most telephone companies rent permanent terminals. For installations of special audio terminals for large groups or unique installations, telephone companies, private manufacturers, and firms supplying equipment to the broadcasting trade offer solutions. Voice-grade telephone lines are sufficient for most audio teleconferences. Some units require four-wire telephone circuits; most use the standard two-wire circuits. To make a connection between two locations, a person at one site simply dials the number of the other terminal. To connect three or more locations re-

TABLE 9.2 Teleconferencing audio equipment comparisons.[a]

Audio device	Suggested no. of people	Cost per month	Cost per hour
Bell 4A Speakerphone	6	$ 9.50	$0.37
Bell 50A1 Portable Conference Telephone	10-12	17.00	0.65
Darome Convener Conference Unit[b]	10-15	18.00	0.69
Northern Telecom Conference 2000[b]	up to 20	33.33	1.28

[a]Table is based on an implementation in which the author took part in the New England area. All hourly rates are prorated, based on only 6 hours of use per week, and are based on tariffs and vendor prices effective in March 1979.
[b]Purchase only; figures are based on five-year, straight-line depreciation.

Completing A Contract Negotiation   A major manufacturer in Boston is negotiating a master purchase agreement with a vendor in the Midwest so that nationwide field sales offices and plants will be able to buy certain supplies at a lower, uniform price. Negotiation is complete except for discussion of several minor insertions and the rewording of several sentences for clarity. The vendor's representative cannot travel to Boston for a face-to-face meeting for another two weeks.

The negotiator from the manufacturer's purchasing administration department arranges a teleconference with the vendor for the following afternoon.

The contract negotiations involve two people from the Boston firm's purchasing administration department, an attorney from the firm's legal department, and the vendor's sales representative, sales manager, and attorney, all in their respective offices. The agreement assumes final form in less than 90 minutes.

---

quires a means of interconnection. Some telephone systems, such as Centrex, permit a three-way connection without operator intervention. More connections require a bridge, described in Chapter 3.

Many internal switchboards are equipped with small bridges that connect a mix of up to 5 inside extensions and outside numbers. Private suppliers of telephone equipment sell bridges. Some are intended for installation at a switchboard site; other, smaller models attach directly within the teleconferencing rooms. The latter can interconnect up to 5 lines but require 4 outgoing lines, since all calls must be placed from the bridge location. Because there is seldom need to connect more than 5 locations, large, private bridges are rarely justified. Telephone company conference operators can interconnect up to 40 separate lines, though audio volume diminishes with more than 25 connections. Several private concerns offer bridging service for up to 100 separate locations in a single conference. At least one firm is planning installation of a bridge with a 300-line capacity, to serve such needs as teleconferenced sales meetings.

Transmission

All audio conferencing terminals are either open-loop (full-duplex) or voice-actuated (half-duplex). A voice-actuated terminal transmits either outgoing sound from the microphone(s) or incoming sound from the loudspeaker(s) but not both at the same time. Voice-actuated units preclude feedback, the electronic howling caused by improper placement of a microphone and a loudspeaker. As soon as a sound within the room enters the audio terminal, a switch turns the microphone on and

Audio teleconference using Bell 50A-1 conference set. Photo courtesy of AT&T.

the loudspeaker off. When the sound has ceased, the switch turns the microphone off and the loudspeaker on again. While local participants are speaking, the microphone is transmitting; those within the room hear no incoming conversation from other locations. To counteract confusion, one person at each location, usually the chairperson and each local coordinator, can wear a lightweight earphone, which is incapable of causing feedback and so remains on at all times. If someone at a remote location speaks while a person at the immediate location has control of the microphone, the person with the earphone will hear the incoming comment even though the local loudspeaker is off. That person can either repeat the remark or ask that it be repeated for all to hear.

Clipping of the first portion of speakers' words or phrases occurs when the electronic switching fails to turn on the microphone fast enough. Voice-actuated terminals hold a microphone open for a predetermined time after a sound to keep it open during the slight pauses in normal speech. If the terminal is preset for too short a lag period, the speaker's microphone will turn on and off continually through his or her presentation. Clipping tires teleconference participants by forcing intense concentration to comprehend the clipped words. Good voice-actuated terminals have very fast microphone switches and proper lag timing that preclude clipping.

In an open-loop system, all microphones and loudspeakers are "on" at all times; every participant, regardless of location, can hear comments from other locations, even when someone is speaking within the local room.

How does a person at one location know who is speaking at another location? This is not a problem when the participants know one another from a prior meeting and when the audio equipment is of high quality. In other circumstances, one solution is the British RCS, the Remote Conference System (still frequently referred to by its former name, Remote Conference Table). The two models provide for either 6 or 8 people at each location, a maximum of 16 conferees. Each person has a separate microphone and a small, table-mounted loudspeaker, labeled with the name of one participant at the other location and placed in the same position the participant occupies at the remote location. Each loudspeaker transmits only the voice of the person whose name is on it; a small indicator light glows on the specific loudspeaker in use.[11]

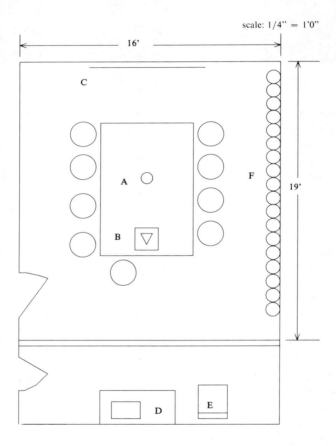

Plan for audio teleconferencing room with graphic support. (A) Microphone and loudspeaker, (B) projector for slides or transparencies, (C) screen, (D and E, in nearby room) facsimile transceiver and photocopier to convert facsimiles to transparencies, (F) acoustic wall treatments. Computer-generated diagram produced by Tymshare, Inc., with AUGMENT software.

In many audio terminal designs the microphones are separate from the loudspeakers. New users, especially, will turn and speak to the loudspeaker just as they would to another person in a face-to-face conversation. In doing so, they often turn away from the microphone and their comments are inaudible. One remedy is to use individual microphones about an inch long, which can be suspended from the neck or clipped to clothing. Such microphones are also useful for speakers who are moving about the room. The Remote Conference System addresses this problem through the provision of microphones and the physical layout of the tables. A third solution is to select equipment with the microphone and loudspeaker in the same enclosure.

Rooms

When it is cost justified, dedicating one or more rooms to audio teleconferencing ensures that necessary equipment will be ready when users arrive. Teleconferencing rooms should be easy to locate, not too distant from users, and in moderately quiet areas, to avoid distraction and the accidental activation of microphones. Relatively inexpensive modifications, such as carpeting, screens, or hangings, can make a room acoustically acceptable. A good teleconferencing room should echo slightly to give the audio a live, natural sound. If a single loud handclap from the center of a room seems to bounce off the walls for a moment and then dissipate, the room is probably well balanced and suitable. Close-speaking microphones, sensitive to a limited spatial pattern and range, can compensate for substandard acoustics.

For displaying graphics, audio teleconferencing rooms should have directional, dimmable, incandescent lighting above the table surface. The zone directly in front of a projection screen should be unlit to prevent washout of projected graphics. Dimmed room lights allow for simultaneous viewing of graphics and note taking.

Operating Security

Security of information in an audio teleconference is the same as in a telephone conversation. Organizations dealing with highly sensitive or potentially valuable information can install voice scramblers in each location to encode spoken words prior to transmission; at the receiving end, a matching unit reconverts the encoded sounds to words. Users may set the scrambling apparatus to encode and decode in hundreds of thousands of permutations. Anyone tapping the line will find transmission unintelligible without the same scrambling equipment and knowledge of the code then in use. In high-security sessions, participants can periodically change the key. Similar security devices are available for analog and digital facsimile units. Equipment is available from vendors of telephone and radio apparatus.

Savings

There are many examples of significant cost reduction and control with audio teleconferencing. In one instance, an installation consisting of two purchased audio terminals and two leased digital fax units connects a Boston office with one in Phoenix and operates six hours per week. The costs of the purchased equipment and the first year's leasing charges for the fax units were amortized in less than 90 days.[12] In another case, NASA, a large-scale, successful user of audio teleconferencing, saves nearly 20 percent in travel costs annually with voluntary teleconferencing.[13]

In a third case, a drug manufacturer held a national sales meeting to introduce new products to 650 salespeople. Shortly thereafter it became necessary to hold a follow-up meeting on short notice. The original meeting had cost about $250,000, and no one was anxious to repeat that kind of expenditure, even though the new meeting would require interaction among participants. Instead, the firm bridged an audio teleconference among 32 locations for $50,000, only 20 percent of the face-to-face cost, and saved participants travel time as well.[14]

Graphically Enhanced Audio Teleconferencing

Graphics improve retention when used with the spoken word and aid comprehension when substituted for text. A simple diagram or graph can help a speaker communicate an idea more rapidly. Either nonelectronic or electronic graphics can be used in audio teleconferencing.

Teleteaching with Graphics   The city of San Diego uses graphically enhanced teleteaching for elementary pupils confined to their homes with long-term illnesses or injuries. Specially trained teleteachers, working from a special conferencing console in the school district's teleteaching room, can confer with groups of pupils studying the same subject, hold confidential discussions, or provide individual assistance. Each child involved is furnished with an electric writer. The teacher can transmit hand-drawn illustrations, and the pupils can perform the electronic equivalent of drawing on a chalkboard or answering a written test. (*Source:* San Diego, California, School District Report, 1975).

Nonelectronic graphics—hard copy, overhead transparencies, and 35mm slides—are inexpensive and generally are already in use or can be quickly implemented. Using them requires making duplicate sets of all materials and mailing them in advance to each of the other locations. Sequential numbering of materials ensures concurrent viewing of the same graphics at all locations during the teleconference.

Noninteractive electronic graphics cost more than nonelectronic graphics but generally require less advance notice to meet teleconferencing needs. They are generated and distributed by facsimile, thermal terminals, communicating word processors, slow-scan TV, or semimotion video units.

Fax units transmit copies to each remote site, where a photocopier is used to make additional copies, overhead transparencies, or both. Multicolor fax transmission is available at substantial cost.

For transmitting 35mm slides, one firm manufactures a remote control, random-access projector. With a Touch-Tone pad and a decoder, a presenter can remotely select a random slide and project it on the distant screen. This system requires a separate telephone connection in addition to the audio circuit; interconnection of three or more points entails establishing a separate conference circuit. Other systems successfully use sound-activated switches attached to remotely located 35mm slide projectors. These units employ the same conference circuit used for discussion.

If graphics material is resident in a computerized file, thermal terminals can directly create black-and-white or tinted overhead transparencies at remote sites. Portable computer terminals are available for such use; one is capable of limited plotting. Prices for alphanumeric terminals range from $1,600, whereas printing/plotting terminals cost about $5,000.

Communicating word processors can transmit and concurrently display alphanumeric material. A few participants can view the material directly on the screen of a display terminal. Some display terminals accommodate video projectors for group viewing. Adequate projectors cost $3,000 or more.

Slow-Scan Television

Slow-scan television (SSTV) like all video has limited application with audio teleconferencing for several reasons. First, most graphics presented at meetings are static images. In an impromptu survey of 46 teleconferencing system planners and users, most felt that slow-scan TV in audio teleconferencing is useful only for displaying a three-dimensional object. Another use, to show who is present at a teleconference, remains controversial. According to proponents, participants tend to re-

Differences in slow-scan TV images at 128 × 128, 256 × 256, and 512 × 512 resolutions. Photos courtesy of Colorado Video, Inc.

lax once they know exactly who is in a remote teleconferencing room. Other planners and users believe the cost is unwarranted for such a limited purpose.[15]

For teleconferencing purposes, basic slow-scan TV units for each location consist of a single camera, monitor, and associated control units. Units with a minimal resolution of 256 by 256 pixels cost about $6,000; better quality units with resolutions up to 512 by 512 pixels cost more. A typical configuration includes two cameras (one on a dolly for use with boards, one vertically mounted on a graphics stand), two monitors (one for the outgoing camera view, one for the incoming signal), a high-quality stereo audio tape recorder, and associated control devices. Image transmissions are analog, permitting the recording of both sight and sound. Such a configuration costs between $18,000 and $20,000 for one location. A similar color configuration costs several thousands more.

SSTV operates by "grabbing" a single frame from a closed-circuit television camera and transmitting the pixels serially through unconditioned, voice-grade telephone lines. This process is also called "freeze-frame TV." The grabber stores the particular frame and, prior to transmission, can also apply compression techniques to save time. Future improvements in compression techniques should bring faster transmission times per image.

Typical transmission time for a black-and-white picture at 9,600 baud is about 32 seconds and for the same image in color is about 120 seconds. On a 1.5 megahertz link (a T-1 carrier) color transmission

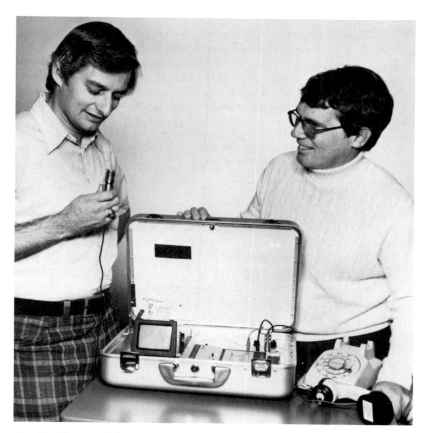

Portable "Convener" slow-scan TV conferencing unit acoustically coupled to standard telephone. Photo courtesy of Darome, Inc.

takes only one half second. If speed is essential, the added transmission cost may be justifiable. Frame-to-frame image time can be greatly reduced through use of a local memory which stores and queues incoming image signals. When an image is called to the receiving monitor, it comes to the screen rapidly from the local memory device.

Optional SSTV equipment includes multiple cameras, either fixed or on small dollies that permit moving from, say, a three-dimensional model to a flip-chart or a blackboard. Other options include additional memory capacity and real-time interactive pointers—bold white arrowheads that can be rotated 360 degrees and moved to any part of the screen. Because the image is locally generated, only the orientation and location control signals for the pointers are sent across the transmission medium. Most SSTV equipment has been designed for use by non-technical personnel and is simple to operate.

Unfortunately, there is little or no compatibility among brands of SSTV equipment: some units scan from left to right, others from top to

Teleservicing with SSTV A German service technician is called to examine a malfunctioning machine designed and built in the United States. The device has been installed for only a few days, and the service manuals have not yet arrived. Unfamiliar with the machine, the technician cannot repair the malfunction. His manager brings slow-scan TV equipment (normally used for administrative teleconferences at the vendor office) to the location and sets up a teleconference with engineers in the United States. The slow-scan TV equipment transmits views of portions of the machine, so the U.S. engineers can both see the physical status of the machine and confer with the technician. The repair is effected in hours.

bottom; black-and-white equipment cannot interact with a unit using color. If SSTV is a requirement, uniformity should be addressed early.

Another limitation is that an SSTV video screen has an aspect ratio of 3:4; that is, the standard vertical image dimension is always 3 units to the horizontal image dimension of 4 units. Consequently, a video screen can accommodate only about two-thirds of a vertically-oriented standard-size page. In addition, lettering on flip charts, mounted graphic images, and chalk and chemical writing boards must be over two inches high for clear viewing.

Finally, color transmission can be important for use with preexisting color graphics or for differentiating color-coded wiring in an electronic chassis, but color SSTV does not produce accurate hues or intensities. It is impractical when differentiation of subtle colors is crucial, as in telemedicine.

Semimotion TV

Semimotion or quasi-real-time video is seldom used in teleconferencing but warrants consideration when motion is necessary. Such units transmit only the portions of the image that have moved since the last scan, reducing the volume of transmitted picture elements and yielding nearly the same impression as full-motion video, though not nearly so smoothly.

Electronic Graphics

Real-time graphic equipment permits immediate creation, alteration, transmission, and remote viewing of graphic images. Real-time equipment may offer only one-way transmission or can be interactive. With interactive graphics, teleconferencing participants at distant locations can create or alter the graphics, with the image visible at all locations as it takes form. Another type of equipment requires predistribution of graphics but permits interactive electronic pointing with a spot of light. Interactive graphics have uses in education, technology, design, and data processing flow charting.

Devices presently available include electric writers, projecting electric writers, the Gemini 100 Electronic Blackboard offered by the Bell System companies, and one or two computer teleconferencing software systems that permit sharing of remotely located terminals.

Electric Writers

Electric writers permit a person to draw or print any symbol or graphic and replicate it in hard copy on a similar remote machine. Generally the replication is by means of a pen harnessed to a mechanism in each machine; when one pen is activated, all others on line move accordingly to create the remote copies. The hard copy is often a printed paper form that can be put to direct use. Talos Systems, Inc., manufactures systems called Telescreen and Forum which use overhead transparency projectors as receiving units and acetate hard copy to permit interactive group viewing of projected images.

Electronic Blackboards

The University of Illinois has used the Gemini Electronic Blackboard since 1974 at its Champaign campus. A number of firms across the state provide employees with access to university engineering courses via teleteaching. Facsimile units can be attached to provide hard copy.[16]

The Gemini 100 can be configured as either a simplex or full-duplex system. A simplex system consists of what appears to be a conventional blackboard connected by telephone lines to the output device, a television monitor. The sender writes on the blackboard with regular chalk. Sensors embedded in the special board cause the chalk strokes to be transmitted to the remotely located television monitor. To clear the blackboard, the sender lifts an ordinary felt blackboard eraser from its cradle on the chalk tray, thus switching the local circuitry into erase mode. The sensors embedded in the blackboard respond to the pressure of the eraser and permit selective erasure of the electronic image simultaneously on all remote monitors.

The sender can thus alter the image without obliterating it. The full-duplex configuration permits users at all locations to draw, write, and selectively erase images. Communication requires use of two telephone lines, one for the voice and one for the electronic blackboard. A stereophonic audio tape recorder can capture both audio and graphic images,

Gemini Electronic Blackboard by AT&T.

since transmission is over analog telephone circuits. The transmission, complete with graphic images, can be replayed later for review by individuals not present at the time of original transmission.

A unique device, the Tele/Pointer, displays predistributed graphic materials on a small, tabletop unit with a translucent screen equipped with a joystick. Via the linking telephone circuit, any user can cause a small light beam to project on any portion of the graphic image, as with a pointer at a blackboard or flip chart. The device provides high security, since the only electrical impulses transmitted are those to the mechanisms that guide the light beam.

Video Teleconferencing

Video teleconferencing with full-motion television is better suited than either audio or computer teleconferencing to discussing complex tangible objects and interpersonal matters. However, video of all types is suitable for only 8 percent of face-to-face meetings for which audio teleconferencing alone is inappropriate.[17] Full-motion television is equivalent to commercially broadcast television. Transmission is either black-and-white or color and, unlike SSTV or semimotion TV, incorporates sound. In the U.S., broadcast TV resolution is 350 horizontal lines by 525 vertical lines. (Resolution in the studio is somewhat higher but is converted for transmission.) The European standard for

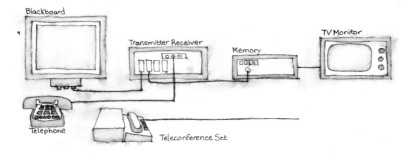

The Gemini blackboard system. Graphics are displayed on TV monitors through one telephone connection while voice transmission occurs simultaneously on a second line. Diagram courtesy of AT&T.

broadcast is 625 lpi; unconverted broadcasts from the United States appear on European monitors with a small black stripe at the bottom of the screen, indicating the missing scan lines. Full-motion television signals require expensive broadband transmission, which restricts its use by private business. With the increased availability of satellite transmission, however, there is growing interest in full-motion television.

Comparative studies of face-to-face meetings and audio, video, and computer teleconferencing show that video teleconferences produce more changes of opinion than do face-to-face discussions but only as many as or fewer than audio conferences.

Conducting a video teleconference parallels conducting an audio teleconference: set up the meeting; reserve the video teleconferencing room; arrange the transmission link; appoint the coordinator at the other location; distribute the agenda, hard copy, and graphic material; arrive a few minutes early to establish the transmission; and hold the teleconference.

A well-designed video teleconferencing room is unassuming and uncluttered yet adequately equipped for its purpose. In 1974 NASA installed a small prototype network of four video teleconferencing rooms, each with a spartan but functional design for use by up to four participants. The rectangular room contained only a small, tripod-mounted video camera for focusing on equipment models or people; two monitors for incoming and outgoing signals; a video camera positioned over a six-foot-long table for viewing opaque graphic materials either prepared in advance or hand-drawn during a teleconference; two portable lights; and four chairs. Just outside the room was a high-speed digital fax unit for transmission of hard-copy graphics.

Such rooms with dedicated basic apparatus can accommodate shared or rented portable equipment, such as video recording and playback units, video hard-copy units, and graphic projectors.

The Picturephone Meeting Service (PMS) rooms, operated by

Video teleconference in an especially equipped room. Photo courtesy of Satellite Business Systems.

AT&T's Long Lines Department, are designed to serve a wide range of clients with varying graphics needs. Each room in the PMS network varies slightly as the result of successive improvements as each was added to the network. The one in Washington, D.C., designed for 12 local participants, has a carefully planned, comprehensive configuration that permits the chairperson or coordinator to override the automatic functions. There are six chairs along one side of the conference table, and each position is equipped with a lightweight microphone on a neck cord. Behind them, on a slightly raised platform, is another row of chairs with a three-foot-high barrier in front. The ceiling lights and light intensity are similar to those in other conference rooms. The chairperson usually sits at one of the two center seats at the table. In the tabletop between those seats is a small panel with buttons which are so clearly labeled that a nontechnical individual can be instructed how to use them to control room equipment in under five minutes.

The front wall of the room has two built-in studio monitors, labeled with the names of the immediate and remote locations. Above the monitors are two small openings in the wall. One contains the camera that views the entire room; the other contains three camera lenses in a concave arrangement. One picks up the two rightmost people in the front

Video Teleconferencing A manufacturing firm acquires another small firm 1,700 miles from its headquarters. The research and development engineers for a particular product line remain at the parent location; the newly acquired firm assumes the role of production engineers for that product.

Just before starting production on a new machine, engineers at the parent firm discover that certain parts are cracking for unknown reasons. The R&D engineers must see the failed parts and witness a failure on a test stand. They schedule a full-motion video teleconference, move a prototype model and a test stand to a storeroom adjacent to the video teleconferencing room, hook up a television camera and a microphone in the storeroom, and mount a close-up lens on the camera to focus on the crucial part.

The video teleconference begins at 1:00 p.m. Fourteen engineers at the parent firm discuss the previous failures with the production engineers, preparing for the test. Then the test begins. The machine operates for several minutes while the two groups of engineers listen and watch. Suddenly the crucial part cracks; the screeching sound of metal on metal fills both rooms. The project manager asks for a replay of the videotape; the failure segment is replayed several times at speed and then in slow motion. Working carefully from the recorded sound track and the video images, the R&D engineers conclude that the tension on four bolts was too high and agree to a change that is still within specification tolerances.

They take a half-hour break while a new prototype is placed on the test stand. In accordance with company practice, an authorization for the tension change is drawn up and word processed at corporate headquarters. Minutes later a vertically mounted document camera displays the image of the document, complete with authorized signatures, to the production engineers 1,700 miles away. A hard copy is also transmitted via a video hard-copy unit.

Thirty minutes later, a second test is conducted using the new bolt tensions. The machine runs 3 minutes, 5 minutes, 11 minutes, and continues to operate. The engineers agree to run the machine through the full 9-hour test and to teleconference briefly again at 9:00 a.m. the following morning to review that test.

At the morning teleconference the participants share the news that the prototype successfully completed the test and reveals no abnormalities.

---

and rear rows; the next, the two people in the center of both rows; and the third, the two leftmost persons in each row. The room microphones can control the cameras electronically. While participants are watching and listening to incoming discussion and no sound is originating in the room, the three close-up cameras automatically show the local participants in sequence, holding each shot for 10–15 seconds. If anyone speaks, the specific close-up camera immediately switches to that speaker. Unless someone else speaks, the automatic camera controls resume sequenced views of the room.

Near the front of the room is a chemical writing board and a large easel with a pad of paper. The tripod-mounted camera at the opposite side of the room can focus on either. Beneath the board is a wall jack for plugging in the microphone of the board user.

On the front wall is a flush-mounted graphics unit about four feet high and two feet square, with a frosted-glass top. A small hood above the cabinet contains a mirror by which a rear-mounted TV camera views the opaque and transparent graphic materials placed on the glass; for an opaque graphic, illumination comes from above; lights embedded in the cabinet provide illumination for a transparency. A built-in 35mm slide projector projects upward onto the ground-glass screen. Videotape equipment is available for both input or recording of teleconferences.

In a rear corner of the room is a video hard-copy unit about the size of a tabletop facsimile. At the push of a button it creates a hard copy of a television image received from the opposite location.

The video conferencing rooms of PMS are linked by broadband circuits. Similar transmission facilities can be arranged through telephone companies or private carriers. An increasing number of vendors offer private satellite video service for teleconferencing. Buildings a few miles apart can use private microwave. An aircraft manufacturer uses such transmission, with a single, intermediate repeater located on a leased tower facility midway between its two sites.[18]

Video teleconferencing equipment and transmission costs more than audio and may be harder to justify. Video equipment for a minimally equipped room costs from $25,000 up; one well-equipped room costs several hundred thousand dollars. But return on investment may overshadow the capital outlay.

Equipment can be purchased outright, privately leased, or rented. Satellite Business Systems and many other commercial sources sell or will assist in the buying of video teleconferencing equipment. On a monthly rental basis the AT&T Long Lines Department will install equipment arrays similar to those in the PMS rooms. Fees vary according to configuration, but a typical on-premises room, such as the one at Ford Aerospace and Communications, costs about $45,000 for the room, including furniture; in addition, there is a $10,200 annual leasing fee.[19]

Public video teleconferencing systems exist worldwide, but on an independent basis, with no interconnection. The charge for the Confravision system between Melbourne and Sydney, Australia, and for the Nippon telephone video teleconferencing service between Tokyo and Osaka, Japan, is $400 per hour, or about $6.67 per minute.[20] The PMS tariff between Washington, D.C., and New York City is $150 per hour or $2.50 per minute (the lowest rate for two points in the system); service between Boston and San Francisco is $390 per hour or $6.50 per minute (the highest rate within the network).

Besides wiretapping outgoing audio and video lines, there are two ways of gaining unauthorized access to video teleconferencing signals. First, anyone with the proper receiving equipment can pick up a satellite signal. Scrambling and descrambling equipment eliminates such access. Second, radio frequency signals radiate from the equipment in the video teleconferencing room itself, the equipment acting as a low-power broadcasting station for a distance of about 200 feet. Installing radio frequency filters and suitably shielding the room itself prevents such electronic eavesdropping.

Computer Teleconferencing

The three major incentives for computer teleconferencing are:

- Time-zone transparency
- Nonconcurrent availability of participants
- A written record of proceedings.

The first two purposes are quite similar. For multinational firms and international transactions, differences in time zones limit or can preclude audio or video teleconferencing. Similarly, busy personnel within the same building who travel or attend many meetings find it difficult

---

Computer Teleconferencing   The expense-control team, a standing committee, consists of a representative and one alternate from each of 11 plants, geographically dispersed among three European nations, five American states in three time zones, and one site each in Puerto Rico, the Far East, and Australia. The team's corporate role is to take practical steps to reduce wastefulness within the firm and thereby keep the firm vigorously competitive despite inflation. Since the group meets every month for only about two hours, they decide to teleconference. There is no concurrent time in their respective working days to permit audio teleconferencing, so they elect to computer teleconference.

Instead of gathering for a two-hour meeting each month, each member allocates a few minutes throughout the month. Working from keyboard terminals connected to the international communications network, they access their expense-control team teleconference at their own convenience. They read the questions, suggestions, and comments of other team members and enter their own, either under their own names or assumed ones for anonymity. Any participant can communicate with any other single participant, combination of participants, or with the group as a whole. The chairperson determines when to poll members and take votes, either of which can be roll-call or anonymous. Results of polls and votes are immediately available to any participant.

---

to get together. A computer teleconference can establish and maintain communication.

When a written record is desirable, a computer teleconference with terminal-to-terminal communication is ideal. The other two forms of teleconferencing require a media conversion to obtain hard copy of the discussion.

Unlike other teleconferences, a computer teleconference permits simultaneous comments. Users can enter the teleconference whenever and as frequently as they desire. Systems are accessible outside normal working hours at the home site to accommodate users in other time zones. A computer teleconference can be as short as a few hours, but often lasts for weeks when it involves standing committees or indefinitely for long-term projects.

The benefits of computer teleconferencing are:

- Time-zone transparency
- Virtually instantaneous exchange of information
- Low cost
- Participation at user's convenience
- Availability of participants
- A written record of proceedings
- Nondiscrimination by rank, age, sex, race, physical attributes
- Continuity after absence (such as a vacation).

Participants in computer teleconferences use a display or hard-copy terminal while in their own offices or at another location, or a portable display or hard-copy terminal while traveling or at home. Most portables operate at 300 baud, and system communications should accommodate both that rate and the customary 1200-baud rate from office terminals. With this dial-up access, computer teleconferencing systems provide geographic freedom. Because virtually all computer teleconferencing systems are strictly alphanumeric, many terminals presently in place are suitable.

Computer teleconferencing systems, though closely related to and often integrated with electronic mail systems, require specialized software providing the following features:

- Restraints on participation
- Option to use actual or assumed name
- System mail
- Selective communication with individual participants
- User-definable survey mail
- Automatic vote tallying
- Discretionary reading.

To ensure a single vote, the system monitors only voting activity of active participants and designated alternates, who may enter comments and read all comments. Those designated as observers may read all comments but are enjoined from entering comments and from voting. Only the chairperson is authorized to delete a message or comment once it has been sent.

Any active or alternate participant can generate comments to a computer teleconference under her or his own name or under an assumed, or pen name. Submitting comments or questions in this way promotes candid and often unrestrained interchanges. An editing facility permits the participants to alter comments until the system sends them to others for reading. At that point the system assigns a unique, sequential identification number to the message.

System mail is software-generated by the presence of a message. The system automatically notifies all participants when a new entry is made in the teleconference. In an independent system, the user receives the message at log-on; in an integrated system, the teleconferencing software inserts the message in the mail queue with other electronic mail. The system determines whether there is a duplicate, unread message still in each participant's queue and will not enter repetitive notices.

Within the computer teleconference system is a subset of the electronic mail system, unassociated with the terminal-based electronic mail, that provides for conversational asides so that a participant can send a message privately to any one or several other participants. These messages also may be edited up to the time they are sent, and are numbered in a different series from the one used for the teleconferencing entries.

User-definable survey mail is used for polls and voting. The chairperson can submit a series of questions to each participant and specify varying formats for response, such as yes/no, numerics (scales of 1–10, or percentages), or freeform comments. After displaying each question or request, the system prompts for the appropriate form of reply. The user may respond at that time or store the material and move to the next question or request; the recipient controls the return of the questionnaire. Some designs incorporate an automatic followup, instituted when the chairperson issues the survey mail: the system software tracks all outstanding survey mail and sends automatic reminders of overdue replies; other designs generate a tickler to the chairperson, who may then decide whether to send a reminder. The system will accept and tally yes/no or numeric replies as they are returned to the chair.

Automatic vote tallying is a less sophisticated version of survey mail. Generally it is limited to yes or no answers and is used only for voting on motions.

Discretionary reading, a unique feature of computer teleconferencing, allows a participant to bypass filed information that is familiar or of little or no value, or to read entries in other than chronological order.

The limited variety of computer teleconferencing software reflects the fact that few middle- and upper-level managerial personnel can or will key. Planet, designed at the Institute for the Future; Forum, COM (a variation of Planet developed by the Swedish National Defense Research Institute), and EIES, designed at the New Jersey Institute of Technology, are among the best known.

Responsibilities of the Chairperson

Most computer teleconferences are established via electronic mail systems. The chairperson or conference leader contacts the system supervisor, who activates the new computer teleconference; a table contains the names of participants and their active, alternate, or observer status. Some systems permit the conference chairperson to add and delete names; this feature allows for sudden changes resulting from promotions, transfers, or other causes.

To permit review of the proceedings at any time by any participant and to maintain a total record of the proceedings, all messages entered in the computer teleconference pass automatically into a chronological system file. Participants of any status have access to the index of this file in its entirety, before or after a specific date, between any two dates, or by parametric search. The chairperson is responsible for filing all text with appropriate natural-language names. A key-word parametric search should be able to scan both the subject line and the body text of an entry.

Once a computer teleconference has concluded, text can remain on line for reference for a time. The chairperson should make arrangements for storing the text, converting it to magnetic media if it will be needed later, but in any case to hard copy or microfiche.

Computer teleconferencing messages tend to be short, about one to five lines, and sometimes consist of phrases instead of sentences. As a result, file storage is small. At the Swedish National Defense Research Institute in Stockholm, 35 participants in six months used electronic storage equivalent to 2,000 typed standard-size pages.[21]

A freestanding system usually controls security of access by requiring a password; a timesharing system can use a second password that will access the table of authorized participants.

Once the terminals have been amortized, computer teleconferencing normally costs less than audio or video teleconferencing. Variations in distance affect cost directly: a call to a distant computer costs more than a call to a nearby network connection or directly into a local computer. Transmission speed and the number of addresses also affect costs.

The Institute for the Future operates a Planet system with a reputed cost in 1977 of $1.50 per message; message length and number of addressees are not known.[22] The Planet system operated by Infomedia, a timesharing company in California, is said to cost the user about 25 cents for each 15 words.[23] Since an average message contains up to 80 words, the cost would range up to $1.33.

The EIES system at the New Jersey Institute of Technology in the mid-1970s charged $8.00 per hour on its 300-user system and $5.00 per hour on the 1,000-user system, including a fixed hourly rate of $3.00 for use of a packet-switching network.[24] Immediate access for all participants eliminates the need to prepare and mail a full hard-copy text of proceedings; using the smaller system became cost justifiable with about 15 people participating.[25]

General Teleconferencing Considerations

Given the turnkey nature and often modest costs of teleconferencing, an investment in equipment and user experience would seem to be wise contingency planning. However, the number of equipment manufacturers remains small and production relatively limited; a sudden increase in market demand may produce long waits for equipment.

It is wise to keep teleconferencing installations as simple as possible. Select equipment with few or no controls to adjust, and make audio, enhanced audio, and video teleconferencing rooms normal in appearance. When choosing a computer teleconferencing system, remember that the users may not be familiar with computer operations and seek a simple system. Acclimation to teleconferencing should begin early by involving potential users in the planning. Once the system reaches pilot or production stage the users will feel comfortable with the medium.

All tools should be conveniently located; people are often reluctant to leave their own building or the immediate environs for teleconferences.

International Considerations

Accessibility through different time zones is the primary international consideration. In addition, international teleconferences must allow for seemingly insignificant cross-cultural differences, which if ignored can acquire major proportions.

Language barriers can be overcome by using interpreters. Such arrangements require a separate communications channel for each language and salaries for interpreters, but still cost less than international travel.

The use of graphics in teleconferencing presents few problems: facsimile devices of disparate national origin are often compatible; slow-scan TV devices compatible with overseas power sources are available from U.S. manufacturers; long-distance full-motion video can be arranged. It is wise, however, to make international transmission arrangements early when using temporary services.

NOTES

1. "Electronic Meetings," *Administrative Management*, December 1979, p.11.

2. Personal correspondence to the author from Lorne A. Parker, University of Wisconsin Extension, November 7, 1978.

3. Anthony H. Marsh, "Technical Developments and Design Considerations for Audio Teleconferencing," joint paper presented at the IGC conference on the Promise of Multi-Media Teleconferencing, Andover, Mass., October 30, 1978; Robert Johansen, Jacques Vallee, and Kathleen Spangler, *Electronic Meetings: Technical Alternatives and Social Choices* (Reading, Mass.: Addison-Wesley, 1980, p. 165; Richard Harkness, *Technology Assessment of Telecommunications/Transportation Interactions, Final Report*, vol. 1, U.S. Department of Commerce, National Technical Information Service (Springfield, Va.: 1977), p. vii; Jacques Vallee, H. Lipinski, and R. Miller, *Group Communication through Computers*, vol. 1 (Menlo Park, Calif.: Institute for the Future, 1974), p. 66.

4. Johansen, Vallee, and Spangler, *Electronic Meetings*, p. 162.

5. Raymond V. Reamer, "IBM Experiences in Teleconferencing," and "MITRE's Experience in Medical Teleconferencing," papers presented at the IGC Conference on the Promise of Multi-Media Teleconferencing, Andover, Mass., October 31, 1978.

6. Roger Pye and J. Springate, "Teleconferencing: The Meeting of the Future—Now," *Management Services in Government*, August 1978, pp. 136–137; Martin C. J. Elton, "Behavioral Aspects of Teleconferencing Systems," paper presented at the IGC Conference on the Promise of Multi-Media Teleconferencing, Andover, Mass., October 30, 1978; Harkness, *Technology Assessment*, vol. 1, p. vii.

7. Pye and Springate, "Teleconferencing," pp. 136–137.

8. Johansen, Vallee and Spangler, *Electronic Meetings*, p. 136.

9. Ibid., pp. 155–158.

10. Elton, "Behavioral Aspects of Teleconferencing," p. 2; Pye and Springate, "Teleconferencing," pp. 136–139; author's experience.

11. "Remote Conference System—2 Site," undated brochure and specification sheet, Plessey Communications Systems, Nottingham, England, p. 2.

12. Author's experience.

13. Samuel Fordyce, "NASA Teleconference Pilot Project," final report, NASA Headquarters, Washington, March 1977, pp. 20–21.

14. H. Bersted, "Teleconferencing: An Easy Way to Increase Telco Revenues," May 28, 1979.

15. Reamer, "IBM Experiences in Teleconferencing," and informal poll of participants, IGC conference on the Promise of Multi-Media Teleconferencing, October 31, 1978.

16. "The Electronic Blackboard for Remote Instruction," *Infosystems*, February, 1979, p. 26.

17. Harkness, *Technology Assessment*, p. vii; Elton, "Behavioral Aspects of Teleconferencing," p. 2.

18. Author's discussions with corporate personnel.

19. Paul Ehrlich, "Users: TV-Phone Alright, But Use Is Limited, Costly," *Management Information Systems Week*, June 18, 1980, p. 15.

20. Johansen, Vallee, and Spangler, *Electronic Meetings*, p. 8.

21. Jacob Palme, "Teleconferencing and Mailing Systems," paper presented at European DECUS Meeting, September 1978.

22. T. Featheringham, "Teleconferences: The Message Is the Meeting," *Data Communications*, July 1977, p. 41.

23. Johansen, Vallee, and Spangler, *Electronic Meetings*, p. 9.

24. Starr Roxanne Hiltz and Murray Turoff, *"Potential Impacts of Computer Conferencing Upon Managerial and Organizational Styles,"* unpublished research paper, 1976, p. 19.

25. Featheringham, "Teleconferences," pp. 40–41.

10

GRAPHICS AND OTHER ELEMENTS

Conversion of data into graphic depiction often helps people to understand complex topics and saves executives and knowledge workers time and effort. The eye is able to take in graphic information at rates equivalent to 72 million words per minute—more than 200,000 times as fast as an average reader. At that speed, you could read this book in one-tenth of a second if all its text and tables could be presented graphically.[1] Conversion to graphics reduces the amount of paper used and lowers printing costs. Three criteria determine feasibility of conversion to computerized graphic format: costs, quality, and time.

Until recently, the only alternative to expensive, hand-prepared graphics was a complex computerized system. In the last decade, however, the decline in computer costs and the introduction of new or improved techniques have made computerized graphics easy and reasonable to produce.

One introduction is a pseudo-graphic capability that permits a user to display ruled lines and define graphic characters of varying radii and angles within dot matrix patterns. Most such terminals require users to provide their own software for arranging the special characters into complete graphic images, something like constructing an automated jigsaw puzzle.

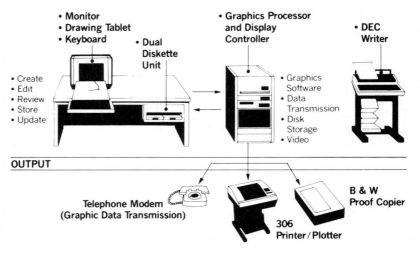

The Genigraphics 100C office slide system. Diagram courtesy of General Electric Company, Genigraphics Equipment Marketing Division.

Another, more important, change is in simplified interfaces between humans and conventional computer graphics devices. Friendly systems now permit the user to select the type of graph (bar, pie, histogram) and then prompt the user for values and scaling. Color systems permit user selection of color for fill-ins of bars and pie chart areas; some also offer a selection of cross-hatchings. Once the user has entered the characteristics, the system creates the graphic image with no further human intervention. The end product can be hard copy, an overhead transparency, a slide, or any of several other options.

One satisfied user is the Bank of America, which provides an active in-house training program. More than 500 of the 70,000 employees use such computerized capability in producing over one hundred different types of graphics.[2] An internationally known manufacturing firm reportedly reduced its average cost per original slide from $55 to $28 after four months of using an in-house computerized slide-making system and anticipated an eventual cost reduction of $22 to $25.

The best-known types of graphs are time plots, bar charts, histograms, scattergrams, and pie charts. The usual graphics application represents one or more sets of similar data as a two-dimensional image. While it is often difficult to depict situations involving multiple variables, with the use of graphic plots it is possible to represent up to four variables within a single graphic image.

Both black-and-white and color graphics have advantages and limitations. Black-and-white is not as appealing to the eye but transmits well in monochrome media, such as fax and black-and-white video, and is

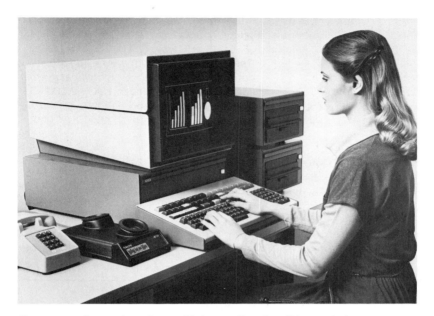

Xerox system for creating color graphic images. Stored on diskettes, the images are transmitted over telephone lines to a graphics center for reproduction as color slides. Photo courtesy of Xerox Corporation.

less expensive. Color is eye-catching but sometimes more complex and always more expensive to create.

Timesharing Graphics Services

Those inclined to keep their graphics installations simple can use dial-up access to service bureaus through CRTs and portable printer/plotters. Computer Transceiver Systems, Inc. manufactures the 4000G portable printer/plotter terminal with black-and-white thermal hard-copy output. The unit features 132-column-wide printing and plotting and can either produce paper output or transfer images directly to overhead transparency material for projection. Software access is available from public or private service bureaus.

Xerox, General Electric's Genigraphics Division, Comshare, Inc., and PW, Inc. offer communicating CRT graphic terminals for black-and-white or color slide production. The user creates graphics locally, then transmits the image files to the remote computer site. Within one or two days the images are converted into slides, hard copy, or overhead transparencies and are returned to the customer. The Genigraphics R-341 offers a selection of 90 colors, with use of as many as 61 on a single slide. A single floppy diskette can store up to 200 images

TABLE 10.1 Resolutions and prices of desktop graphics systems.

Model	CPU	Resolutions graphics	Alpha	Average price($) for typical system
Apple II	6502	280 × 192	40 × 48	1,000–2,000
Chromatics	Z80	512 × 512	85 × 51	6,000–12,000
HP System 45B	Dual Custom 16-bit	560 × 455	80 × 25	12,500–34,000
HP System 35	Custom 16-bit	Plotter	80 × 24	10,000–23,000
IBM 5110	Custom	Plotter	64 × 16	8,500–28,000
ISC 8090	8080	160 × 192	80 × 48	4,500–12,000
TEK 4051	6800	1024 × 780	72 × 35	6,000–12,000

Source: Adapted from P. J. Kirby, "Desktop Graphics," Datamation, May 1979, p. 166.

locally for later retrieval or modification. The Xerox 350 and the Genigraphics R-341 rent for about $800 per month plus a per-slide charge of $9 and up depending on volume. Both remote terminals offer a choice of display types, point sizes, and graph types.

A medium-size real-time system, the Genigraphics Full-Spectrum Office Slide System serves the user requiring 1,000 or more slides per year. The user selects from among four type styles in an almost infinite number of sizes and creates full-color title and/or image graphics; the color CRT interactively displays up to 8 colors from a color palette of some 8 million colors. The completed graphic images are locally stored on diskettes and are transmitted to a Genigraphics service center for conversion to slides. The system, which has no camera, can be leased for $1,300 per month or purchased for about $50,000.

On-Site Systems

Those with a large production volume or high security requirements can use either of two on-site system approaches: in-house timesharing or standalone systems. Such systems range from simple black-and-white to comprehensive color systems able to create animated color films.

Firms such as Apple and Hewlett Packard offer compact standalone graphics systems at modest prices. Table 10.1 lists several models. The H-P System 45B is typical: it provides a graphics display screen, keyboard, logic, magnetic storage, and a thermal printer/plotter in a single desktop unit. Options such as a four-color pen plotter can be attached.

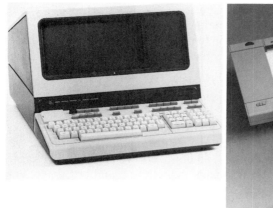

HP2647A color graphics terminal and plotters. Photos courtesy of Hewlett Packard.

The Genigraphics 100C, a very sophisticated system, is for generating color graphics, including animated films. It consists of a minicomputer, an operator's console with color CRT and joystick (for image positioning and editing control), a camera unit, and a black-and-white copier for quick draft copies of images. Using a tablet digitizer with an electronic pen, an operator can enter freehand images; computerized, stored preexisting sketches; or finished artwork from other sources. A basic unit comes with a library of over 1,200 standard graphic images and provision for more. Standard images include all two-dimensional geometric shapes, images of people, map outlines, and so forth, all of which can serve as either foreground or background images. For example, an outline map of a country can be screened into the background in a faint color, with national statistics overlaid in positive colors in the foreground. Calling geometric forms to the screen, the user can enlarge or reduce them and move them to any location on the screen. Color capability spans the spectrum, since the hue and intensity of any color are under direct operator control. Any area can be filled with any color of any intensity and altered at will. The entire process is interactive.

Once the image is complete and all labeling is in place, it is sent to the camera subsystem, a 4,000-line-resolution graphics tube facing a camera housing. Output can be slides, 35mm animated film, overhead transparencies, or color photos. The purchase price of the Genigraphics 100C artist's unit ranges from about $65,000 to $88,000. The graphics unit is more costly and is priced at about $243,000.

Standard Oil of Indiana procured the first Genigraphics 100B in

1975. By 1976 the system was generating 1,400 slides per month, about two-thirds of the total slide volume. For the slides still created by vendors, the mean cost was $110; for those still created from hand drawings internally, $33; for slides created on the 100B, $12.[3]

Digitizers

When it is desirable to modify a preexisting graphic image, digitizers are used to convert and store such images in computerized graphic systems. The three most commonly used digitizers are scanners (similar in operation to an OCR or fax scanner), free cursors, and pen types. The typical free cursor is a ring several inches in diameter containing a magnifying lens and a set of crosshairs for alignment. Hard copy is placed on a tablet containing an embedded matrix of wires. The user aligns the crosshairs with the image and moves the cursor along the lines on the image. When a pushbutton on the ring is pressed, the matrix of wires embedded in the tablet picks up the signal. The computer to which the digitizer is attached records the coordinates magnetically. Once recorded, the image can be recalled and manipulated as needed

VT125 monochrome graphics terminal for business and scientific use. Photo courtesy of Digital Equipment Corporation.

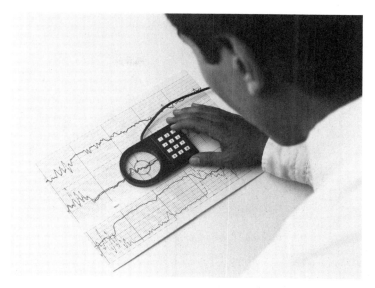

Talos digitizer for conversion of graphic images. Photo courtesy of California Computer Products, Inc.

according to the capabilities of the system. Prices of digitizers vary according to type and complexity, from under $1,000 to over $300,000.

Hard-Copy Graphic Output

Hard-copy graphic output devices are available with either black-and-white or color capability. The black-and-white types include ink-jet, impact, thermal, electrostatic, and xerographic printers plus plotters. The color types include color ink-jet, impact, pen plotters, and color copiers. Color output is also available through color camera systems as 8 by 10-inch color photographs, color overhead transparencies, 35mm slides, color microfiche, and 16mm or 35mm motion picture film.

Some popular dot matrix printers can be used for graphics. Selanar Corporation, for one, offers a hardware/software conversion for under $2,000 that permits the hard-copy terminal to plot graphics; print in standard, boldface, and double-width characters; print individual characters upright, upside down, left-oriented, or right-oriented; position characters at any location in quarter-line steps; and perform microprocessing within the terminal. Daisy wheel printers, with ability to print in increments of a hundredth of an inch, can also be used for low-resolution graphic output in conjunction with appropriate software.

Graphic terminals with add-on/add-in, electrostatic and electrographic options also convert graphics to hard copy. Terminals with

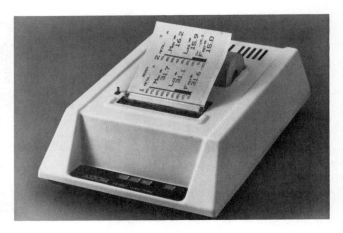

Compact video printer for converting computer graphics to hard copy. Photo courtesy of Axiom Corporation.

built-in options are manufactured by Texas Instruments, Digital Equipment Corporation, and others for $4,000 and up. Axiom manufactures the EX-850 Video Printer which connects directly to a CRT, video monitor, or TV set, and exactly reproduces the images displayed on the screen. It sells for under $1,300. There are also black-and-white plotters from such firms as Versatec, CalComp, and Tektronix. They come in many sizes; some can produce hard-copy graphics up to six feet wide.

Among the color devices, Xerox manufactures the Model 6500 color photocopier, which can interface with a computer or a graphics terminal. Priced at $25,000, it uses the three primary colors to produce on bond paper up to 192 high-resolution color prints per hour. Xerox does not market interfaces to other devices, and the user must arrange for interconnection.

Several firms, including Dunn Instruments, Matrix Instruments, Image Resource Corporation, and Hewlett Packard, manufacture special cameras that interface with color or black-and-white graphic CRTs to produce various hard-copy media. The Dunn 631 Color Camera System can produce as many as 30 eight-color 8 by 10 photos or overhead projection transparencies or 35mm slides per hour from any raster-scan CRT. The camera is available with various output options such as a Polaroid kit, etc. A competitive camera system by Matrix Instruments can produce 8 by 10 Polaroid color prints, overhead transparencies for backlit displays and projection, 35mm color slides, 60-image color microfiche, and either 16mm or 35mm color animation films; it permits multiple image formats. Such systems have base prices of around $11,000 before adding optional attachments.

The Videoprint 5000 by Image Resource Corporation and the system 45C Camera Hood offered by Hewlett Packard offer fewer output options at correspondingly lower cost. Both can be made to accommodate 35mm film output for slides or small Polaroid prints. The equipment is available at prices ranging upward from $1,000.

Hybrids

Hybrid equipment, which combines into one unit two or more functional devices formerly available only individually, includes intelligent copiers and OCR/fax units (see Chapter 6).

Intelligent copiers are manufactured by such firms as Honeywell, Xerox, IBM, and Wang. Purchase prices range from $32,000 to about $300,000, depending on the brand and options selected. A cross between a photocopier and a mini- or microcomputer, an intelligent copier can create multiple copies without an original; some, including the IBM 6670, can also function as a conventional copier. In an on-line or off-line mode, it can image hard copy directly from the magnetic files of word processors or computers. The intelligence permits automated insertion of logos, shading, signatures, and form-ruling lines, which can be imaged concurrently with data to produce a final document. The copiers offer a selection of type styles and sizes, and either vertical or horizontal printing on hard copy at an average speed of two standard-size pages per second. The Xerox 9700, in addition to paper output, can accommodate a microfiche subsystem with a choice of $24\times$, $42\times$, or $48\times$ reduction ratios.

Voice Recognition

Voice-controlled terminals that can convert spoken words into commands or even into encoded document files are being developed and improved by firms such as Threshold Technology, Interstate Electronics, Heuristics, and Nippon Electric. The two main drawbacks are limited vocabularies and, with the exception of a Nippon Electric unit, inability to contend with continuous speech. Most units today have a vocabulary of around 100 words; some have as many as 500. All but one of these devices must be "trained" to recognize the speech of the individuals who will use them; most will not respond to the spoken commands of others, which provides an added degree of system security. A user typically repeats a word as many as six times to train the system, thus providing a sample of variations in voice patterns; the voice recognition memory records a series of recognition factors for each word. The system then identifies a spoken word by comparing it with its table of prerecorded words.

A Practical Use for Voice Recognition A Midwestern commodity exchange has equipped people on the exchange floor with portable radio headsets. As they utter commodity names and price changes into their microphones, a ceiling-mounted antenna picks up the sounds and transfers them to the voice-recognition unit of a computer in an adjoining room. The computer converts the speech to signals and sends them to the computer-controlled commodity price boards overlooking the floor of the exchange. The entire process takes only a few seconds.

Increased awareness of the potential uses of voice recognition has intensified the rate of technological advances, resulting in decreased cost-per-word of such units. A typical unit with a vocabulary of 100-plus words, such as from Interstate Electronics, costs in the vicinity of $2,000, significantly lower than just a few years ago. Ultimately increasing technological capabilities and decreasing costs will lead to development of the longed-for voice-recognition typewriter, which now exists in prototype form and is said to be 90 percent accurate.

Voice Response

Interfacing people and computers is the most important aspect of office automation. One way to make the initial acquaintance easy is with voice response, the creation of audible responses by some stimulus, such as entering a code into a computer through a terminal keyboard or a telephone keypad. A few units produce sounds by magnetic recordings; in others the sound is generated by solid-state technology. Most units operate from a limited but often expandable vocabulary. Burroughs, Cognitronics, Interface Technology, IBM, Master Specialties Inc., Periphonics, and Wavetek are among manufacturers that offer such devices. Vocabularies range from one word to as many as 10,000. Prices vary from $400 to a rare extreme of $500,000. Most hardware costs less than $50,000; the user must either purchase or develop the software.

Other units, referred to as voice synthesizers, operate with a set of sounds called phonemes. Every word in the English language can be constructed from 66 phonemes. Normally a program sends impulses to the voice-synthesizer unit, directing both the sequence in which the phonemes will be audibly re-created and the pauses that provide inflection and the separations between words. Voice-response units that operate with phonemes have unlimited vocabularies. If correctly programmed, they can read directly from text files and convert the contents to audible sounds. Two firms manufacturing these units are Interface Systems, with DAVID, and Federal Screw Works, which offers the Votrax series. Their base cost is about $1,200.

Another type of phoneme-based voice synthesizer is self-contained, requires no special programming, and costs upward from $400. Such units are connected directly to a terminal rather than to a computer, permitting audible verification of keyed input and audible responses from the computer. Unlike other audio output devices, they are inaccessible by telephone.

Mechanical Devices

A device classified as a robot delivers and picks up mail and packages, freeing people for more meaningful tasks. The Central Intelligence Agency has a machine of its own design in use at its headquarters in McLean, Virginia. A commercially available device called the Mailmobile is manufactured by Bell and Howell.

The battery-powered Mailmobile follows an invisible chemical line or path across nearly any type of floor at a speed of about one mile per

Mailmobile in office use. The self-propelled unit follows an invisible guide path and makes predetermined stops.

hour. For safety, the device generates a soft sound every second or two and has flashing blue headlights. Mechanical switches embedded in a sponge-rubber bumper ensure immediate braking. The unit is said to be incapable of upsetting a man on a stepladder.

As the unit makes its rounds, invisible markings on the chemical path cause it to stop at predetermined points for removal of mail and packages. Strip switches along the top of both sides of the unit can also halt it; another set of strip switches will set it in motion again. The manufacturer offers various options: sensors that detect the presence of obstacles in its path and halt it before any contact, multiple-car units for high-volume use, and apparatus that permits the Mailmobile to summon an elevator and indicate the floor at which it is to disembark.

Banks and insurance companies have a number of successful installations; one New York City bank reputedly has more than 50 units.

The base price of a Mailmobile is under $15,000. It is available in industrial models and in fine finishes for offices.

NOTES

1. Bill Mitchell and Rich Ferguson, "Computer Graphics for Business," *Modern Office Procedures*, April 1981, p. 82.

2. N. Kelly, "Computer Graphics: Info at a Glance," *Infosystems*, December 1979, p. 38.

3. R. C. Anderson, "Computer Graphics: A New Era of Slide Production," *The Professional Photographer*, August 1978, pp. 50–52.

To be master of any branch of knowledge, you
must master those which lie next to it; and
thus to know anything, you must know all.

Oliver Wendell Holmes, Jr.
Lecture, Harvard University

INTEGRATED
OFFICE AUTOMATION
SYSTEMS

An integrated office automation system (IOAS) is a combination of
functionally related computerized subsystems. An IOAS deals with the
communication, processing, storage and output of data, text, graphics,
and, recently, audio. An IOAS can contain text management, computer-based message systems (a type of EMS), store-and-forward facsimile (another type of EMS), electronic filing, electronic calendars
and appointment schedulers, tickler (reminder) files, alarms, graphics
capabilities, computer teleconferencing, and dozens of other tools.

Integrated office automation systems generally are designed to accommodate extended functions. Sometimes they permit individualized
tailoring of preexisting IOAS functions. At even modest levels of integration, they support the individual knowledge worker by providing
automation through the six stages of documented information life:

1. Creation—the capture of thought in an initial, draft mode
2. Conversion from draft to final mode
3. Replication—the generation of duplicate copies
4. Distribution

5. Filing and retrieval
6. Disposition—the ultimate discarding or destruction.

Integrated office automation systems assist knowledge workers in three ways:

- Acceleration of the perceptual/cognitive process
- Augmentation of the substance of a task
- Delegation of the task to an information system.

Two examples of the use of IOASs demonstrate the benefits of implementing such systems.

From July 1976 through March 1978, a National Science Foundation program office conducted a production test of an IOAS. The group of four officers and a secretary was typical in staffing size and configuration. The function of the office was also typical, in that the group supported a specific scientific field through grants; it was atypical in that the field was information science. The four officers had display terminals at their workstations and portable terminals for use outside the office; the secretary had a letter-quality terminal for document production. In the course of the evaluation, each member of the group eventually operated each of the other types of workstation terminals.

The intended pilot period of one year was abridged for reasons beyond the control of the office to six months, from September 1977 through February 1978 for the officers and for the secretary, eleven months, from April 1977 through February 1978.

An Air Force Office Automation Project The U.S. Air Force Systems Command's Electronic Systems Division (ESD) at Hanscom Air Force Base, Bedford, Massachusetts, has produced some facts showing that office automation can deliver its promised payload. Findings of the three-year Project Impact (Improved Administrative Capability Test) show that:

- Among clerical personnel, the system produced a 60 percent savings in the time previously allotted to tasks.
- Professionals doing clerical work realized a 50 percent time advantage in performing tasks.
- The professionals doing professionals work spent 33 percent less time performing such work than previously.

All this adds up to a savings well in advance of the $12.8 million (FY 1979 dollars) annual cost avoidance estimated (in 1979, by ESD and Booz, Allen & Hamilton Inc., the N.Y.-based consulting firm) to accrue if all ESD were to install automated office equipment.

That estimate was made on the basis of a reduction of 75 percent in time spent by professionals doing clerical work and 47 percent more "free time" for clericals doing clerical work. It did not include the time savings mentioned above for professionals doing professional work.

Project Impact has also accomplished other things:

- It managed to combine several different manufacturers' word processing systems on a local area network designed by Mitre, Inc.
- It created a methodology for measuring productivity that the National Bureau of Standards turned into a handbook (Special Publication 500-72, NBS, Department of Commerce, Washington, D.C.).
- A spin-off project for CMIS (Command Management Information Systems) graphics created a prototype audiovisual/printing center that is already planned for installation at six Air Force bases around the United States.

Impact was organized from its inception in mid-1978 by Booz, Allen and the American Institute for Research (AIR). The first phase of the project, according to program director, Bob Kent, was data collection, to establish a cost base line.

Approximately 140 managers, technicians, and support personnel were involved in the data collection stage. Out of this grew two different forms of data: a measurement of the professional and clerical man-hours needed to produce "business products" (i.e., reports, documents, etc.); and a traditional work measurement, primarily at clerical locations. About half the time required to produce each of about 30 products was spent on professional work, the other half on clerical work (typing, filing, dictation). About 24 percent of the clerical tasks were performed by professionals.

"That gave us targets of opportunity for automation," Kent said. These included a large return on investment, the potential for electronic mail, filing, and facsimile transmission to make clerical life easier, the possibility of freeing the professional from clerical work, and the addition of a new dimension to the professional's ability to perform.

Phase II of the project, completed in April 1979, included a cost/benefit analysis, and established the priorities and the candidates for automation. A total of 225 users were involved, at a ratio of about 9 professionals to each clerical.

The report on Phase II said that "automated office operations offered the potential for increased productivity" at a value of "approximately $60 million over five years." Depending on whether equipment was leased or purchased, a net benefit of $24 million to $29 million was estimated for the same period.

Phase V will update the Phase II report and document Project Impact results. A preliminary observation noted that "during the test, a secretary who originally handled eight people could handle twice that number with the automated systems."

Phases III and IV, dating from May 1979 to the present, involved preparing an MIS plan, designing the prototype system, and establishing user procedures, then installing the prototype, testing it, and finally evaluating the results.

The heart of the design was a large central processor (a Prime 550) driving various office automation devices over a local area network connected by CATV-type cables. (A fiber optics link used just for connections in the Project Impact headquarters building was also designed by Mitre for the test.)

Twelve system program offices, which develop Air Force military technology, and headquarters staff offices were linked to the Project Impact headquarters site on the base for the test. The central computer worked through modems, emulating TTY to talk to the office automation equipment.

Two different concepts for word processing were utilized:

The first was use of standalone units for each secretary with a dial-up modem to the central computer, plus intelligent terminals and dial-up modems. The other involved use of a WP terminal plus an OCR (optical character reader) and a modem to the computer, electric typewriters with a font acceptable to the OCR, and a modem to talk to the computer.

Both concepts are being considered for base-wide implementation. The distributed concept was easier and cheaper to install for the prototype, but for the whole base a centralized scheme would cost about the same. For the prototype, the cost of hardware, software, and consulting fees totaled about $1.6 million.

Source: Abridged from Richard D. Hoffman, "Air Force Test May Boost Office Automation," *Information System News*, May 4, 1981. Printed with permission of the publisher.

Productivity was measured in units of time. Each member reviewed his or her activity record in 16 activity categories for the third week of each month. Working from lists of specific tasks, each program officer estimated the number of hours worked on each task, the number of hours required to complete such work without the IOAS, and the amount of activity that would not have occurred without the computerized tools. The results indicated an average work week of 34.5 hours, about three-eighths of which was related to preparation of written documents, half to communication of other types, and the remainder to miscellaneous activity. The program officers indicated a productivity improvement of 22 percent, subject to a deviation of $\pm$ 5 percent, or 7.6 ($\pm$ 1.8) hours of additional production per week.

The secretary measured five work categories in much the same way as the program officers. The average work week of 36.7 hours consisted of about 12 hours of typing and stenography, 4 hours of filing and retrieval, 11 hours of general tasks (mail, telephone answering, greeting visitors, photocopying, and the like), and the balance in other activity. The study indicated a productivity improvement of 33 percent, subject to a deviation of $\pm$ 8 percent, or 12 ($\pm$ 2.9) hours of production per week.

These results are in conformance with studies of more than a hundred other users of the same IOAS system, performing a variety of work in more than a dozen diverse NSF organizations. By early 1979 nearly every National Science Foundation office was employing the same system.[1]

The U.S. Air Force has achieved dramatic cost reductions through use of IOASs. One case involves the Maintenance Policy and Procedures Division at Air Force headquarters, which maintains and publishes documents on maintenance policy and procedure. In 1972 one of the last nonautomated updates, a consolidation of all maintenance management systems material into a 12-volume manual required 8 months, some 49 man-years of officer effort, and 2 1/2 man-years of clerical effort to produce 643 pages at a total cost of $2,010,315. The cost per page, adjusted to 1979 dollars, was $3,126. The high cost was due in part to the need to bring dozens of people from distant duty stations to Washington, D.C.; the influx of 200 people at one time or another required providing 80 percent of housing off base.

In 1975 the division implemented an IOAS to assist in document production, primarily in preparing document text but also in graphic support. The system remains in use today. In a typical year, 1978, some 240 pages of one regulation were updated at a total cost of $69,045, for a cost of $288 per page, a saving of $2,838 per page over the former nonautomated cost.

In 1979 the Air Force conducted a study of the IOAS installation to ascertain the results of use. In four years the system updated 2,324 pages, an average of 581 pages per year. A cost analysis, using 1972 nonautomated cost factors adjusted to 1979 dollar values, indicates that the IOAS installation resulted in net savings of $2,815 per page, or a total of over $6,500,000 since 1975.[2]

In addition to direct cost benefits, productivity improvement ultimately resolves into cost reduction. An IOAS that enables one person to supervise, for instance, eight people instead of seven will eventually decrease the number of positions required within a management structure. That was the original motive for the Citicorp office automation project, as part of its ultimate goal: a $150 million reduction in wages and fringe benefits over a ten-year period.

Other benefits of the Citicorp installation include:

- Time/cost savings in media transformations
- Time/cost savings in combined file operations (a single search, for example, searches every file, regardless of medium)
- Time/cost savings over logging in/out of individual systems many times each day
- Geographic transparency of mixed-media file location.

Limitations arise from individuals' reluctance to key, which system designs can overcome by limiting keying and simplifying the means of system inquiry, and from intersystem incompatibility, which both hardware and software products can now overcome.

In international implementation of an IOAS, language and cultural differences are the major considerations. A word made up of the same combination of alphabetic characters may have two different meanings in two languages. To avoid confusion, it is best to avoid slang and colloquialisms. The single most desirable tool—a fully automated natural-language translator—remains unavailable. Simple awareness that one is exchanging information with a person from a different cultural background, together with common sense and basic etiquette, avoids many problems.

System Components

At a minimum, an IOAS consists of a computer, peripheral devices, and an IOAS software package. The host computer may range from a small minicomputer to a large mainframe. Some IOASs are based in single computers, some in "smart" front ends, and some operate in network fashion.

IOASs can use intelligent front ends in two ways. In one, the front end is a minicomputer that functions as a communications controller. In the other, the role of the minicomputer is broader: all communication lines are attached to it, all IOAS application software is resident within it, and all computation activity takes place within it. The back end, a large mainframe of different manufacture, contains all the files and data bases created and used for IOAS operations. No computation takes place within the mainframe.

Two types of computer networks are often used in IOASs. One is a series of minicomputers, none of which is superior to any other; a second-level communications system, operating on a 15-minute cycle, interconnects the nodes, and not all functions are shared among the IOAS nodes. The other network is a ring of minis hard-wired together. One mini controls all the others; all exterior communications lines are linked to it, and all computation takes place in it. Each of the other minis serves only as a file controller for each of the attached disk drives.

Peripherals are those devices not located in the host computer. They include keyboards and display terminals, graphics devices, hard-copy terminals, plotters, printer/plotters, intelligent copiers, line printers, micrographic retrieval units, fax units, portable hard-copy and plotting terminals, voice-recognition and voice-response devices, and video projectors.

A Writing Project The coordinator of a writing project divides the sections to be written, assigns them to several people, and enters the milestone dates in the IOAS. These reminders will go to both the coordinator and the writers at the outset of the work, just before each milestone date, and again after the due dates if work is overdue. The initial message to each person contains the general directive and the milestone and project completion target dates.

During the writing process, each author enters the outline and text into the IOAS in much the same way. The originator completes the first draft, either by keying it or by dictating it for keying by a secretary, transcriptionist, or clerk. The originator then proofs the draft by calling the text file to the screen of a display terminal, replicates the file electronically, and electronically transfers one copy to the coordinator.

The coordinator, who is essentially an editor, makes notations to the file contents. (Some IOASs incorporate the editor's notations and corrections in the text; others maintain notations separately while automatically making note of the appropriate location.) The coordinator then retransfers the text file to the originating writer for review and possible reworking. Once the text is in order, the editor transmits the draft to reviewers or management—either serially, with each person adding comments electronically, or simultaneously—with reviewers' respective comments automatically labeled by name and merged into proper sequence in a single electronic file listing. The coordinator can incorporate the comments directly into the draft, but in this case chooses to pass them on to the originating writer for consideration. Eventually the writer returns the completed document to the coordinator ready for release as an internal electronic publication. For use outside the IOAS user community, the coordinator sends the document to a phototypesetter for conversion to hard copy.

IOAS software is as varied as its users. The best software is modular, open-ended, and open-sided. Modularity and open-endedness permit the addition or removal of functions; open-sidedness, also referred to as "profiling" or "tailoring," permits the ready shaping of a module to the specific need of each user without altering the manner in which that function operates in relation to other users. For example, one user of an actual IOAS, although no longer associated with a particular project, continued to receive electronic mail in regard to it. To keep this user from being bothered by unnecessary reading and responding, a simple program routine was added to the IOAS system to automatically search electronic mail messages for key words, phrases, and project numbers pertaining to the prior project. When such a message is detected, the system sends to the originator a standard message that Mr. P. is no longer associated with that activity and that inquiries should be directed to Mrs. M. The system then automatically deletes both the incoming message and the automated response. Mr. P. is not only relieved of unnecessary effort, but by his own choice is never even aware that such messages are received or sent by the system.

Functional Structure

The first IOAS was developed at the Stanford Research Institute during the 1960s. Since then, enough systems have evolved to disclose certain structural patterns. An IOAS generally comprises:

- Basic components
- Optional components
- Extended-application components.

The classification of components may vary somewhat depending on the installation and the functions served. For ease of presentation, this discussion assumes that each category is discrete and that there is no overlapping of components. In actuality, there is no hard line distinguishing the categories of use. Basic components are broad-based tools so common that they apply to nearly every possible situation and user. Optional components are still relatively comprehensive but are not necessarily applicable to every installation. Extended-application components are those with rather narrow use, perhaps by only a single department or one person. These consist of data processing application software and personalized computing, which permits individuals to create specific applications that operate under the control of or in conjunction with the IOAS.

Each of these groups contains elements that serve three functions:

- Action
- Control
- Inquiry.

An action element permits the conduct of some activity: a word processor permits words to be captured and edited; a business graphics module permits the creation of graphs for either transmission or conversion to off-line presentation media.

A control element guides or monitors some activity. Electronic calendars and project management modules are examples.

An inquiry element accesses preexisting file information. Such elements provide for automated searching of an electronic message file, accessing stock market reports, or browsing through an on-line personnel manual.

The accompanying outlines show how some IOAS components and their functional elements may be grouped. No single configuraiton would be appropriate for all applications, nor would all planners or specialists agree on the choice of the various elements.

The functional elements in an IOAS are limited only by user need and the inventiveness of system planners. This section briefly reviews the most common functional elements, which are discussed in detail in Chapters 4 through 9.

Word management (word processing) and computer-based/terminal oriented message system modules are both a means of inputting text to an IOAS. A CBMS module generally automates the formatting of the text in some predefined manner, whereas a word management module permits a variety of formats. A link should exist between the two so that a user can freely manipulate and transmit text through the IOAS.

An IOAS should provide for natural-language file naming comparable to hard-copy filing conventions, system-controlled maintenance of file names in alphabetic order, system-controlled indexing of individual documents within each file, and a means of displaying an index of personal and shared file names and contents. Users should be able to perform bulk refiling and cross-filing of documents and to rename any file.

Electronic calendars are essentially individualized files containing appointment information; sometimes they are established as shared files, accessible to others. Exchanges of information about appointments generally occur via the computer-based message module.

Tickler files are personalized files, not usually shared. Sometimes they are part of the CBMS module; in such cases, a user enters a self-addressed, postdated message. The system may be designed so that en-

---

Basic IOAS Components

Action Elements
- Word management (keying and editing)
- Terminal-oriented computer-based message system
- Automated file indexing
- Electronic filing and retrieval
- Off-line connection to computer-operated micrographics (for system purging)

Control Elements
- Electronic calendar
- Electronic tickler file

Inquiry Elements
- Automated file searching and retrieval
- Directory of users (names, addresses, telephone numbers, etc.)
- Capability for open-loop computer-aided retrieval (CAR) of micrographics
- Capability for input/output control of physical files

---

try of the name of another IOAS user will ensure that the addressee receives the tickler on the stipulated date. This is a helpful feature for project or report production management.

Automated file searching is handled in any of three ways. Some systems search only the contents of the subject line; some search for key words; others search the entire contents of both the subject line and the body of text. Even with only a subject-line search capability, it is possible to operate an open-loop computer-aided retrieval system or to control the checkout of hard-copy files or library books. The subject line can contain the number of the file, document, or book; the user's name and extension; and perhaps a due date. An automated file search readily produces the location of a specific document, file, or book. A daily search of files can use the previous day's date to produce a listing of overdue files or books, with the names and extensions of those who checked them out. Overdue book notices can then be sent electronically via the CBMS to library patron users of the system.

User directories are almost universal. IOAS directories can include all employees in an organization and indicate whether each one is a user. If input is continually maintained, an IOAS directory can be particularly helpful to switchboard operators and receptionists.

Optional Elements

Optional elements generally provide functions needed by more than one group but not by all system users, such as interconnection to external message systems and data bases, store-and-forward fax, soft-copy fax, and interconnection to fax devices and/or systems external to the immediate IOAS. Preferably, all such interconnections occur without user intervention. The IOAS software should handle the transfer of both textual and graphic messages to relieve users of repetitive tasks.

Depending on the size of the textual and on-line, soft-copy micrographic data bases and the structure of the computerized file, it may be advisable to provide users with search options for either or both data bases. Users should be able to retrieve part or all of a micrographic data base for inclusion in a new document being created with the word management facility and to forward all or part of a micrographic data base as part of a document file or a message. The recipient(s) must have a compatible terminal.

Organizational documents that require frequent updating, printing, and distribution are directly convertible to electronic media by means of an IOAS. A terminal-oriented CBMS can provide an approximation to electronic publishing: the master copy of the text resides in a word processor document file, where it can be repeatedly updated and a

Optional IOAS Components

Action Elements
- Interconnection to other terminal-oriented, computer-based message systems
- Interconnection to public teletypewriter systems
- OCR (optical character recognition) input
- Digitized, hard-copy input (temporary; for incoming mail)
- Store-and-forward fax
- Soft-copy fax
- Interconnection to external fax devices and networks
- Audio output electronic mail (digital-to-audio conversion)
- Business graphics (black-and-white)
- Electronic calculator
- Sorting capabilities
- Photocomposer output
- On-line output of computer-operated micrographics (COM)
- Computer teleconferencing

Control Elements
- COM format previewing
- Project management and control
- Management of multiauthor document preparation

Inquiry Elements
- Soft-copy CAR
- Electronic publishing (manuals, price lists, news, etc.)
- Interconnection to other internal systems and data bases
- Interconnection to external research data base services

copy forwarded to the usual recipients as an attachment to a CBMS message. In such a system each recipient must delete the previous copy from his or her files and then file the most recent one.

True electronic publishing operates with a shared file. Documents reside in files, rather than being sent in message form. As with other computer-based electronic files, only a single copy of a file exists within a single system node. Access to each file is controlled through the user directory, either by a code entered by the system supervisor or by membership in a group address, which may entitle the user to access a file on a "read only" basis. One or more authorized persons have access to update the file contents.

Electronic publishing with an IOAS makes it simple to organize and maintain control of documents with multiple authors by permitting the electronic transfer and editing of outlines, drafts of text, and illustrations. The person supervising creation of the document can assign tasks, set target dates, transfer segmented outlines and draft text to writers, editors, reviewers, and management, and monitor progress.

Project management in an IOAS is much like that in a freestanding system. Milestones control activity flows; when deadlines are not met, the system notifies those responsible for the work as well as the project manager. The system automatically monitors overdue project elements for the manager; it also tracks completion percentages by element and in terms of the entire project. It compiles project summaries of individuals' hours and of hours and percentages over- or underestimated. Properly designed and executed, an IOAS project management function can automatically adjust the completion date for a project and provide improved information regarding future project estimates.

In computer teleconferencing, discussed in detail in Chapter 9, the teleconference takes place in a joint file area containing the series of messages exchanged among participants. Special software supports the chairperson by monitoring progress: each time a participant enters a comment, the software automatically notifies all participants via an electronic mail message. A single such notice exists in the electronic message queue of every participant regardless of the number of times it is sent. Once she or he accesses the referenced teleconference, the message should automatically be deleted from the message queue. Another software tool assists the chairperson with surveys or votes by transmitting preformatted individual or serial questions to participants, tallying the responses, and returning them to the chairperson.

Extended-Application Elements

Extended-application functions in an IOAS generally are those that are limited to one operating group within the user community. The extended-application capability provides a means of handling jobs considered too insignificant or too costly to warrant effort by centralized systems and data processing departments. These functions are so diverse and numerous that a fully representative list is impossible.

Functionally Integrated Office Automation

Working alone, individual office automation tools can do only a part of the job; intelligently combined, they provide a comfortable and efficient means of information management. The preceding portion of this chapter has dealt with integrated office automation systems, which are software, and part of the array of office automation tools. The balance of this chapter pertains to functionally integrated office automation: how the tools discussed in the earlier chapters and the first part of this one are combined.

Office automation planners devise specific combinations of hardware, software, and procedures to meet the needs of a particular user

Extended-Application IOAS Components
Action Elements
- Automated departmental billing for IOAS usage
- Individual applications
- Personal computing (permits individual to program)
- Unit applications
- Departmental applications
- Divisional applications
- Regional applications
- Line-of-business applications
- Functional applications (mathematical formulas)

Control Elements
- System usage monitoring (departmental level)
- Specialized applications (as above)

Inquiry Elements
- Specialized applications (as above)

---

community. Customized programming is not always necessary, however. A number of office automation software systems, packages, and utilities on the open market can be used individually or in concert with other software. The handful of typical office automation systems described in this section are based on existing installations or on working components from more than one installation. All the hardware is commercially available; most of the software is or soon will be.

With office automation, the whole is often more than the sum of the parts: two elements, each of value in its own right, when combined form a new tool. Some electronic mail systems, for example, prevent the editing of messages once they have been sent; updatable material undergoing revision therefore has to be rekeyed into the system. Storing the master document magnetically in a communicating word processor, however, permits easy updating and subsequent transmission to any number of persons through the electronic mail system. Joining a communicating word processor and a terminal-based electronic mail system creates an additional tool: electronic publishing.

The systems described below offer a broad spectrum of real choices but represent only a few of the almost limitless possibilities. The purpose of these examples is to provide modular concepts that organizations can modify to suit their specific needs. In reviewing these illustrations, planners should keep in mind the distinction between designed functions and creatable functions. Designed functions are those intentionally programmed to perform some action or task (e.g., terminal-based electronic mail, word processing); creatable functions are those that planners can provide, either through creative use of programmed functions (e.g., using parametric file searching for open-loop CAR) or by incorporating two or more items of standard hardware or software in a single system (such as combining word processors for off-line updating and terminal-based electronic mail for distribution). Through creatable functions, planners have access to hundreds of design possibilities with no expense for customized software or hardware, and with little or no delay between decision and implementation.

A Single-Mode Terminal-Based Electronic Mail System

Simple in concept as well as in configuration, a single-mode CBMS serves several functions and is well suited to organizations of any size. The hardware consists of stationary and/or portable terminals used to access an electronic mail system. The software has multidocument natural-language filing capability and automated retrieval. Altogether the system offers electronic message handling, filing, retrieval, automated file searching, and open-loop computer-aided retrieval.

Though not specifically programmed into the software, it is possible to use a form of automated tickler by creating self-addressed messages (with or without sending) and filing them under "Ticklers," "Reminders," or some other name. Access is self-initiated, either through the system-generated index for that file or through parametric search, since the software is not designed to trigger the appearance of the messages on the specific dates.

The open-loop CAR is easy to implement. The automated retrieval

---

A Single-Mode Computer-Based Electronic Mail System

Software
- Electronic mail timesharing service / software

Features

Text
- Computer-based electronic mail (CBMS)
- Portable electronic mail
- On-line document preparation (CBMS terminal)
- Multiauthor document preparation (CBMS terminal)
- Electronic document distribution
- Categorized multidocument natural-language filing
- Automated file searching (parametric searches)
- Tickler function (manually operable; not programmed)
- Telephone message file (using CBMS)
- On-line user directories
- Computer teleconferencing (manually operable)
- Computer-aided retrieval (CAR)

Data
- Access to coresident data processing (DP) tasks and files in CBMS system
- Access to outside data bases and DP services

Text / Graphic
- Not applicable

Graphic
- Video projection of terminal screen images
- Open-loop CAR (off-line micrographics)

Audio
- Not applicable

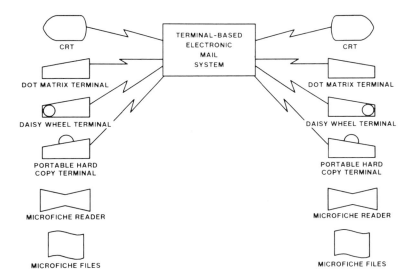

Computer-generated diagram by General Electric's Boston Genigraphics Service Center.

functions of the software system include a parametric search. The user enters key words, microfiche numbers, and frame coordinates in the subject line of self-or group-addressed messages. Those messages reside in a single file, named, for example, "Fiche" or "Database." The parametric search feature of the electronic mail system locates specific file entries. The index displays the entire subject line, including the numbers and frame coordinates of each referenced microfiche. The same procedure can be used with hard-copy files or reference libraries.

A number of such systems are presently in use, usually only for electronic mail. The system software is commercially available.

Though similar to the previous system, a two-mode word processing/electronic mail system includes standalone word/data processors, which considerably expand the functions. The word processors can be used off line to prepare messages and update materials (price lists, policies, etc.) as well as for all the usual word processing tasks. They also serve as conventional terminals, either with the electronic mail system or with data processing applications on a timesharing basis. Although on-line message handling is cost efficient for brief communications, the use of word processors in off-line preparation and editing of long documents reduces line charges and access time to the electronic mail system. When there is an in-house electronic publishing system, the use of word processors for off-line work on long documents provides more efficient use of the system communication ports.

Because the word processing system has both word and data processing capabilities, it can be used in conjunction with the electronic mail system for roll-ups. In a roll-up, data and text from several sources are assembled and edited into a summary for presentation to higher levels of management. Assuming a sales roll-up is needed on the first day of each month, the process could work as follows.

Sales data addressed to the national sales manager from the field sales managers enter the electronic mail system in specified formats. The national manager's secretary electronically copies the incoming messages into a single word processing document, uses the word processor off line to format and edit the data, then uses the mathematical software package to summarize results. The software can not only automatically generate subtotals for each sales representative, but also subtotals by office and region with a grand total for each column. The word processor can also be programmed to process the document file as if it were a data processing file—editing, tabulating, subtotaling, and totaling without secretarial intervention. The secretary enters a cover

---

A Two-Mode Word Processing/Electronic Mail System

Software
- Electronic mail timesharing service/software
- WP software with asynchronous ASCII communications

Features

Text
- Standalone communicating word processing
- Point-to-point electronic mail (communicating WP systems)
- Terminal-based electronic mail (CBMS)
- Portable electronic mail
- On-line document preparation (CBMS)

- Off-line document preparation (word processor)
- Multiauthor document preparation (CBMS)
- Electronic document distribution
- Categorized multidocument natural-language filing
- Automated file searching (parametric search)
- Tickler function (manual, using parametric search)
- Telephone message file (using CBMS)
- Electronic publishing
- On-line user directories
- Sort utility (in WP software)
- Math utility (in WP software)
- Computer teleconferencing (using CBMS)
- CAR

Data
- Access to coresident DP tasks and files in CBMS system
- Dial-up access to other computers

Text / Graphic
- Not applicable

Graphic
- Video projection of terminal screen images
- Open-loop CAR (off-line micrographics)

Audio
- Not applicable

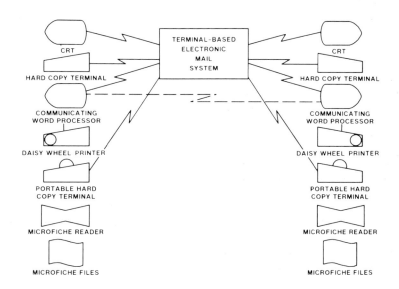

Computer-generated diagram by General Electric's Boston Genigraphics Service Center.

memo as the first page of the document. After the principal reviews the document, the summarized report can be disseminated electronically to the electronic mail system users and in hard copy to others.

This system exists at a number of locations. It is a basic configuration that can accommodate OCR page readers or photocomposers. The software is commercially available.

A Three-Mode Integrated Mini/Mainframe System

A three-mode integrated mini/mainframe system represents one of the few installed office automation systems to meld two normally incompatible computers: a minicomputer of one manufacturer with a mainframe of another.

The front-end minicomputer handles all communications, contains the software for an integrated office automation system, and performs all computing related to the IOAS. The mainframe, with its greater disk file capacity, serves as the file processor to the IOAS as well as serving conventional data processing uses. There is dial-up access to the minicomputer via dumb terminals, intelligent terminals, intelligent graphic terminals (remote, timesharing graphics), or portable dumb terminals, although not all terminal types are presently in use.

Some unusual software tools are incorporated, including one for scanning text files at various levels of detail. A user may scan 64 levels of headings and subheadings within a document, or may have the system display specified levels of headings and the first lines of each paragraph that follows. Another feature permits the user to split the screen vertically at any column; one side can display an outline while the user writes or adds material to the document on the other. The user can also

---

A Three-Mode Integrated Mini/Mainframe System

Software
• Integrated office automation system timesharing service or software
Features
Text
• Terminal-based electronic mail system (CBMS)
• Portable electronic mail
• On-line document preparation (CBMS terminal)
• Split-screen displays
• Multiauthor document preparation (CBMS)
• Electronic document distribution
• Categorized multidocument natural-language filing
• Back-end filing in mainframe computer
• Automated file searching (parametric search)

- Telephone message file (manually operated)
- Sort utility (in WP system)
- Math utility (in WP system)

Data
- Full DP capability within same computer
- Sort utility (IOAS and DP)
- Math utility (IOAS and DP)
- Electronic calculator (in integrated system)

Text / Graphic
- Commingled text / graphic creation and transmission

Graphic
- Computer output microfilm (COM) previewing on display terminals
- Timesharing graphics

Audio
- Not applicable

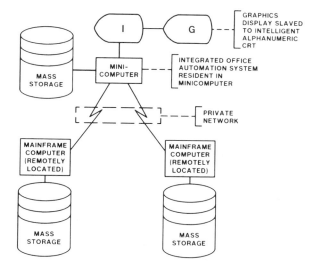

Computer-generated diagram by General Electric's Boston Genigraphics Service Center.

compare two documents or files by displaying them simultaneously. Each side of the screen can be individually scrolled forward and backward. Still another tool permits previewing the formatting of microfiche, prior to sending documents to the computer output microfilm (COM) device.

The system has a graphics feature that may be unique: it can transmit graphics between nodes via the electronic mail facility within the system on a store-and-forward basis, just like text and data. Normally, computerized graphics are either local (standalone), remotely accessed (timeshared), or transmitted point-to-point, but are not directly transmittable as message images.

The basic IOAS software and all the tools mentioned are available on the open market; the software that interconnects the mini with the mainframe is proprietary.

A Three-Mode Integrated System

A three-mode integrated system provides text, graphics, and audio capabilities. Substitution of a word-and-data processing system would make this a four-mode system. Text is served by a standalone communicating word processor that can prepare off-line electronic mail and provide magnetic capture and storage. The system also contains dumb display terminals with built-in or attached video hard-copy equipment. This arrangement permits the user of a terminal to produce hard copy by depressing a single button.

The graphics in this system are produced by freestanding fax units that communicate among themselves. They can be conventional units transmitting one on one; of the broadcast type (capable of transmitting to more than one other unit); or multiple autopolling units, which automatically dial other units to determine whether there are documents awaiting transmission for the calling system.

The third mode resides in the audio teleconferencing, which both the text and graphics equipment support. The EMS transmits any material needed for an audio teleconference. Fax transmits any required graphic material for local production of multiple hard copies or conversion to overhead transparencies. Printing text pages in a large typeface prior

---

A Three-Mode Integrated System

Software
• Electronic mail timesharing service / software
Features
Text
• Standalone communicating word processing (WP)
• Point-to-point electronic mail (communicating WP systems)
• Computer-based electronic mail (CBMS)
• Portable electronic mail (optional)
• On-line document preparation (CBMS)
• On-line document preparation (word processor)
• Multiauthor document preparation (CBMS)
• Electronic document distribution
• Categorized multidocument natural-language filing

- Automated file searching (parametric search)
- Tickler function (operable manually; not programmed)
- Telephone message file
- On-line user directories
- Sort utility (in WP system)
- Math utility (in WP system)
- Computer teleconferencing (operable manually)
- Off-line phototypesetting (optional via WP system)
- COM output (optional from WP diskettes)
- CAR

Data
- Access to coresident data processing (DP) tasks and files in CBMS
- Access to outside data bases and DP services
- Sort utility (in WP and DP systems)
- Math utility (in WP and DP systems)

Text / Graphic
- Graphic electronic mail—fax
- Store-and-forward fax (via timesharing service)
- Portable fax (optional)

Graphic
- Video projection of terminal screen images
- Open-loop CAR (off-line micrographics)

Audio
- Audio teleconferencing

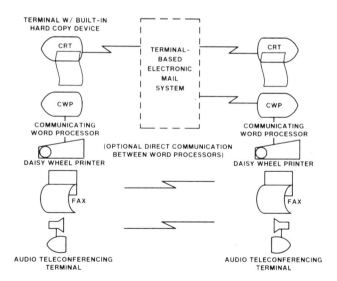

Computer-generated diagram by General Electric's Boston Genigraphics Service Center.

to creating the transparencies makes the projected text much easier to read.

This common basic configuration can be expanded to accommodate OCR page readers, photocomposing hardware, portable terminals, or audio recorders for the teleconferencing system. The electronic mail software is commercially available.

A Four-Mode Nonintegrated System

A four-mode nonintegrated system differs in three major ways from a three-mode integrated system. First, there are no individual terminals for principals; secretaries and word processing operators handle all input and output, using both typewriters and WP systems. This design serves principals who are unable or unwilling to perform their own keying. Second, the addition of OCR page readers permits typewriters to function as input devices; the text is scanned onto the magnetic media of the word processors, freeing the latter to do what they do best: edit. Third, there is no terminal-oriented computer-based message system; the electronic mail is point-to-point via communicating word processors, and principals receive incoming mail in hard copy printed by the word processing equipment.

The word processors have both word and data processing capabilities. In addition, the fax devices sometimes operate in conjunction with the word processors in support of audio teleconferencing.

A Four-Mode Nonintegrated System

Software
• Word Processing with communications
Features
Text
• Standalone communicating word processing (WP)
• OCR input to word processor
• Point-to-point electronic mail (communicating WP systems)
• Electronic document distribution
• Tickler function (operable manually; not programmed)
• Sort utility (in WP system)
• Math utility (in WP system)
• Off-line phototypesetting (option)
• COM output (option)
Data
• Dial-access to timesharing computers (not illustrated)
• Sort utility (WP used as dial-up terminal)
• Math utility (WP used as dial-up terminal)

Text / Graphic
* Graphic electronic mail—fax
* Portable fax (optional)

Graphic
* Fax

Audio
* Audio teleconferencing
* Dictation—local
* Dictation—dial-up (optional)
* Dictation—remote control (optional)

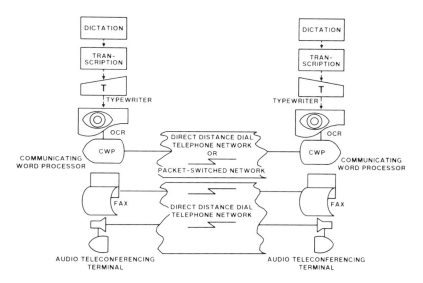

Computer-generated diagram by General Electric's Boston Genigraphics Service Center.

A Four-Mode System with Shared-Logic Word Processors

A four-mode system with shared-logic word processors serves principals who do their own keying. The terminals of principals are part of the shared-logic word processing systems. Principals can restrict use of their personal terminals by dictating input, which secretaries or word processing operators key into magnetic files. They can review drafts of messages and documents via their terminals, dictating editorial changes to the person doing the keying. All CRTs have direct, hardwired access to the on-line word processing files and provide optional dial-up access to both the electronic mail system and remote word processing systems for direct transmission and receipt of documents. Principals use their terminals to read incoming messages, scan files, and initiate parametric file searches. Their keying barely exceeds that required to operate a pushbutton telephone.

The basic system, illustrated here, provides great flexibility in both function and configuration. Although only two terminals are depicted per shared-logic word processing system, more terminals can be added. The shared-logic word processors can use both diskettes and optional hard disks, providing considerably greater on-line file capacity. Users can employ any combination of display or hard-copy terminals, either stationary or portable, to communicate via the electronic mail system.

A Four-Mode System with Shared-Logic Word Processors

Software
- Word processing software with communications
- Electronic mail timesharing service / software

Features

Text
- Shared-logic word processing
- Point-to-point electronic mail (communicating WP systems)
- Computer-based electronic mail (CBMS)
- Portable electronic mail
- On-line document preparation (CBMS terminal)
- Off-line document preparation (word processor)
- Multiauthor document preparation (CBMS or WP system)
- Electronic document distribution
- Categorized multidocument natural-language filing
- Tickler function (operable manually; not programmed)
- Telephone message file
- Electronic publishing
- On-line user directories
- Sort utility (in WP system)
- Math utility (in WP system)
- Computer teleconferencing (pseudo version using CBMS)
- Open-loop CAR (optional)

Data
- Access to timesharing computers
- Sort utility (in WP system or via timesharing)
- Math utility (in WP system or via timesharing)

Text / Graphic
- Graphic electronic mail—fax
- Portable fax (optional)

Graphic
- Open-loop CAR (off-line micrographics)

Audio
- Audio teleconferencing

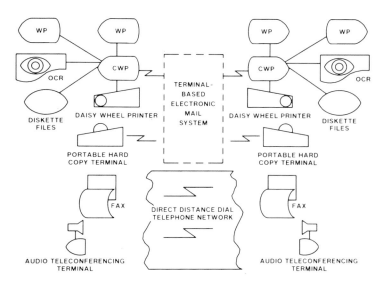

Computer-generated diagram by General Electric's Boston Genigraphics Service Center.

Both word processing and the electronic mail software are readily available commercially. Optional word processing software may include math, sort, and records management utilities.

A Four-Mode System with Timesharing Graphics

Considerably more sophisticated than the preceding examples, one four-mode system incorporates an IOAS package with interactive business graphics. The complete set of IOAS tools includes a terminal-oriented computer-based message system with interconnection to TWX and Telex through a manually-operated paper tape switching center, electronic filing and retrieval, automated parametric file searching, tickler files, word management/document subsystem, electronic calendar with automated appointment scheduling, a user directory/personnel locator subsystem, and interactive timeshared graphics. Both fax and audio teleconferencing are electronically discrete, but attaching a video projector to a display terminal located permanently in the teleconferencing room permits group viewing of any text transmitted from another location for audio teleconferences. Data and plotting specifications can be similarly transmitted to other locations for local re-creation and projection of graphics.

A Four-Mode System with Timesharing Graphics

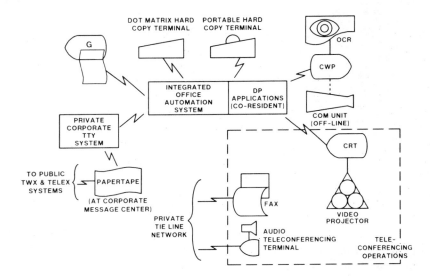

Software
- Word processing software with communications
- Integrated office automation system timesharing / software

Features
Text
- Standalone communicating word processing (WP)
- OCR input to word processor
- Point-to-point electronic mail (communicating WP systems)
- Computer-based electronic mail (CBMS)
- Portable electronic mail
- On-line document preparation (CBMS)
- Off-line document preparation (word processor)
- Multiauthor document preparation (CBMS)
- Electronic document distribution
- Categorized multidocument natural-language filing
- Filing in medium / large minicomputers (optional: from WP system)
- Automated file searching (parametric search)
- Tickler function
- Telephone message file
- Electronic calendar
- Automated appointment scheduling (multiperson)
- Electronic publishing
- On-line user directories
- Personnel locator system (names, telephone numbers, etc.)
- Torn-tape message center connection to TWX and telex
- Direct interconnection to TWX / telex networks
- Sort utility (in WP system)

- Math utility (in WP system)
- Computer teleconferencing (pseudo form using CBMS)
- Off-line phototypesetting
- COM output (off-line)
- Open-loop CAR

Data
- Access to coresident DP tasks and files in CBMS
- Access to outside data bases and DP services
- Sort utility (in WP and DP systems)
- Math utility (in WP and DP systems)

Text / Graphic
- Graphic electronic mail—fax
- Portable fax

Graphic
- Video projection of IOAS graphic images (local)
- Slow-scan video (black-and-white)
- Open-loop CAR (off-line micrographics)
- Local computer graphics (color pen plotter)
- Timesharing graphics (black-and-white)

Audio
- Voice-response electronic mail
- Audio teleconferencing
- Dictation—local

Computer-generated diagram by General Electric's Boston Genigraphics Service Center.

The IOAS shown here also connects to a separate minicomputer that serves as a corporate teletypewriter switching system; all messages sent outside the firm are addressed to the corporate message center, where they are output in paper tape and fed into a TWX or Telex terminal without rekeying. This system affords IOAS users communication worldwide, either directly to other IOAS users or by telegram, cablegram, or Telex to other individuals.

Computer output microfilm is used to purge text files in word processors and the IOAS.

This multinode IOAS system can operate with a number of intercommunicating minicomputers. If messages are awaiting transmission to other nodes, the IOAS software activates an automatic telephone dialer that contacts the appropriate network node (computer). The calling system then transmits the message(s) and simultaneously accepts mail from the called system.

Several powerful and cost-effective options are available with this design. One alternative is to substitute a communicating desktop graphics system for one or more system terminals. Such a device serves both as a conventional interactive terminal and as an off-line, local means of creating business graphics. In the system illustrated, the desktop graphics system could incorporate a plotter capable of producing business graphics in up to eight colors on either paper stock or overhead transparency material. Another alternative is to hard-wire the optional standalone graphics system to a camera system (see Chapter 10) for local production of slides, graphic microfiche, overhead transparencies, or photos. Any department that requires a large volume of presentation materials or works with short lead times on such materials would find such a unit advantageous. Other departments might share a unit.

A system like this, but with fewer features, began in June 1980 to incorporate voice-output electronic mail, which converts the headers and text of messages to audible form. Users may dial into the IOAS from any tone-operated telephone and hear their electronic mail "read" to them by software operating through a phoneme-based voice-synthesizer. Because the module operates with phonemes, the vocabulary is unlimited; the system has demonstrated a remarkable ability to pronounce surnames. The software for the IOAS and the voice-output electronic mail remain proprietary.

NOTES

1. Harold E. Bamford, Jr., "Assessing the Effect of Computer Augmentation on Staff Productivity," *Journal of the American Society for Information Science*, May 1979, pp. 136–138.

2. U.S. Air Force, Maintenance Policy and Procedures Division, Directorate of Maintenance and Supply, *Maintenance Directives Development Cost Analysis*, (Washington, D.C., 1979), pp. 1–12.

THE INDIVIDUAL
WORKSTATION

An office workstation is the environmentally controlled space and apparatus provided to a worker for the performance of assigned tasks. Most workstations consist of three elements: furniture, nonelectronic equipment, and automated equipment. This chapter discusses components that are either automated or are directly associated with automated devices. The discussion is oriented toward workstations for professionals, though anyone who handles information should be considered for some type of automated station.

There is no such thing as an average knowledge worker, an average task, or an average workplace. No single product suits every person, every task, and every location ibecause employees require varying degrees of automated capability. The ideal solution is to give each knowledge worker the precise tools with which to optimize his or her own task—no more and no less. Every task array requires individual assessment to ensure that utilization of both human and automated resources benefit the organization as a whole. Given that individual needs vary over time, the modularity of the workstation is frequently essential.

Certain tasks are common to virtually every knowledge worker, such as sending and receiving memos and letters, preparing reports, communicating with fellow workers, and attending meetings. Combining task arrays with information such as physical location, employee density, and organizational size can lead to a basic set of workstation specifications useful to all, or nearly all, employees in an organization. Tools used most frequently are at the personal workplace; those used less frequently or justifiable only on a shared basis are conveniently located in the immediate vicinity; infrequently used or high-cost/high-speed devices are either centralized or dispersed on a per building basis. However, a careful cost analysis may indicate that quantity purchases of many units of a single design at a discount may be more economical than implementing an array of customized units.

Terminals

The most frequently used office automation tools manage alphanumerics and audio. Since 90 percent of the nonspoken communication is alphanumeric information, and 10 percent is graphic, for some workers, a dumb display terminal will suffice. It is capable of simple alphanumeric input and output accommodating text management, terminal-based electronic mail, interconnection to Telex and TWX networks, electronic calendars, tickler files, access to internal and external data bases and news services. Combination alphanumeric/graphic displays will be needed by others. As many as 10 or 15 people can share such a terminal. Those with frequent needs require a dedicated terminal. Table 12.1 lists a representative selection of existing workstation terminals available today in the open market.

Professional workstation combining computing, editing, graphics, and communications. The Xerox Star system includes a simple to use two-button control device. Photo courtesy of Xerox Corporation.

TABLE 12.1   Cost and features of selected workstation equipment.

Equipment/Features	Cost ($)
Display terminal	600-2,000
Uppercase only	600
Video capability	1,500-2,000
Black-and-white graphics tube	4,000 and up
Screen dump printer/plotter	
for text and graphics	850 and up
Freestanding full-color graphics	
with plotter	15,000 and up
Standalone word processor	
Dual floppy disks and	
letter-quality printer	6,000 and up
Communications option	1,000
Acoustic coupler	
300 baud	200
1,200 baud	900
Fax unit	1,500 and up
OCR unit	10,000 and up
Audio teleconferencing terminal	500 and up
Interactive pen-type graphics unit	5,000 per location

Work space must accommodate the terminal both physically and electrically. Surfaces intended to support keyboard devices such as typewriters and terminals are 26–27 inches high, a few inches lower than conventional writing surfaces. The difference in height is small but very important to reduce user fatigue. Altering the height of the keyboard even slightly results in errors, decreased output, and physical discomfort.

Telephones

In the audio mode, the telephone not only remains a viable tool but is growing in importance. Locating it on a wall, partition, or panel eliminates intrusion on the work surface. Loudspeaking telephones in open-plan offices afford no privacy and disturb others; instead audio teleconferencing terminals in dispersed teleconferencing rooms can be used as loudspeaking telephones in one-to-one telephone calls.

Dictation Machines

As a growing number of managers and professionals key their own information and voice electronic mail and voice recognition evolve, use of dictation machines will decline in offices, but portable units will remain practical.

Graphics

Graphic communications are primarily via shared fax units, that is, interactive or standalone computerized graphics terminals. Few are installed for exclusive use at individual workstations. Some compact fax devices, such as those manufactured by Burroughs and Alden, fit easily on narrow shelves in desk organizers. Most units are slightly larger and require space for separate stands, tables, and work surfaces so that individual writing surfaces remain clear for paperwork. In some display terminals, computerized graphic options coexist with alphanumerics; some have optional, built-in hard-copy printer/plotters while others require added space for a separate hard-copy device.

Meeting Individual Needs

Implementing new tools with minimal disruption to individuals or office routines requires tailoring them functionally to the knowledge worker. Cabinetry with a pleasing appearance increases the user's receptivity to the device.

Table 12.2 lists a selection of equipment and options for upper management through clerical personnel. As a rule, the more general the task structure, the broader the tools; the more specific the task array, the more limited the range of tools.

There is seldom a need to provide a keyboard-type terminal to upper management who cannot key. Instead, a display terminal with a ten-key pad, touch-screen, or voice recognition feature is more suitable. Any necessary keyboard input can be handled by executive secretaries in such cases. For both aesthetic and acoustical reasons, output devices for executives are best located at the secretarial workplace or in an adjoining equipment room. Since upper management often uses graphic information, such as line graphs and block diagrams, the terminals they use should be capable of displaying soft-copy fax, computer-generated graphics, and/or video.

Depending on individual circumstances, middle management terminals may be equipped with a keyboard or another means of control similar to upper management terminals, and have graphic display capability, with graphic input optional at the managerial terminal or at the secretarial workplace. Again, fax input and hard-copy output devices are likely to be at the secretarial workplace or in an equipment room.

Table 12.2   Workstation equipment and some available options for different categories of personnel.

	Tool	Options
Upper management	CRT terminal	Keyboard
		Ten-key pad
		Touch-screen
		Custom cabinetry
		Soft-copy fax
		Computerized graphics
		Video
	Loudspeaking telephone with automatic dialer	Audio teleconferencing terminal
Middle management	CRT with graphics	Keyboard
		Ten-key pad
		Graphic input
		Special cabinetry
	Loudspeaking telephone with automatic dialer	Audio teleconferencing terminal
Professionals	CRT terminal	Keyboard
		Dedicated, shared or secretarial graphics
		Soft copy fax
	Conventional telephone	Automatic dialer
Technical personnel	CRT with keyboard and soft-copy fax display	Computerized graphics
	Nearby FAX input	
	Standard telephone	Automatic dialer
Secretarial personnel	Alphanumeric word processor with keyboard and soft-copy fax display	Computerized graphics
		OCR/fax input, dedicated or shared
	Hard-copy printer/ plotter	
	Standard telephone	Call director
Clerical personnel	CRT with communications capabilities	Microfiche viewer
		Standard telephone

Creating a Line Graph A consultant, reading his mail just before 11:00 a.m., finds updated material which considerably alters a manually created graphic he plans to use that afternoon in a 1:30 presentation. Knowing that another consultant just down the hall has recently installed an integrated office automation system with a graphics capability, he requests his assistance in creating a new graphic.

Dialing into the system, selecting the GRAPHICS option from the numbered menu, the second consultant enters a series of revised monthly values for a twelve-month period, each in response to a question style prompt by the system. At the thirteenth question he enters nothing and presses the RETURN key to signify the end of the data input. The system immediately displays a menu of numbered graphics options, from which the second consultant selects LINE/TIME PLOT. The computer system asks a series of questions about the scaling to be used, whether it should label the scales, and so forth, all in conversational style questions. Finally the question OK? YES or NO (Y or N)? appears and is answered with Y. Approximately a minute and a half later a completed plot is signaled to the consultants by a short, quiet buzz emanating from the terminal. Since the plot scaling is too compressed vertically, the formatting information dealing with the vertical scaling is re-entered, and a new plot, properly scaled, is produced on the screen within 2 minutes. Since the terminal is equipped with a built-in electrographic hard-copy unit, pressing the single key labeled PRINT produces a hard copy of the graph in about 30 seconds. The departmental secretary converts hard copy into the required overhead transparency, a process completed within another 3 minutes. Total time from start to finish, under 20 minutes.

An administrative support secretary can use a shared device at the support location.

Professional personnel who work constantly with information need access to soft-copy text via personal terminals. Provision of individual, shared, or secretarial graphic input and output devices depends on frequency of use. Most personal terminals should have the ability to add soft-copy fax capability.

Technical personnel generally have more need for graphics, and they tend to require terminals with alphanumeric, graphic, and soft-copy fax display capabilities. Alternatively, technical personnel may need a shared computerized graphics facility and shared fax quite close to the workplace.

Personal and administrative support secretaries are apt to have intelligent terminals in the form of word processors, with soft-copy display of fax, computerized graphics, and a printer/plotter for hard-copy production. These units must have communications capabilities. Personal secretaries are unlikely to have dedicated hybrid OCR/fax input devices; administrative support secretaries will have shared devices.

Graphics display terminal for professional workers, *left*, and the Termiphone, a hybrid terminal combining telephone, keyboard, and single-line display. Photo courtesy of Human Designed Systems and Micon Industries.

Clerical employees have more narrowly defined task arrays, and their workplaces reflect their specializations. They almost certainly require terminals with keyboards for alphanumeric input and output. A customer service clerk may have a microfiche viewer alongside the CRT, permitting open-loop computer-aided retrieval of billing information, telephone numbers, addresses, and so forth. When lookup speed is important, the terminal can have the ability to display digitized images from an on-line micrographic data base, perhaps including graphic contents such as signatures.

Current Workstation Configurations

In Fort Worth, Texas, the home office of Equitable General Insurance Company, service and claim representatives have uniform workstations consisting of a CRT display terminal beside a microfiche viewer. The microfiche contains images from original documents, an authoritative information source. Combined access to computerized data bases and to micrographic copies of original documents has resulted in an average turnaround time of one day on claims.[1]

London Life in London, Ontario, has 200 CRT display terminals connected to a mainframe computer; another 300 terminals are in branch offices. The terminals are used both for interactive inquiry and for a broadcast type of individually or group-addressed electronic mail.[2]

A large, multinational manufacturing firm in New England has been using a broad range of office automation tools since the mid-1970s. Beside the desk of the firm's chief executive officer is a video display terminal that provides access to terminal-based electronic mail from his staff. The terminal also provides an electronic calendar with scheduling

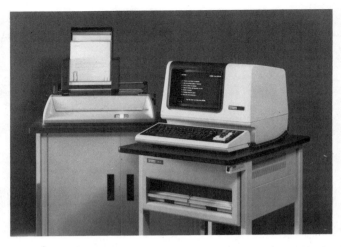

Multipurpose DECmate workstation for office specialists, independent professionals such as lawyers and dentists, and small businessmen. Photo courtesy of Digital Equipment Corporation.

functions and provision for adding local graphics and video display capability. The executive often performs his own keying. The workstation of his secretary consists of a communicating word processor equipped with a letter-quality printer. Also at the secretarial workplace is a fax unit with automatic answering capability to accommodate numerous overseas office communications. The adjacent executive conference room is equipped with multiple telephone lines for audio teleconferencing; audio terminals are brought in as needed.

Workstations of vice presidents and their secretaries are similarly equipped, except that few have fax units, relying instead on shared units throughout the firm.

Middle management workstations vary. Some have display terminals in their manager's office; others have them at secretarial workstations. Most are alphanumeric display terminals; many also have timeshared graphics capability and can convert screen images to hard copy via built-in printer/plotters at the touch of a single key marked "print." Many private offices are equipped with loudspeaking telephones; the firm has also begun an international program of installing audio teleconferencing rooms belonging to individual departments but shared by adjacent ones. Most managerial workstation terminals have dial-up connections to the computer via telephone handsets over a leased network. Most managers feel that subordination of incoming calls to the use of terminals causes few problems: most telephone communications are internal, and many of the knowledge workers now use the integrated office automation system.

Technical and professional personnel have numerous display terminals, most of which are alphanumeric, and a few dedicated hard-copy terminals. Individuals with soft-copy terminals share hard-copy terminals and use secretarial or shared communicating word processors for hard-copy output. Fax service is via 200 units installed worldwide. A handful are in message centers; most are shared within departments.

Some secretarial workstations are equipped with freestanding or shared-logic word processors with communications capability. Other secretarial workstations have only typewriters and share self-service word processing systems in the immediate vicinity or in the internal word processing center for work that requires revision. Still others have both a typewriter and a dial-up CRT equipped with graphics and built-in printer/plotter. Those secretaries are able to enter text through the IOAS and output either draft-or letter-quality hard copy through the local, self-service word processing system or a shared hard-copy terminal. A handful of secretarial stations have either fax or micrographic devices. All have telephones.

Many clerical workstations have micrographic viewers; few have dedicated computer terminals. Access to the IOAS is through shared terminals located within departments.

All office automation terminals are compatible with the centralized and dispersed data processing systems; a number of hybrid word and data processing systems are also in operation.

Square footage and furnishings are much as they were prior to automation. Individual workstations have terminals; dispersed here and there are cubicles or rooms that house shared word processors, soft-copy and hard-copy terminals, and fax units. Conference rooms have overhead transparency units, projection screens, audio teleconferencing terminals or loudspeaking telephones.

The firm has a central computerized slide-making facility with a high annual volume and a large COM center.

Costing of Automated Workstations

To compare the cost of automated to nonautomated workstations, and make the comparison valid, the cost factors for each must be the same.

The workstations themselves should be costed in two parts: the individual workplace, and a proration of shared facilities such as teleconferencing rooms, shared word processors, fax units; centralized services such as word processing; and automated audiovisual service facilities, such as computerized slide making. Rented equipment, telephone service, and electric power must also be costed.

Prospective users must also take into consideration the inflating effect of the cost of pilot operations. If only 20 or 30 workstations are to be installed and supported by a dedicated computer, distributing the cost of the computer among so few workstations will significantly distort the mean cost. One solution is to average the cost of the computer and software according to the maximum number of workstations they will ultimately support and then add that figure to the cost of each workstation. A medium-scale minicomputer, for example, can support about 500 users with access to an integrated office automation system plus data processing applications.

International Considerations

Social norms in other nations require careful scrutiny; involvement of local management and users is advisable. Planning and costing workstations outside one's own nation requires consideration of compatibility. Many data and word processing firms market international versions of equipment that are compatible with local power sources and legal requirements. But the introduction of newer models of equipment is slow, and it is sometimes possible to install compatible devices of local origin. Another solution is for an organization to purchase and export equipment itself. Some firms solve resulting maintenance problems by stockpiling spare units and returning nonfunctioning units to the country of origin for servicing. Acquisition costing in such cases should include the cost of self-acquired power converters, shipping, and import duties.

NOTES

1. N. Kelley, "Computer Graphics: Info at a Glance," *Infosystems*, December 1979, p. 38.
2. N. Knottek, "Display Copier Survey," *Datamation*, July 1979, p. 162; C. F. Schmid and S. E. Schmid, *Handbook of Graphic Presentation*, 2d ed. (New York: John Wiley, 1979), p. 276.

13

THE HOME AND
PORTABLE OFFICES

Millions of people conduct their daily business activities at home or on the road. Residential offices, whether permanent or temporary, may range from a kitchen table to a room dedicated to business use. Portable, mobile offices are far more diverse. Sales, service, and delivery personnel and police officers spend many of their working hours in mobile offices. Others occasionally travel on business; at such times, their portable office may be a desk in another firm's office, a hotel room, or even the front seat of a car.

In both the office at home and the portable office, people create and process information, and they often use similar automated equipment to do so. Working from home is called "telework," and it may become more prevalent as the cost and scarcity of fossil fuels increase and as skilled individuals confined to their homes join the active work force. Firms such as Arthur D. Little, Control Data Corporation, and the Continental Illinois National Bank and Trust Company are presently involved with telework.[1]

Increasingly compact, multifunction portable devices now emerging in the marketplace will likely take and hold a sizable market share until the 1990s. The market for portable hard-copy and portable display terminals, estimated at $200 million in 1980, is projected to advance to

$3 billion by 1990.[2] By then, voice-recognition and voice-response hardware and software may be well enough developed to convert the standard telephone handset into an even more important and versatile audio input and output terminal.

Purpose and Value

An automated residential office can fill virtually every information processing need. With automated tools it is possible to maintain interactive contact with and control over projects elsewhere, to communicate with colleagues in other time zones, and to gain rapid access to immediately required information, regardless of weather conditions.

The Continental Illinois National Bank and Trust Company in Chicago uses two kinds of residential offices. Terminals in the homes of Continental executives provide permanent, part-time links to the bank's terminal-based electronic mail system.[3] The other link is between the bank and two operators who work at home full time with communicating word processors and a telephone dictation system. When input keying is complete, documents are electronically transmitted to the bank, where the hard copy is printed.[4] During a severe snowstorm that almost totally closed the bank, the two teleworkers continued to word process vital work from their homes.

An automated residential office provides:

- Full-time accessibility to files
- Full-time communication with colleagues
- Imperviousness to weather conditions.

An automated residential office that supports telework provides:

- Work force stability
- Reduced turnover and training curve losses
- Savings in energy resources, commuting time, employee clothing costs, and expenses
- Reduced overhead for office space.

Portable offices likewise make the physical location of the permanent office immaterial. They provide access to electronic mail, personal files, policy manuals, and research material. Information can flow in both directions in all four modes. Traveling executives can make policy decisions, sales personnel can enter orders, and attorneys can transmit contract-closing announcements moments after transactions are complete.

Any automated tool of a reasonable size can be installed in a permanent office at home. Alphanumeric terminals are often a first choice, usually with some provision for hard copy. A hard-copy terminal requires limited space. Display terminals can be equipped with either a screen dump printer, able to produce a hard copy of whatever is displayed on the screen, or an intelligent terminal with storage and a printer.

The array of portable equipment differs, but not necessarily its functions. Table 13.1 lists typical equipment, options, and prices.

Portable printing terminals weigh from 14 to 20 pounds. More sophisticated units have bubble memory and editing capability. Printing/plotting terminals, such as those manufactured by Computer Transceiver Systems and Computer Devices, Inc., can print alphanumerics with superscript and subscript and can plot graphics as well as function as conventional portable terminals.

Portable CRT terminals display from 1 to 18 lines and up to 80 characters per line. Most come with acoustic couplers. Some are available with miniature hard-copy printers and European acoustic couplers and modems. Portable smart CRTs provide an array of capabilities. The Scrib, manufactured by Bobst Graphic, Inc., has internal editing and a

Hand-held computer and peripheral devices. Photo courtesy of Panasonic.

TABLE 13.1   Automated equipment for the portable office.

Tool	Features/Options	Weight	Cost Range ($)
Hard-copy terminal	Up to 80-character lines	14 pounds up	1600 up
	Bubble memory and editing capability	16 pounds up	3,000
Printer/plotter	132-column print, superscript and subscript; graphics plotting	14 pounds up	5,000–6,000
Display terminal 1-18 line display	Hard-copy printer Acoustic coupler/ modem	5 1/2–23 pounds	5,000 up
Smart CRT	7-inch screen Internal editing Removable storage Alternative power sources	20–23 pounds	under 6,000
Fax unit	Up to 8 1/2 by 11-inch pages	25 pounds	1,500 up
	Models for outside North America		1,600 up
Microfiche viewer			
Pocket	Single frame	4 ounces up	30 up
	Battery light	6–10 ounces	10 up
Attache style portable		5 pounds up	150 up
Pocket dictation unit	W/single-use battery	6 ounces	65 up
	W/rechargeable battery	4–8 ounces*	85 up
Dictation/ tel. ans. units	W/remote control	—	300 up

* With batteries, 8–15 ounces.

7-inch diagonal screen with 18 lines of 64 characters, a control information line, a split-screen capability, removable cassette storage, and a 224-character set. The terminal can be powered from 110V 60Hz AC, 220V 50Hz AC, or from internal, rechargeable batteries, giving the user two hours of independence and mobility.

Many fax units marketed for stationary installation in offices can serve as portables. Most portable fax units can transmit and receive documents up to standard-size pages. All are powered by conventional AC current. Some models are manufactured for use outside North America. Fax units can also be installed in vehicles. Both radio transceiver models built for law enforcement agencies and AC portable fax

Rear view of portable printer-plotter terminal showing optional communications connections. Execuport terminal courtesy of Computer Transceiver Systems, Inc.

Portable terminals: *top*, model with crypto device for security; *lower left*, 17-pound unit with many of the attributes of a wõrd processor; *lower right*, communicating hard-copy terminal. Photos respectively courtesy of Technical Communications Corporation, Telcon Industries, and Texas Instruments.

units can be used from vehicles. During an intensive manhunt by the New York City Police Department in the 1970s, task force cars were equipped with 110V current supplied from the vehicle engines. Long wires attaching the fax units to acoustic couplers made it possible for task force members to connect with any pay telephone or police callbox and receive up-to-the-minute composite drawings of suspects and hard copies of signed directives. Repair personnel and salesmen could use the same type of installation. Salesmen could transmit facsimiles of orders within minutes of a sale; repair servicemen could receive work orders without returning to the office or transcribing them during a telephone call.

Portable microfiche equipment, discussed in detail in Chapter 8, comes in a variety of sizes. Dictation units are now so small they can easily be carried in a pocket or a small purse. Most units allow the user a choice of power sources and are available with miniature earphones for listening privacy. For limited applications, a remotely controlled dial-up dictation unit installed at a permanent location can receive input from any telephone; some hybrid units can also serve as telephone answering units with remote control message playback.

While writing this book, the author maintained both an office at home and a portable office. Three stationary and three portable devices (the portable tools served while traveling and in the residential office)

Author's automated home office equipped for writing this book.

Equipment for Author's Automated Office at Home and Portable Office
Stationary devices
  Word processor
    DIGITAL WD-78 (word and data)
    Dual floppy diskette drives
    LQP-78 Diablo printer (letter quality)
    Communications option
  Modem
    Vadic VA355 with handset
Stationary/portable devices
  Terminal
    Execuport 4000G printer/plotter
  Facsimile
    Qwip 1200 fax transceiver
  Microfiche viewer
    77R-GLM Taylor Merchant pocket viewer

---

helped demonstrate the viability of office automation for this type of work.

International Considerations

International travelers carrying terminals continue to face problems of incompatibility. Some portable terminals are available with the standard acoustic coupler, but an optional European acoustic coupler or modem is often required.

Most electronic equipment is manufactured for power sources in the country of sale. Unless a device has been manufactured to accommodate voltages and cycle rates operative in the country of use, it will not function according to specification or may incur damage. Some electronic and radio hobby stores sell small, inexpensive converters that eliminate such problems. These small cube-like units have several different types of plug prongs and outlets for varying power needs.

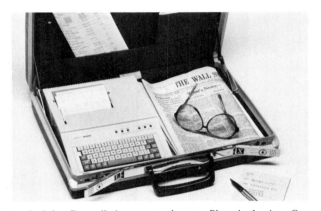

A compact terminal that fits easily into an attache case. Photo by Lexicon Corporation.

NOTES

1. Tom Nicholson, Pamela Abramson, Donna Foote, and Diane Weathers, "Commuting by Computer," *Newsweek*, May 4, 1981, p. 58.
2. "Portable Terminals Shipments Seen at $3B by 1990," *Computer Systems News*, April 14, 1980, p. 36.
3. Rick Minicucci, "Profile: Electronic Mail," *Corporate Systems*, December 1979/January 1980, p. 12.
4. "WP by Moonlight," *Word Processing World*, August 1979, p. 12–13.

It is a bad plan that admits of no
modification.
                    Publilius Syrus
        Moral Sayings (first century B.C.)

THE END IS
THE BEGINNING

The implementation of a system of office automation tools is not an
end, but a beginning. It is a mistake to think of office automation as a
project, with a definite point of completion. Office automation is a
healthy, dynamic adolescent looking ahead to a long life. Because it is
still growing, it warrants continued attention. Organizational groups
planning for office automation should become permanent departments
whose task will be to stay abreast of rapid technological improvements
in both products and ideas. These groups must examine a wide range of
influences: business markets change; new products appear and others
vanish; executive changes signal new directions. Changing needs will
require changes in office automation systems. A flexible system should
be continually updated.

The information age is one of astounding technological growth. New
means of exploiting worldwide sources of information are burgeoning.
Data banks are increasingly a feature of business operations; in the
home, personal computers, video discs, and videotex will change the
way we conduct our lives; universities offer degrees in computer science and courses accessed through electronic media; government projects worldwide are promoting nationwide automated information systems. In many respects the process in self-sustaining: one new discovery

unlocks yet another. In such a world, office automation systems will inevitably become less than perfect over time as other planners launch better systems. The greater one's knowledge of what is happening, the more successful the system improvements are likely to be.

Flexibility

Because electronic publishing is still limited, the written word remains our best source of information about office automation. Many information management trade periodicals run feature articles and regular columns dealing with various aspects of office automation. Most concern themselves primarily with office automation, office systems, and telecommunications; but audiovisual, video, general business, educational, photographic, news, foreign affairs, alumni, and other periodicals are also concerning themselves with the subject. Many of the systems and information periodicals are issued free of cost to those involved in the field, subject to certain conditions: some are offered only on a subscription basis, others are available with membership in an organization.

Several looseleaf information services are now available on a subscription basis. Most cost several hundred dollars per year; a few offer free examinations of their product prior to a subscription decision. They have potential worth beyond their cost, but any planning group should evaluate them in relation to its needs before choosing any one.

Also of value are newsletters and bulletins; some are published commercially and some by institutions of higher education; many are government publications. Prices range from $15 to several hundred dollars; most are under $200.

Finally, a few books deal with office automation. Most are on specific subjects, such as facsimile, micrographics, records management, and word processing. Single books (sometimes issued as three-ring binders) range from about 8 to over 600 dollars; most of the latter are market studies and trend analyses.

To maintain a broad and clear perspective, planners should constantly review a representative body of publications. An annual outlay of several thousand dollars is not unusual. Each member of the planning group can be responsible for reading specific publications, mark items of value, and circulate them to the others. Consideration should also be given to automated indexing of such information on a yearly basis, for later references to support the efforts of the group.

Joining Special Groups

Most business and professional societies have special-interest groups concentrating on office automation; many such societies deal exclusively with one aspect of the field, such as general management, information management, data processing management, micrographics, word processing, and electronic mail. Annual dues range upward from $50.

Two kinds of groups deal specifically with office automation. Both of these tend to keep membership small and have expensive annual dues. Both hold periodic meetings with both intraorganizational and outside speakers. Some concentrate on policy issues, others on technical and planning aspects. The first type of group is commercial, profitmaking, and international and tends to comprise very large corporations. Annual dues are up to $10,000; the fee covers many of the expenses related to the periodic meetings, such as the cost of accommodations, meals, beverages, and publications. There are similar local and regional groups of a commercial nature. The second type of office automation group tends to be nonprofit, local or regional, and comprises end users with noncompetitive lines of endeavor.

Seminars, Conferences, and Trade Shows

An increasing number of seminars and conferences deal with office automation. Some are commercial ventures; others are sponsored by established business and professional organizations, by publishers, or by institutions of higher learning. Experienced OA users and fellow members of business and professional groups can furnish guidance about which presentations to attend. Those who are unfamiliar with office automation will benefit from attending one or two that cover the subject in general, thereafter relying on those with a particular focus, according to need, such as computer graphics, electronic mail, word processing, or teleconferencing.

Trade shows, many with concurrent seminars, offer planners a chance to see most of the new products, compare competitive models, and witness demonstrations.

Sharing Information

Much information comes from asking questions, not only of colleagues, fellow planners, and members of professional societies, but also of neighbors or members of civic, social, fraternal, and religious groups. Office automation has already affected so many fields that only rarely does someone not have some knowledge of it. There is an unmistakable camaraderie among office automation planners—an unusual willingness to share discoveries, successes, adversities. Telephone calls to total strangers find friendly receptions within the limits of professional ethics and institutional confidentiality.

Criticism, whether self-generated or external, is another means to improvement. Each of us may secretly criticize our own efforts but find it difficult to accept identical advice from others. Valid criticism from any source, be it a differing point of view or a response to an error, results in corrective change.

An office automation group that engages in group critiques will more quickly and easily uncover weaknesses in a plan, system, sub-systems, a presentation, or any other relevant concern. By the time the planning group finds itself facing such questions, perhaps in a hostile environment, the answers are ready and the weaknesses corrected.

Creativity in planning requires time. An office automation group that is large enough to allow members time to think in addition to per-forming assigned functions can engage in brainstorming sessions. Once participants are relaxed about the technique, the application of group thinking can produce valuable creative results.

Because there are still many unanswered questions about office auto-mation, a bit of calculated daring is often valuable: daring to ask the unaskable question, daring to try something new. Each venture stretches the boundaries of the mind, the discipline, and the potential gains in ways that pure logic cannot.

Success requires both knowledge and effort. Close up, office auto-mation tools are nothing more than an assemblage of wires, glass, elec-tronic waves, photographic film, lenses, and other inanimate objects, skillfully crafted and integrated by human intelligence. Viewed this way, the tools become manageable. There is no magic in office automa-tion; the magic is in the people who use it effectively.

TRADEMARKS

A.B. Dick Company, Magna SL. Amdax, Inc., DAX. American Tele-
phone and Telegraph Company (AT&T), Bell 50A-1, Comm-Stor II,
Gemini 100 Electronic Blackboard, Picturephone, Picturephone Meeting Service, Speakerphone, Touch-Tone. Bell and Howell, Mailmobile.
Bobst Graphic, Inc., Scrib. Buscom Systems, Inc., Soft-Touch. Com-
pression Laboratories, Inc., CLI-441. Computer Transceiver Systems,
Inc., Execuport 4000G. Darome, Inc., CONVENER. Diablo Systems,
Inc., Diablo LQP-78. Digital Equipment Corporation, DECmate,
DF02, VT125, WD-78. Exxon Information Systems, Quip, Qyx. Feder-
al Screw Works, Votrax. General Electric Company, Genigraphics
100B, 100C, R-341. Hewlett Packard Company, HP2647A, HP9872C,
System 45B. Institute for the Future, Planet. Interface Systems, DA-
VID. International Business Machines Corporation, IBM 3278, Dis-
playwriter, 6670, IBM 75. Micon Industries, Termiphone. Minnesota
Mining and Manufacturing (3M), Advanced Local Area Network.
Network Resources Corporation, Localnet. Northwest Microfilm, Inc.,
NMI PRO. Panafax, MV3000. Planning Research Corporation, Tele-
fiche. Prime Computer, Inc., Prime 850. Racal-Vadic, Vadic VA 355,
871. Ragen Information Systems, Ragen System 95. Talos Systems,
Inc., Forum, Talos digitizer, Telescreen. Taylor Merchant Corporation,
77R-GLM. Teknekron, Inc., Automated Records Management System

(ARMS). Teletype Corporation, Teletype 33, 35. Terminal Data Corporation, DocuMate II. Texas Instruments, TI 787. Tymshare, Inc., AUGMENT, Tymshare. Ungermann-Bass, Net/One. Western Union, Telex, TWX. Xerox Corporation, Ethernet; Star Information System; Xerox 850, 6500, 9700; Telecopiers 455, 495. Zilog, Z-net.

INDEX

Burroughs Corporation, 98, 176, 210
Buscom Systems, Inc., 48

CalComp (California Computer
    Products), 174
Calendars, *see* Electronic calendars
Call diverters, 46. *See also* Telephone
Cameras:
    CCD (charge-coupled device), 113
    graphics system, 171, 173, 174–175
    microfilm, 109, 126, 128–130
    SSTV, 150–151
    See also Micrographics; TV
Canada: Telidon system, 99–100. *See also*
    TV
Capital investments, *see* Costs
CAR (computer-aided retrieval) systems,
    see Electronic filing and
    retrieval
Cassettes, 55, 67
Cathode ray terminals, *see* CRTs
CBMS, *see* Computer-based message
    systems
CB radio, 40
CBX, 44. *See also* Networks; Telephone
CCITT, *see* Comite Consultatif
    Internationale de Telegraphie
    et Telephonie
Central Intelligence Agency, 177
Centrex system, 144. *See also* Telephone
CIM (computer input microfilm), *see*
    Micrographics:
    microfiche/microfilm
Circuits, 42. *See also* Telephone;
    Transmission, modes of
Citicorp, 183
Coaxial cable, 37, 45–46
Codes and coding, 6, 34
    conversion of, to phonemes, 91,
        176–177, 206 (*see also* Voice
        response)
    digital, 33–34, 114, 127
    fax, 98
    graphics, 100
    micrographics, 109, 127
    OCR and, 66
    in transmission, 40, 41
    in telephone bridge connections, 47
    See also Transmission security
Cognitronics, Inc., 176
Color:
    -coded microfiche headers, 131
    CRT options, 54
    fax systems/transmission, 93, 96, 149
    graphics, 168–174 *passim*, 206
    ink-jet printers, 72, 75, 173
    OCR, 66
    TV full motion, 40, 154

TV slow scan, 150, 152
Columbia Broadcasting System, 99
COM (computer output microfilm), *see*
    Micrographics:
    microfiche/microfilm
COM (Swedish teleconference system),
    162
Comite Consultatif Internationale de
    Telegraphie et Telephonie
    (CCITT), 92, 93, 94
Command mode, 84
Comm-Stor II, 34
Communications, 31–49
    as basis of office automation, 20, 31
    consultants, 48–49
    data (defined), 31
    means of, 37–41
    networks, *see* Networks
    speed of, 13–14 (*see also* Transmission
        speed)
    telecommunications (defined), 31
    units of measure in, 32
    word processor capabilities of, 57, 65
        (*see also* Word processing
        systems)
    See also Transmission, modes of
Compression Labs, Inc., 98
Compuscan (Company), 98
Computer(s), 3, 6, 31, 33, 91
    "host," 57, 66, 184
    -human interface, and importance of,
        168, 176
    IOAS networks, 184 (*see also*
        Networks)
    mainframe, 184, 196
    minicomputers, 56, 170, 184, 196, 205,
        216
    personal, 225
    telephone input to, 48
    word processors as, 77 (*see also* Word
        processing systems)
Computer-aided retrieval (CAR), *see*
    Electronic filing and retrieval
Computer-based message systems
    (CBMS), 66, 106, 122, 203
    advantages of, 83
    costs of, 82, 83, 84
    electronic filing and retrieval in, 88–91,
        105–108, 187–188
    as element of IOAS, 187, 188–189, 192
    functions and use of, 84–91
    graphics in, 91
    modes of operation, 84, 86 (fig.)
    tickler functions, 121
    See also Electronic mail system(s)
Computer Devices, Inc., 219
Computer input microfilm (CIM), *see*
    Micrographics:
    microfiche/microfilm
Computer output microfilm (COM), *see*

word processor, 51, 52, 53, 55, 203
See also Cameras; Printers
Harder, D. S., 1
Hardware, 3, 34, 192, 218
word-management, 55, 56
Hardwired transmission, 37. *See also* Transmission, modes of
Health effects of CRTs and VDTs, 17–18
Hertz, 32, 37. *See also* Measurement
Heuristics, Inc., 175, 176
Hewlett Packard Company, 170, 174, 175
Holofiche, *see* Micrographics: microfiche/microfilm
Holofile Industries, Ltd./Technology, Inc., 114
Home, office in, 217–222, 223 (fig.)
Honeywell, Inc., 175
Hub network, *see* Networks
Hunt groups, 48. *See also* Telephone
Hyphenation, *see* Word processing systems

IBM (International Business Machines) Corporation, 34, 98, 175, 176
Professional Office System, 121 (fig.)
Image Resource Corporation, 174, 175
Incompatibility, 18–19, 34, 77, 184, 196
facsimile system, 92
film type (in micrographics), 126
power source, 223
SSTV equipment, 151–152
See also Interface; International considerations
Index(es):
CBMS file, 106, 108
IOAS, 187
microfilm retrieval system, 109, 130–131, 193
tickler file, 117
word processor, 67, 68, 105
Infomedia (Company), 163
Information, 2, 3, 6, 11–12
Infrared transmission, 39
Input, 3, 12, 48, 200, 201. *See also* Dictation systems; Digitization/digitizers; Keying; Optical character recognition (OCR); Transmission, modes of; Typing; Voice response
Institute for the Future, 163
Integrated office automation systems (IOAS), 6
basic elements of, 184–186, 187–188
benefits of, 7, 179–180, 182–184
costs of, 183, 194, 205
defined, 179
electronic mail system (EMS) and, 179, 185, 192–206 *passim*

joined with word processor, 23, 65–66, 91–92, 191, 192
extended-application elements of, 186, 190, 191
functionally integrated, 190–192
and graphics, 197, 198, 203, 205–206
National Science Foundation use of, 180, 183
optional elements of, 186, 188–190
project management in, 189–190
U.S. Air Force use of 180–182, 183
user directories, 188
workstation access to, 215
See also Office automation
Intelligent copiers, 175
Intelligent terminals, *see* Terminals
Interactive Systems/3M, 45
Interface Technology (Company), 176, 177
International considerations:
in fax system, 92
in IOAS implementation, 184
in micrographics use, 126
for portable equipment, 223
in scheduling appointments, 120
in teleconferencing, 163–164
in telephone service, 48
in word processor use, 79
for workstations, 216
International Data Corporation, 137
International Record Carriers, 48
International Word Processing Association, 15
Interstate Electronics, Inc., 175

Job security, 21. *See also* Work force

Keying:
of four-mode IOAS, 202
managerial attitude toward, 17, 83, 162, 184, 200, 210
See also Typing
Keypad:
advantage of (over full keyboard), 17
of CB radio, 40
telephonic, 17, 48, 176
ten-key numeric, 17, 210
Knowledge workers, *see* Work force

Labor, *see* Work force
Labor, U.S. Department of: labor force statistics, 10–11
Laser-beam recorders (LBRs), 129. *See also* Cameras
Laser transmission, 39–40
Leahy, Emmett, 10
Letters, 10, 52, 62

Telemetry, 40. *See also* Transmission,
  modes of
Telephone, 3, 31, 209
  answering machines, *see*
      recorders/answering systems,
      below
  as audio input/output terminal, 100,
      101, 209, 214, 218
  automatic dialers, 46
  bridge connections, 46–48, 144, 148
  call diverters, 46
  CBMS replacement of, 82, 83
  CBMS used with, 91
  circuits, 33, 37, 44
    in teleconferencing, 143
  hunt groups, 48
  keypads, 17, 48, 176
  outside North America, 48
  in portable office, 218, 221, 222
  private exchanges (PBX, etc.), 44–45,
      84
  recorders/answering systems, 46,
      100–101, 222
  teleconference use of, 142–143,
      153–154
  tone-operated/Touch-Tone, 48, 91, 101,
      117, 149, 206
  in transmission, 36–37, 40, 43
    private systems, 44–45
    shadow functions, 12, 100
    (*see also* Transmission, modes of)
  word processor use of, 57
  See also Voice response
Tele/Pointer, 154
Telescreen system (Talos Systems, Inc.),
      153
Teletypewriter (TTY) systems, 31, 41,
      91–92, 205
  protocol, 34
  TWX and Telex, *see* Networks
Television, *see* TV
Telex, *see* Networks
Telidon (videotex) system (Canada),
      99–100. *See also* TV
Terminal Data Corporation, 128
Terminals:
  alphanumeric, 149, 160, 213, 214, 215,
      219
  costs of (vs. printing/plotting), 147
  audio, 142 (*see also* Teleconferencing;
      Transmission, modes of)
  blind, 52
  buffered, 34
  display (soft-copy), 51, 52, 91, 149, 208,
      210, 214, 219
    cathode ray, *see* CRTs
    plasma panel, 114
    Telefiche system, 113
    video, *see* VDTs
  (*see also* graphic; portable, *below*)

graphic, 91, 98, 169, 170–171, 174,
    203, 210
hard-copy, 90, 215, 219
intelligent, 52, 88, 196, 219 (*see also*
    Word processing systems)
key pad operation of, 17, 210
portable, 5, 142, 149, 160, 169, 219,
    221 (fig.), 222 and *fig.*
printing/plotting, 149, 219, 221 (fig.),
    222
reading on, 90
for residential office, 218
shared (vs. dedicated), 208, 211, 215
telephones as, *see* Telephone
thermal, 149
voice-actuated, 144–145, 210
word processing systems as, 66, 194,
    200
workspace for, 209
Texas Instruments (Company), 174
Text-editing systems, *see* Word processing
    systems
3M (Company), 45, 112
Threshold Technology, Inc., 175
Tickler files, *see* Electronic tickler files
Time:
  and length of meetings, 117
  and productivity, 3, 12–13, 100, 101,
      116
  utilization of 12–13, 15
Timesharing services:
  graphics, 169–170, 198, 203
  word processing, 52, 53, 77, 194
Time zones, 120, 159, 160, 163. *See also*
    Electronic calendars;
    Teleconferencing
Touch-Tone, *see* Telephone
Translations, 78, 184. *See also*
    International considerations
Transmission, modes of, 34–48, 38 (table)
  analog, 33, 44, 96, 150, 154
    -digital conversion, 36, 37 (fig.), 98,
        101
  audio systems, 100–101, 139, 142, 198,
      209, 218
  circuit flexibility in, 42
  computerized fax systems, 96–99
  computerized text systems, 91–92
  consultants for, 48–49
  digital, 33, 37, 44, 96
    -analog conversion, 36, 37 (fig.), 98,
        101
  directional capability, 41–42, 94, 144,
      153
  line-of-sight, 39, 40, 41
  media, 37–41
  networks for, *see* Networks
  nonsynchronous, 82, 96, 139
  outside North America, 48 (*see also*
      International considerations)

synchronous/asynchronous, 34, 35, 82, 139
for teleconferencing, *see* Teleconferencing
videotex systems, 99–100
voice apparatus in, 40, 46–48, 91, 101, 144–145, 175–177, 206 (*see also* Telephone)
wired, 37, 44–45
See also Bandwidth; Electronic mail system(s) (EMS); Graphics
Transmission security:
audio teleconference, 147–148
CBMS, 84
computer teleconference, 162
fax options for, 94
video teleconference, 159
word processor, 77
See also Codes and coding
Transmission speed, 34, 36, 37, 41, 42, 45
CBMS, 91
fax, 93–94
measurement of, 32
OCR, 67
printer, 71
SSTV, 150–151
videotex, 100
See also Baud rate
Transparencies and slides, *see* Cameras; Graphics; Hard-copy output
Transponders, 40–41. *See also* Transmission, modes of
TTY, *see* Teletypewriter (TTY) systems
TV, 31
broadcast resolution (U.S.), 154
European standard, 154–155
full motion closed-circuit, 96, 154–155, 164
and Picturephone (PMS), 100, 141, 155–156, 158
satellite transmission of, 40
slow-scan (SSTV) and semimotion, 96, 139, 149–152, 154, 164
in teleconferencing, 139, 149–152, 154
VHF signal, 32
and video printers, 174, 175
and Videotex systems, 99–100, 225
TWX (Teletypewriter Exchange Service), *see* Networks
Typesetting: "poor man's," 75. *See also* Phototypesetting/ photocomposition; Word processing systems
Typewriters, 52, 66, 176, 200
electronic, 52–53 and *figs.*
See also Typing; Word management
Typing:
costs, 59, 66
vs. word processing, 53, 57, 58, 59, 66
managerial attitude toward, *see* Keying

time occupied in, 15
See also Letters; Reports

Ultrafiche, 127. *See also* Micrographics
Ungermann-Bass, Inc., 44
United Nations, 92
University of Illinois, 153
University of Wisconsin, 138

Value-added Network (VAN), 43. *See also* Networks
Value Line (data bank), 109
VDTs (video display terminals), 18, 203, 214–215. *See also* TV
Versatec, Inc., 174
VHF broadcast signal, 32. *See also* TV
Video display terminals, *see* VDTs
Video teleconferencing, *see* Teleconferencing
Videotex systems, *see* TV
Voice response:
calendars, 117
CBMS, 91
code conversion to phonemes, 91, 176–177, 206
drawbacks to, 175
hardware, 218
software, 206, 218
terminals, 144–145, 210
and voice filing systems, 101
See also Telephone; Transmission, modes of

Wall Street Journal, The, 96
Wang Laboratories, 175
Wavetek (Company), 176
Western Union International, 91, 92
Women: career opportunities for, 14
Word management, 51–79
components, 54–55
defined, 51
electronic filing and retrieval used in, 62, 105
internal operating instructions and capabilities, 55–58
in IOAS, 203
systems and types of devices for, 51–55, 71–75
See also Word processing systems
Word processing systems:
and administrative support teams, 14–16
basic design of, 51–52
capabilities and applications of, 52–54, 57–59, 62–71, 75
communicating, 57–58, 65, 66, 75, 82, 88, 91, 149, 191, 198, 215, 218

About the Author and This Book

David Barcomb is a pioneer in the field of office automation. He designed and implemented some early word processing applications and has served as consultant on office automation projects for major multinational firms. This book is a product of his experience with automated systems. It was composed on a communicating word processor and electronically transmitted in part to the publisher. Author and publisher often corresponded by means of an electronic mail system that is part of an integrated office information system. Several diagrams used as illustrations were computer generated, some from rough drawings transmitted from the author's residential office by a facsimile device. The type was set from the word processed copy by means of an automated translation program.